D1146147

a reluctant memoir

Robert Ballagh is an Irish artist, painter
and designer. He lives and works in Dublin.

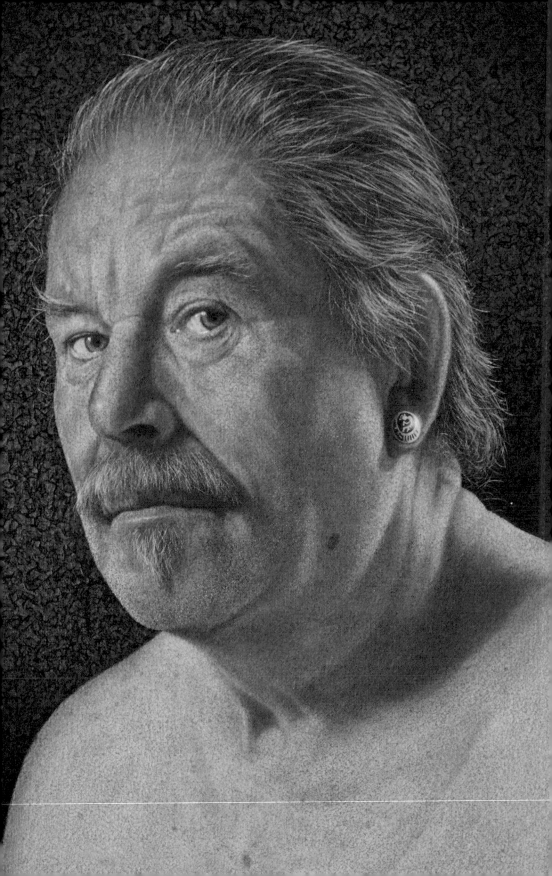

robert ballagh

a reluctant memoir

HEAD
of ZEUS

An Apollo Book

This is an Apollo book, first published in the UK in 2018
by Head of Zeus Ltd

ISBN (HB) 9781786695314
ISBN (E) 9781786695307

Designed by Heather Bowen
Printed and bound in the UK by Gomer Press

Frontispiece: *Man with a silver earring*, detail, oil on canvas, 2017

Head of Zeus Ltd
First Floor East
5–8 Hardwick Street
London EC1R 4RG
WWW.HEADOFZEUS.COM

a reluctant
memoir

Contents

Prologue

If you are reading these lines then you have either bought, borrowed or stolen this volume, an acquisition indicating a level of interest that surprises me considering my scepticism about writing it in the first place.

Let me explain. Years ago, I sent several essays that I had written on art and politics to a few publishers, wondering if they might consider them for publication. With probable justification they all rejected my efforts, but a number of them indicated that if I was to give some thought to writing a memoir they might be interested. I felt both disappointed and embarrassed. As far as I was concerned, only self-indulgent pricks write memoirs. Just look at any list of bestselling books at any given time: soccer managers, models, teenage pop stars and B-list celebrities are all telling their life stories or, to be more precise, someone else is usually telling their stories for them. The memoir today has become a fucked-up literary form driven by hubris and crass commercial interests. My late wife Betty would certainly have endorsed this negative assessment. She had no time at all for people who prattle on about their achievements. She could spot a spoofer a mile away.

Occasionally, if some windbag succeeded in persuading me of their genius, Betty would fix me with a withering stare, not unlike an exasperated teacher losing patience with a dopey pupil, and utter a dismissive, 'What a complete load of shite!'

She not only policed the pomposity of others; she also made quite sure I didn't resort to similar self-serving blather.

For example, whenever I was interviewed on some radio or television programme, my own response afterwards was always one of relief that I had not made a complete fool of myself.

Betty, on the other hand, was always more measured, greeting me with something quite positive like, 'Well, that wasn't too bad,' before following fairly swiftly with 'Perhaps a little too much of the *me business*.'

As you can imagine, this attitude would not have made Betty a great fan of the memoir as a form: a great deal of the *me business* bound between two covers.

One obvious consequence of such negative attitudes to the writing of a personal narrative was that I instantly consigned the idea to the nethermost regions of my mind, which of course now begs the question, 'Why did it not stay there?'

In truth, the explanation is simple enough. Over the last few years a steady stream of art historians and journalists have been seeking my take on various individuals that I might have encountered, and incidents that occurred in the course of the last half-century or so. What I remembered was not recorded in most official accounts of the period and some of these erudite researchers urged me to write my own story to set the record straight; usually tacking on the depressing admonition, 'Before it's too late!' As one of them said, 'When you're gone, you're gone and all that store of knowledge will be gone too.'

Nonetheless, whether through laziness or philosophical principle, I maintained my resolve not to get involved in the memoir business.

It was only when one person introduced the hazard of moral blackmail that I finally conceded that further resistance was futile. Her argument was simple enough; she said that I had a clear responsibility to tell my story so that future generations would have access to the full facts, at least as I remembered them.

With heavy heart I began to consider the task of compiling a memoir. However, in order to avoid boring myself, the first decision I made was to shun conventional narrative: the *and then* school. 'I was born on such and such a date *and then* I went to school, *and then* I met so and so *and then* I did this *and then* I did that,' and so on ad nauseam. In the words of Samuel Beckett, 'Mortal tedium'. Instead I decided that I would recall individuals and events that proved significant in my life, write about them in no particular order and trust to fate that the unfolding narrative might make some sort of sense. So I decided to start this reluctant memoir at its end.

CHAPTER 1

The Beginning of the End

The end, or in my case, the beginning of the end commenced at lunchtime one fine day in March 2010, when I managed to get all shades of shite beaten out of me. Allow me to explain. For years my usual routine was to return home in the middle of the day to have a chat and a bite to eat with my wife Betty. Normally I walked the short distance between my studio in Arbour Hill and my home in Broadstone, a journey that often included a stroll through the well-maintained grounds of James Gandon's masterpiece, the King's Inns, where Ireland's barristers are trained.

However, having decided to drive rather than walk on that particular day, architectural splendours were far from my mind as I turned into Temple Cottages, a short cul-de-sac of twenty-eight terraced houses, and found my way home blocked by a big white van.

Frustrated by this obstruction, I walked over to the van and asked the driver, 'You know you're parked on double yellow lines?'

His response was curt and to the point: 'You think I give a fuck!'

Now if I had some previous experience of such offensive behaviour I might have acted differently and simply walked away, but in all my sixty-seven years, believe it or not, I had never been involved in violence of any kind, so failed to spot the clear signs and unwisely prattled on in my best pedantic manner, 'Oh, that's simply not good enough. I'll have to call the Gardaí.'

Without warning and quick as lightning he turned on me and unleashed three or four vicious jabs to the chest. I collapsed immediately into a feeble heap. The last comment I remember hearing from him was, 'Report that to the fucking police!'

Feeling utterly broken I lay prostrate on the ground before gathering the strength to drag myself home.

When I told Betty what had happened she was incredulous at first, because she could see no evidence of the assault: no marks, no blood; but it slowly dawned on us that this guy had, in fact, exhibited a certain malicious expertise. Probably he had done something similar in the past and in all likelihood would do it again. To prevent that possible outcome I decided to go to the Bridewell police station and report the incident.

I was able to provide the officer on duty with the registration number of the van. This was amazing, because normally I'm useless at recalling numbers. If you asked me for my own car number I wouldn't be able to tell you.

The officer wrote everything down and promised that later that day a community policeman would call at my house to take a full statement. I waited and waited that afternoon but nobody turned up. The next day when I woke up I was stiff as a board and aching all over, and as the day progressed my condition didn't get much better. Twenty-four hours later, when what felt like paralysis had set in, I decided that it was time to pay a visit to my doctor. After a short physical examination he pronounced that I had suffered two fractured ribs and a fractured jaw. He said that there was little he could do other than prescribe painkillers and leave the rest to nature.

Fuck me, I thought to myself, before nervously asking, 'How long will nature take to fix my broken bones?'

'About three months,' came the ominous reply.

Nonetheless I resolved that this misfortune would not deter me from my work. As soon as it was physically possible to do so, I returned to the studio and began to paint again.

Then one day, a few weeks after starting back, the phone rang. It was a journalist from a tabloid newspaper who was following up the story of my assault. He asked if I had anything to add to the information he already had on file. After insisting that I had nothing more to say, he quickly changed tack and asked, 'Did you report the incident to the police?'

'Yes,' I replied.

Literally an hour later the phone rang again, but this time it was a garda from the Bridewell. He told me he had been put in charge of my case and that he just wanted to check a few facts.

'For example,' he asked, 'when did the incident occur?'

With what sounded like a fair degree of caution, I replied, 'On the same day that I reported it at the Bridewell.'

'And did you manage to note the registration number of the vehicle?'

'Yes,' I responded, 'and I passed it on to the officer on duty.'

There followed a moment's hesitation before he muttered, 'Eh… I'm afraid we seem to have mislaid the file; would it be possible for me to call later today and discuss the matter further?'

We agreed a time and I patiently waited once again for a policeman who failed to show up. After such an obvious lack of interest I thought to myself, 'Well, that's the last you'll hear from the bloody Gardaí.'

About a month later, at around eleven-thirty at night, the phone rang. 'Hello, this is Garda So-and-so; I'd like to pop up and have a chat about your assault.'

I replied, 'Fine, when?'

'Oh, now would be fine.'

As I was about to go to bed, my immediate reaction was to say, 'Ah, would you ever fuck off!' but of course I didn't; I simply replied, 'Oh, that's terribly inconvenient.'

His response was a little unexpected. 'You see, I'm on nights so I can only interview you between the hours of midnight and six in the morning.' Again, I was itching to tell him where to go but instead I politely made the following suggestion: 'When you are back on day duty again, give me a call.'

Years later, I guess he is still prowling the streets of Dublin at night, because I never heard from him again.

True to my doctor's word, after about three months all my injuries were healed, but I was left with something I had never experienced before – an acute feeling of vulnerability. Obviously, in a physical sense, I had learned a very practical lesson in human frailty, in how easily health and wellbeing can be snatched away. So, in spite of feeling fine, but just to be sure, I decided to book myself in for a full check-up. My GP informed me that everything seemed well, but since both my parents had died from heart-related ailments he said he was sending me to a cardiologist who, in turn, arranged for a whole batch of tests, including several fairly sophisticated scans.

On receiving the results, he let me know that, 'For a man of your age' – a phrase, by the way, that I have grown to hate – 'your heart is fine,' but then disclosed that when examining the coronary CT scan, he had noticed that my lymph glands were enlarged. I hadn't a clue what this meant and said so. He admitted that such matters were not his speciality, so he was making an appointment for me to see a haematologist.

This resulted in more tests; and, it might appear naïve, but it was only when I entered St Benedict's ward in the Mater Private Hospital and spotted a plaque proclaiming that *This oncology ward was opened by President Patrick Hillery* that the seriousness of the situation became apparent. On my return visit, the haematologist explained that I had chronic lymphocytic leukaemia, but immediately added that I was not to be alarmed by the technical term. He defined chronic as 'continuing for a long time', exactly what it says in the dictionary, and therefore not something that was immediately disastrous. He explained that CLL is a cancer of the white blood cells called lymphocytes, which normally die off naturally at the end of their life span, but that with CLL those cells live on even when they can no longer fight infection. They build up in the bone marrow until there is no space for normal blood cells to develop. This causes problems with fighting infection, carrying oxygen and blood clotting. The exact cause of CLL is unknown but it mainly occurs in people aged over fifty. Chemotherapy is the most common form of treatment, and it aims to stop the bone marrow making abnormal white blood cells. When this happens it is called 'remission', a desirable state to be in. He claimed that the recently developed treatment for CLL was remarkably effective.

Nervously, I inquired, 'When do we start?'

'Oh, right away,' he replied.

The only emotion I felt was one of complete shock. In all my life I had never spent a day in hospital, so I had arrived at the simple-minded conclusion that it was only other people who got sick.

I surprised myself by accepting the diagnosis with a perplexing fatalism. For example, I didn't indulge myself in questions like 'Why me?', blaming fate, or myself; in fact, quite the opposite. I faced my

The 'hungry' tree in the gardens of the King's Inns.

treatment fully convinced that there would be only two possible out-comes: I would survive, or I wouldn't – as simple as that!

The following Monday I checked in for my first chemotherapy session. It wasn't as bad as I might have expected, especially since I didn't have an aversion to hypodermic needles and there were plenty of those to deal with. In the days and weeks that followed I didn't suffer any measurable side-effects like nausea, hair loss or mouth ulcers, which, I was told, were a distinct possibility. I suspected that I was merely fortunate, a conjecture confirmed when I witnessed some of the ghastly side-effects endured by several of my fellow patients.

There was one distinctly unpleasant procedure: the extraction of a bone marrow sample from my pelvic bone. In the interests of good taste, I will spare the reader a detailed description of how this is effect-ed. Thankfully it only happened twice in the course of my treatment.

Eventually, after six months, my consultant came to my bedside.

'I have some good news,' he told me. 'You're in remission.'

However, there's always a sting in the tail. Before he left, he told me that another doctor would like to speak to me. This doctor disclosed that in monitoring my blood sugar levels, they had come to the con-clusion that I had Type 2 diabetes, a piece of news I could have done without. Nevertheless, ever since, with the constant care and attention of my medical team and the pharmaceutical industry, I have managed to maintain good health.

The one unexpected feature of the whole experience was that I never felt ill at any stage, nor exhibited any recognizable symptoms; in fact, it was only by chance that my varied ailments came to light. One obvious consequence of being a cancer survivor is the recognition of the inescapability of one's mortality. This can be depressing, but it can also be liberating, particularly if one opts to take full advantage of a precious future, yet to be lived.

As bad luck would have it, as soon as I got the all-clear, Betty, who had been so supportive during my treatment, fell ill herself. Normally Betty never complained; she was a stoical person who suffered in silence, but towards the end of 2010, she began to express quiet concern about abdominal pains. Her GP prescribed medication but she didn't seem to feel much better for it, so when I attended my own GP on 17 January 2011, I took Betty with me and asked him to have a look at her. He said he was worried about her condition and arranged an appointment with a gastroenterologist at Beaumont Hospital for the next day. This consultant organized blood tests, an abdominal scan and later a chest X-ray. Seven days later, Betty attended the Bon Secours Hospital for a colonoscopy, an endoscopy, scans of her abdomen, pelvis and thorax, plus pathology tests. The following day her consultant instructed her to submit herself for admission to Beaumont Hospital at the A & E department. She arrived at 2.30p.m. to discover that all they could provide for her was a chair – all the stretchers and trollies were occupied; so this sick woman was forced to sit waiting on that chair until 6.30 the following morning, a total of seventeen hours, before a trolley became available. I returned to the hospital after lunch to find that she had been transferred to St Patrick's Ward. Initially I was relieved, but then discovered that this facility was what was known as a holding ward, where no medical treatment was provided. In my opinion, this was no more than a political stunt to reduce the quoted numbers of patients on trollies waiting for treatment. Eventually, in the evening, she was transferred to St Lawrence's Ward, which was part of the proper hospital system.

While on this ward, Betty was under the care of a consultant colorectal surgeon. During a visit with Rachel and Bruce, our children, he explained that there was an intestinal blockage and that surgery was necessary. The probable outcome would be a colostomy bag for about three months and then corrective surgery. Naturally, we were concerned, but were encouraged that at last something was going to be done.

We all awaited what we assumed would be the next stage in Betty's treatment – namely surgery to remove the intestinal blockage; but then I had a phone call from the hospital on 4 February, informing me that Betty was being discharged on the instructions of her gastroenterologist. I was baffled. How could someone who so obviously required immediate surgery be discharged from hospital? I could not get anyone to give me any explanation for the decision.

When I brought Betty home she rapidly came to the conclusion that she would be far better off in hospital with proper nursing care, and not dependent on my incompetent efforts. But this was not to be.

On 15 February she reacted badly to the preparation for another colonoscopy that was to be carried out in Beaumont the next day. The only good news following the procedure was that there was no sign of malignancy, but Betty continued to deteriorate – vomiting, losing weight and not eating. I became extremely concerned. On 22 February we met her gastrologist. I was more than surprised by his flippant opening remark, 'How's the mystery girl?'

He weighed Betty and seemed to agree with me that she required immediate attention. He said he would contact the surgeon so that surgery could be arranged. Finally he told us he was travelling to Edinburgh for the Ireland vs. Scotland rugby match, but that the surgeon would look after Betty.

The next day, when I came home at lunchtime, Betty was quite distressed. She had called the admissions department in the hospital to be told that she was not on any list. I phoned myself, only to be told the same story. I then called the consultant's secretary who suggested that I contact the surgeon's secretary. She in turn recommended that I phone admissions again. I asked her to phone them herself, but she claimed that the private sector cannot contact the public sector. We were stuck in a bureaucratic web.

I was frantic; for two days I continued to phone admissions but received no response, and the two secretaries were of no help at all. No one returned my calls.

In desperation I phoned David Hickey, a senior consultant and a personal friend, who said he would look into the matter. On 25 February I continued making calls, but Betty was not placed on any consultant or surgeon's list. David Hickey phoned back, the only person in Beaumont Hospital to do so, and said he had spoken to some people and hoped that this might help.

The next day I managed to contact the surgeon who was supposed to be responsible for Betty, but he cautioned me, saying that, 'All the phone calls you are making are not helping,' and that I was not to worry as everything would be all right.

On Sunday morning, 27 February, there was still no bed in Beaumont for Betty; but at lunchtime I received a call to say there was a bed in St Joseph's Hospital in Raheny, and that after spending the night there she would be taken to Beaumont for surgery.

In the late afternoon Betty took a shower, and because she was so weak she asked me to help her dress. I was shocked by her emaciated condition. I took her to St Joseph's at around six o'clock and helped with her admission forms. I stayed until roughly 7.30p.m. then gave her a kiss, wished her well and promised to see her later the following day. I felt that Betty, though terribly weak, was in good form, probably because she hoped that, at last, she was going to receive some proper treatment.

When the phone rang at two in the morning on 28 February, I immediately sensed that the tone heralded very bad news. It was a nurse at St Joseph's, asking me to come to the hospital. When I got there I was told by the doctor and nurses on duty that Betty had died roughly an hour earlier.

I am still amazed at how calmly I accepted the desperate news, but I was probably in some kind of shock. I was left in private with Betty and bizarrely found myself feeling quite happy at how content she looked. Obviously her face no longer reflected the discomfort and pain that had been her recent experience, and when I touched her, even though I knew it would be the case, I found myself surprised by how cold she felt – unmistakable confirmation that she was gone.

Later I was asked to sign documents giving permission for a post-mortem and for organ retention. I was also asked to return at 9.30a.m. to identify Betty's body before members of An Garda Siochána. I did so, but had to wait for over an hour for the guards to turn up. During Betty's time in St Joseph's, no one from Beaumont Hospital visited her, no tests were taken and no medical notes were provided. Later that day the surgeon phoned to say, 'It was the worst possible outcome,' and asked for my permission to release Betty's body for the post-mortem. The coroner, Dr Tan Chien Sheng, formed the opinion that death was due to sudden cardiac arrest. But it was surely a striking failure of medical care not to have evaluated Betty's cardiovascular status in view of her age, her history of smoking and a family history of stroke, especially before a planned operative procedure.

David Hickey also called that day to convey his condolences and to say that, tragically, Betty was not the first person to die in such circumstances and would not be the last. He described the health system as totally dysfunctional.

Dr Eoin O'Brien, an eminent cardiologist, in examining Betty's case, was of the opinion that 'the delay in dealing with a benign diverticular stenotic lesion of the bowel, that had debilitated the patient by causing abdominal pain, vomiting, inflammation, weight loss and electrolyte disturbances, predisposed the patient to the combination of circumstances (severe hyponatraemia, anaemia, oxygen desaturation and probable heart failure) that culminated in her death. The question must be asked as to why there was a delay of two months between her presentation with significant and debilitating symptoms of bowel disease and surgery that would have been curative had the patient not died prior to intervention.'

The funeral took place on Thursday 3 March. Betty arrived in a simple wicker casket, something I'm sure she would have appreciated. A huge crowd gathered at Glasnevin cemetery, too large in fact for everyone to cram into the small oratory. Right from the start, I was unsure how to conduct the proceedings. Obviously, since both of us were non-believers, it would have been the height of hypocrisy to engage in any religious ceremony, but what to do? Then it struck me. I remembered being at a Quaker meeting many years before and, right away, decided to follow their example. After the gathering settled and musician Cormac Breatnach played a moving version of 'Mná na hÉireann' ('Women of Ireland') on low whistle, I got up and spoke about Betty. I finished with these words: 'Betty was an exuberant, lively, funny, friendly, loving, challenging and sometimes difficult woman. It is hard to accept that her incandescent life has been quenched. But it has. We draw comfort from the fact that the pain she suffered has also been extinguished. She is at rest. We will miss her.' I then invited anyone who wished to say anything about Betty or even recite a poem or sing a song, to come forward. After what seemed like an eternity of silence I began to speculate that I had made an enormous error of judgement, but I needn't have worried. Slowly, friends, relatives, neighbours, even people I didn't know got up and said kind things about Betty; after that Máire Breatnach sang her beautiful yet poignant song, 'Éist' ('Listen').

The proceedings were brought to a close with the haunting sounds of 'Caoineadh Uí Néill', the lament for O'Neill, played on the uilleann pipes by Peter Browne. It was a fitting send-off. I believe Betty herself would have thoroughly enjoyed the occasion.

*

Several months later, rather reluctantly, I gave several media interviews in which I described the tragic circumstances of Betty's death. I must admit I had not anticipated the enormous public response to my unhappy account. It seemed to me that almost every family in the country shared a similar grim story. There and then I decided to take a case against those I considered responsible for their failure to provide Betty with adequate medical care. I embarked on this course for two reasons. In the first place, I wanted those whose job it was to look after Betty to be held responsible for their negligence, and secondly, I hoped that by highlighting her case other patients might be spared the indignity and pain that Betty endured at the hands of the Irish health service.

For several years the Heath Service Executive or HSE completely stonewalled all attempts at seeking justice. Of course, from their point of view, this made sense. After all, many people faced with interminable delays simply give up the struggle. And if a settlement is delayed, the final damages are paid not by the HSE but by the redress board – in other words, by the exchequer. Consequently, there is no incentive for the HSE to speedily resolve difficult issues. In my case, however, it became obvious that I was not going away.

Finally, almost six years after Betty died, the defendants – namely the HSE and the two consultants – offered to settle. They accepted the charge of negligence and paid damages plus legal costs. A victory of sorts, I suppose; but as far as my hope of improving the health service for other patients, I reluctantly accepted that the settlement would have zero impact on the way the HSE conducts its business. In the years since Betty's death, things have gone from bad to worse. The figures for people on waiting lists for treatment and for people forced to lie untreated on trolleys are higher than ever. The present Irish health system is not only unfit for purpose but also appears to be institutionally unreformable. Is it not time to create a replacement scheme specifically designed to serve the interests of the Irish people?

For the sake of Betty's memory, I had hoped that compelling those who were responsible for her care to accept the blame for their negligence would help bring about some kind of closure to that heart-rending chapter, but of course it didn't.

And, as I was to discover, there are stories that simply never seem to end, and instead go round and round in circles. Some time later I was invited on to a prominent radio programme and, during the broadcast, the presenter reminded the listeners that I had experienced some tough times. I sensed that he wanted to revisit Betty's story, so to deflect attention, I spoke about my assault in 2010 and the bungling efforts by the guardians of the peace to solve the crime. The presenter found the story hilarious, exclaiming, 'You can't be serious.'

The next day, when I was back working in my studio, the doorbell rang. I opened it and beheld two men in dark blue uniforms: one a rather tall sergeant, the other a smaller garda.

'We've come to talk to you about the assault.'

Flann O'Brien couldn't have made it up.

CHAPTER 2

Grief

G rief is difficult to understand – impossible to explain.
Some time after Betty died I encountered the writer Dermot
Bolger, whose own wife, Bernie, died in not-too-dissimilar
tragic circumstances. He offered his condolences and then, curiously,
welcomed me into an exclusive club that, for certain, has no eager
waiting list for membership – the society of the recently bereaved.

We both agreed that the essential benefit of membership is the full
understanding that, even if the rest of the world can't possibly appreciate
our unique anguish, we, the bereaved, intuitively empathize with one
another; this in spite of the fact that no two individuals' experience
of grief will be exactly the same. Obviously, death is something that
every being on the planet will experience at some time or another,
yet strangely, we never seem prepared when it makes a personal call.

There are no apprenticeships – no dress rehearsals. I believe it's
important to recognize that grief is not one specific emotion, but a
powerful combination of uncontrollable responses to a traumatic
life event: no wonder the bereaved are characterized as grief-*stricken*.

Incredibly, many people who suffer the death of a loved one find
the numbing effect of shock quite enabling as a way of dealing with

such a dire experience. Certainly, in my case, this conjecture offers the only possible explanation for how I was able to conduct myself with reasonable propriety during the hectic days that followed Betty's death. I recollect that on a few occasions, when alone, I succumbed to a giddy, lightheaded feeling of spurious liberation, based on the contradictory notion that, being dead, Betty was far better off, since she no longer had to endure illness or pain. I understand that such an outlandish response, resulting from shock, is not uncommon.

And then there's anger. For the bereaved, anger seems an inescapable reality. Some feel aggrieved with the person who has died, who has abandoned them. I have to say that this was not my experience. Others rage at God: 'Why did He allow this to happen?' Since I didn't even accept his existence, I considered that particular response totally irrational. My anger was directed solely at those responsible for Betty's health, who failed miserably in their duty of care. However, in order to retain some semblance of sanity, I decided to withdraw from the day-to-day struggle for justice and instead request that my solicitor pursue the case.

If I hadn't done that, I'm convinced that I would have simply burned up with rage. When a loved one dies, the survivor unavoidably surrenders to acute feelings of guilt. For example, I still find myself asking, 'Could I have done more?' and especially, 'Why wasn't I with Betty during her last moments?'

Of course, I can't alter the past, but those corrosive thoughts will haunt me for the rest of my days.

Naturally, when one of a couple dies, the survivor experiences a keen sense of loss; and the depth of that feeling is often in direct proportion to the length of time they were together. I met Betty when she was sixteen and she died aged sixty-one, so we were a couple for forty-five years. We were an enduring partnership.

After Betty died, I became aware very quickly of the many practical tasks that she performed. For example, she looked after all money matters. She dealt with the bank, insurance companies and other financial institutions as well as paying all the bills. If we were a company, she would have been both chief executive officer and financial controller.

In the beginning I was at a complete loss, but I had no choice. I had to jump in at the deep end and attempt to manage the monetary situation myself. In the home, to my shame, Betty discharged most domestic duties. She took on responsibility for cleaning, washing and, most significantly, cooking. She was an excellent cook. After she died, I received sympathy letters from several people who grew up on our street, admitting that everything they knew about food they had learned from watching Betty in her kitchen.

I was obliged to take on the execution of all those necessary home duties, with, as it turned out, varied levels of accomplishment. I found that there was no alternative but to learn how to cope on my own.

Unfortunately, as I was to discover, there were other more significant losses that were not so easily overcome.

In our lifetime together we must have done a lot of talking, because one of the aspects of our relationship that I miss most are the many conversations we shared. We discussed everything from the banal to the most serious subjects, and when we tackled critical issues I always valued Betty's opinion. In a way, she was my moral compass. Without her, I am adrift.

And, in the course of almost four decades as an artist, I cannot think of a single picture of mine that wasn't improved by constructive comment by Betty on the work in progress. She was the only art critic that I ever listened to; but sadly now I can only surmise what she might say – a poor substitute!

One fairly obvious aspect of a life lived alone following the death of a loved one is the loss of intimacy. Now, by intimacy, I don't necessarily mean copulation – after all, in older couples this can be occasional enough. What I am referring to here is much more casual, but is nonetheless an essential part of any special relationship. It consists of, for example, the occasional hug, a considerate arm on the shoulder, an affectionate kiss on the cheek or the tender clasping of hands. The treasured memory of such small personal intimacies persists long after the loved one has gone.

It's important to accept that grief is not a medical condition – there are no pills to cure it – in fact, it is a natural process, and thankfully healing is part of that process.

There can be no doubt that nature helps us get through these traumatic experiences. For example, today I find that when I think of Betty my memory banks swell with recollections of the many good times we had together, whereas thoughts of dark and difficult experiences seem to sink to the bottom and become almost impossible to retrieve.

Nevertheless, in spite of nature's best efforts, I still have a Betty -shaped void at the centre of my life; there seems to be a portion of me missing, the part that went to form the couple we once were.

CHAPTER 3

Suffer the Little Children

Ifucking hate exams. Even today, whenever I observe the serried ranks of young unfortunates being herded into examination halls around the country, an involuntary spasm of queasiness strikes me. Considering that over half a century has lapsed since I sat my last exam, it's amazing that such emotional scar tissue still chafes.

The Leaving Certificate marks the climax of a young person's schooling in Ireland. Unfortunately, I made a balls of it, especially the drawing exam. In those days art was not an approved subject. Instead we were taught drawing, and our ability to draw or sketch was examined at the end of each year. When I first entered John Coyle's art class in Blackrock College I observed a circle of boys gathered around a pile of disparate objects, each attempting to translate what they saw in front of them onto a sheet of paper using only a pencil and a rubber or eraser. I immediately noticed copious use of the rubber as clumsy hands attempted to correct awkward scratchings. I joined the circle of fumblers and in no time at all, unearthed a buried talent for making sense of what I saw and conveying that knowledge to the paper in front of me. After a few more weeks creating rudimentary still-life drawings, I felt a tap on my shoulder and was quietly instructed by John Coyle to gather my belongings, go to the top table and join a few other lads who were beavering away at something else. John Coyle explained that since I had demonstrated that I could draw, now was my chance to show if I could do something imaginative with that talent.

The art class was a life-saver for me because, at last, I was able to appreciate that I was good at something. This was real compensation for being utterly hopeless at what was considered to be the greatest achievement possible at that school – the ability to play rugby football. For me, John Coyle's art class was an oasis of enlightenment in a desert of ignorance and stupidity.

It was expected that I would do well in the Leaving Certificate drawing exam; what was not expected was the chain-smoking habit of the supervisor. Every few minutes he slipped out of the room where the exam was taking place.

In no time at all the lads deciphered a definite pattern, so during his frequent absences individuals pleaded with me to start them off by sketching in the lines of the still life from their particular perspective. One result was that I probably helped a few inept draughtsmen pass the drawing exam. On the other hand, because I spent so much time on this illegitimate activity, my own efforts were a fucking disaster, resulting in failure to achieve an honour in my best subject.

Another unexpected intervention occurred at the beginning of the exam cycle. Because I was always a quick finisher, I was delighted with the Department of Education rules which stated that any student could leave the exam hall after twenty minutes. Certainly I took this to mean that I was no longer bound by college rules, which insisted that everyone remain in place until the bitter end.

After I finished the first exam I packed up my things and left, only to find a priest, the dean of discipline, pacing about the corridor outside the exam hall.

'And what do you think you are doing?' he bellowed.

I nervously quoted the Department of Education rules as my excuse.

'This is not the Department of Education,' he thundered. 'This is Blackrock College and while you are in Blackrock College you will obey Blackrock College rules!'

Probably because of naked fear, no further early exits were attempted; however, as the end of the exams approached I became emboldened and, having finished the final exam well within the designated time limit, decided to clear out. When I exited the exam hall, there he was, once again lurking in the corridor.

He addressed me with menace in his voice: 'Follow me!'

Opening a nearby locker room, he ushered me into the small space. Naturally I was expecting a severe bollocking, but I have to admit I was gobsmacked by what followed. He quickly turned his back to me, locked the door then spun about, throwing back his cape; and like one of *The Three Musketeers*, unfurled his bamboo cane and began making wild jabs in my direction. I was so surprised by this turn of events that my immediate response was simply to cower and raise my arms in pathetic self-defence. This instant reaction did prove somewhat successful, as only the odd lunge broke through and nipped me on the ear or slashed across my hands. After a few minutes the reverend gentleman, his face flushed and his glasses all steamed up, was spent. He turned rapidly away, unlocked the door and stormed out, muttering something like 'Let that be a lesson to you!'

I reflected with some irony, *What a fitting clerical farewell to a decade of care in the hands of Holy Mother Church.*

From my first encounter with the reverend fathers I found their attitudes and particularly their pronouncements puzzling, although my own personal circumstances probably played some part in this. I was the child of a 'mixed marriage'. In most places that phrase might imply a difference in race, but in holy Ireland it meant only one thing: a difference in religion – and, fuck me, did that bring complications.

My mother was a Roman Catholic and my father a Presbyterian, so in order to get married my father was obliged to sign up to what was called the *Ne Temere* decree. The main effect of this was a promise that any child from the union would be handed over to the Catholic Church to be educated. In my case, uncertainty and confusion emerged at an early stage. For example, during religious knowledge class we were told frequently and enthusiastically that only Catholics could pass through the pearly gates into heaven. Can you imagine how, as a six or seven year old, I was affected by that pronouncement? I wanted to scream, 'What about my da?' but because I felt utterly powerless, I kept my mouth shut.

Another idiotic diktat informed us that it was a sin to enter a Protestant church. Again this was a problem for me, as I lived opposite St Bartholomew's Church, a branch of the (Anglican) Church of Ireland, and among my playmates were the vicar's children. One of our favourite games was 'hide and seek', and obviously the old church was a perfect location for concealment. In order to be successful in this innocent pastime I was obliged to deny the rules of my religion and hide in the actual church building. Even as a small child I was learning fast that the Roman Catholic Church was a bit like a stern parent, strong on rules but short on love and affection. But worse was to come.

Before we had a bull's notion of what they were talking about we were being cautioned by the reverend fathers against the dangers that sex posed to our immortal souls. Very quickly we picked up a whole new lexicon dealing with an area of human activity that for most of us was a complete mystery. In spite of this initial bewilderment, we soon found ourselves able to ponder such infelicitous topics as 'bad thoughts', 'heavy petting' and 'nocturnal emissions' without a moment's hesitation.

Another destructive attack on our innocence was a fierce determination to cast at least half the human race as a source of demonic temptation. The instructions we received on this tricky subject proved unhelpful, if not contradictory. On the one hand we were informed that since girls were 'temples of the Holy Ghost', we should treat them with the utmost respect; yet at the same time, it was suggested that best practice might be to avoid them completely, as they presented the danger of terrible temptation.

In my experience, the holy fathers advocated the latter, since I was threatened with expulsion from school on several occasions for daring to talk to girls whenever that rare opportunity arose. Once, at a football match, a few of us met some girls from a nearby convent. Unfortunately some eager cleric noted our behaviour, and as a result our parents were summoned to the school to account for our 'immoral conduct'.

On his return, my puzzled father wondered what had happened.

'We were talking to some girls,' I honestly explained.

'That's all?' was his disbelieving response, followed by a barely audible, 'Bloody priests!'

As if fashioning a moral straitjacket to encourage sexual continence wasn't enough, the Holy Ghost fathers had other instruments of torture for the young boys in their care. Their religious order came to Ireland from France in the nineteenth century, tasked with educating the new middle-class Catholics who were taking their place in society following Catholic Emancipation. There is no evidence to suggest that their zeal in that regard had diminished in any way by the time I encountered them in the 1950s.

At the end of each week day boys were obliged to take home a *Judgement Book*, get it signed by a parent and then return it to the school. This book contained marks of assessment for each subject and if, terror of terrors, the total for any two subjects added up to less than nine, the unfortunate pupil was consigned to the Black List. Frequently this mortification gave rise to pathetic attempts at forgery and erasure, whose ineptitude only resulted in further torment.

In my own case this nonsense caused me little concern, as I always managed to gain sufficient marks to remain safely outside the danger zone. However there were two categories at the top of each page devoted to conduct and deportment that to my untutored mind were a total enigma; but since I seemed to automatically receive top marks every week, I decided to pay them scant attention.

Out of such complacency disaster looms.

Some time later, as we all sat at assembly in the Jubilee Hall listening to our weekly results, I was shocked and dismayed to hear my name announced in public as part of the dreaded Black List. I had received dismal marks in both conduct and deportment. Apparently a nosy priest had spotted a few of us in a nearby park talking to some girls, smoking cigarettes and, worst of all, wearing trousers of the 'blue denim variety'.

For some reason the reverend fathers seemed to take grave exception to such garments, and never tired of reminding us that the material involved might make suitable work clothes for tradesmen, but was totally inappropriate for Blackrock College boys.

The president of the college, seizing on the revelation of this unfortunate affair, began to drone on about the dangers of 'company keeping' and 'corner boy' conduct, when suddenly, warming to his topic, he changed tack and began to stress the fact that we were not Christian Brother boys, destined to be 'hewers of wood and drawers of water'. Our fate was to become the future leaders of Irish society, and for that reason alone each and every one of us carried an onerous responsibility to behave in an appropriate manner on all occasions. As I sat dumbfounded in the hall surrounded by hundreds of impressionable young men, I remember thinking, *Has he gone completely fecking bonkers? Surely he recognizes, like I do, that most of my schoolmates are messers and eejits and as such can never amount to much.*

But of course, as was often the case, I was mistaken; and the passage of time witnessed the vindication of the president's hypothesis, with most of the messers and eejits gaining entrance to the ranks of Ireland's professional elite.

In our society, privilege always wins the race. As I prepared to walk out through the front gates of Blackrock College for the last time, John Coyle came up and wished me well, suggesting that if I wanted to become an artist I had the necessary talent. That generous assessment had some bearing on a family conference that was convened some time later. As often happened on such occasions, my mother did most of the talking.

She began by assuring me of my parents' wholehearted support for whatever choice of career I fancied – with one exception: art was simply out of the question. The life of a painter was not an option for her only son. Strange as it seems, I appreciated my mother's attitude. She was a very conservative woman with social pretensions and would have viewed the life of a painter as foolhardy and reckless. Also, the tragic suicide of my cousin Noah Durley, himself a talented artist, would have wholly confirmed her negative appraisal of the artist's lot. My mother and Noah's mother were sisters. Ruth Durley was not only a well-known performer on the Dublin stage of the 1950s, but also published a biography of the celebrated actress Sarah Siddons. As a kid I was always in awe of my cousin Noah's prodigious talents for drawing and painting; his abilities seemed far in advance of his years. He also played the drums and his music of choice was jazz. After finishing school, Noah travelled to London to seek his fortune, but while there tragedy struck. Apparently, when his girlfriend left him he fell into a deep depression and, broken-hearted, took his own life.

Even though my mother was dead set against me going to art college I wasn't too disappointed. There was a simple explanation. I had already surreptitiously embarked on my own chosen path as a rock 'n' roll musician, and this boisterous commitment sucked up all my creative passion. Of course my parents would have judged things differently, and would have assessed the music thing as no more than a passing fad; so naturally they still hoped that I would make an acceptable career choice. I opted for architecture and this turned out to be a providential decision.

My parents on their wedding day.

Because of the mess I made of the Leaving Cert, my exam results proved insufficient for me to gain entrance to the architectural course in Bolton Street College of Technology, but much to my surprise I was called for an interview. After this, even more curiously, I was offered a place. Naturally I assumed that my interview must have gone really well, but on my first day in college I figured out the real explanation for my successful admission. There were supposed to be thirty students in the first year but the complete tally only came to twenty-eight.

We all nervously gathered in the college auditorium for our very first lecture, only to be taken aback by our tutor who, holding aloft a small item, solemnly declared, 'This is a pencil.'

After explaining, in some detail, the correct manipulation of the pencil, he went on to demonstrate the proper utilization of both the T-square and the setsquare. We were then let loose in the studio to discover if we had picked up anything from our initial instruction. Eventually, after many false starts, most of us found ourselves sufficiently proficient to take on our first major project, which was to draw and

A bunch of cousins: Noah Durley is on the left and I'm on the far right.

render in watercolour a Doric column, capital and entablature. This turned out to be an impossibly difficult task, which almost broke my spirit; but, with dogged persistence, I managed to just about complete the required drawing.

In the course of our first year, most of us ended up becoming reasonably competent draughtsmen. This training proved invaluable in my later work as an artist, for I always design a painting rather as an architect designs a building. Everything is calculated and worked out using tracing paper and T-square, setsquare and pencil on a drawing board, before being transferred to canvas. Nothing is left to chance.

For my first two years in Bolton Street I was most fortunate that my main tutor was the architect Robin Walker, who had worked with Le Corbusier in France and Mies van der Rohe in Chicago. He had just returned to Ireland from the United States and was a passionate proselytizer for modernist architecture.

It was like Moses coming down from the mount. We were getting the message first-hand. His lectures were enormously exciting. Robin Walker laid emphasis on a practical approach to problem solving. There had to be a logic and a reason behind everything: essentially the Miesian principle, 'Form follows function.'

Unfortunately, however, when I advanced to my third year Robin Walker did not follow and, as a result, certainty was replaced by confusion. At the time, all the energies of the profession seemed to be concentrated on creating more and more office blocks; yet at the same time, Dublin had an appalling housing shortage. Every week the homeless were out on the streets in protests organized by the Dublin Housing Action Committee. I was becoming involved in a profession that seemed to be totally cynical. Architects wouldn't acknowledge that they had a social role. They insisted that a building was a building and that their only responsibility was to ensure that it was well designed. That was a delusion; in reality the profession was a hostage to the greed of developers and speculators.

As I pondered whether to persist with my architectural studies, a curious occurrence towards the end of my third year helped me make up my mind.

While in college I played music semi-professionally and, as ill luck would have it, the night before an important building construction exam I found myself in Derry performing with a band.

Arriving back in Dublin at nine in the morning, I was deposited outside the college and promptly fell fast asleep in the course of the exam. Naturally I failed, but permission to repeat the exam and advance to the fourth year was refused. I was told that I would have to repeat the entire third year, in spite of having passed everything except the building construction exam. I felt that this was terribly unfair, so I opted instead to exchange my life as a student for that of a full-time musician.

CHAPTER 4

Rock 'n' Roll Daze

One evening in 1956, when I was just thirteen, my father issued an unexpected invitation: 'Come on, let's go to the pictures!' And then, out of my mother's earshot, he whispered, 'We're going to *Rock Around the Clock* at the Carlton.'

I detected a shiver of excitement in his voice, probably caused by the not inconsiderable controversy already surrounding the film. Like all youthful crazes, *Rock Around the Clock* was greeted by an almost totally negative response from the older generation. Newspapers were full of wild stories of dancing in the aisles, slashing of seats, riots inside and outside cinemas and as if to confirm such a dangerous possibility, when we arrived in O'Connell Street we noticed something really unusual: policemen standing guard outside the cinema. Undeterred, we made our way through the modest cordon, bought our tickets, took up our seats and nervously awaited the screening. Unlike my father, who hadn't a clue, I did harbour an inkling as to what we were about to experience.

One year before, I'd been to see the film *Blackboard Jungle* starring Glenn Ford as a harassed teacher dealing with unruly schoolkids. It wasn't a bad movie, but the one element that caught my full attention was the song played over the opening credits. I'd never heard anything like it before. Its jump band beat with dramatic rimshots, thumping double bass and twanging guitar breaks briefly opened a door to new musical horizons that cruelly slammed shut moments later.

Like all fresh addicts I craved more. That song was 'Rock Around the Clock', and unbelievably there I was, once again in a Dublin cinema, about to see a movie of the same name. Of course I wasn't the only person in the cinema breathlessly awaiting the start of the film. The whole audience seemed to be quivering in restless anticipation. And, on cue, the first flickering images prompted raucous shouting and cheering. Braver souls, mostly Teddy Boys and their partners, could barely wait for the music to kick in before rushing to the aisles to jive and jitterbug. This enthusiastic exertion continued unabated until the end of the final reel. You can appreciate how unlikely it would have been for a thirteen year old in the presence of his father to join the unfolding mayhem, yet as a passionate witness I eagerly absorbed it all.

For a start, I adored the style of the Teddy Boys. I loved their drain-pipe trousers, their shoes with thick crepe soles called 'brothel creepers', and their three-quarter-length Edwardian-styled jackets. The whole conglomeration was topped off with a magnificently oiled coiffure that featured a fascinating combed effect at the rear known as a DA or 'duck's arse'. Sadly, at the time I could only dream of such attire, because of wardrobe constraints imposed both at home and at school.

As we left the cinema my father remarked that the film wasn't too bad, if a bit loud, and thankfully there was no real trouble. I felt that for him it was a one-off experience, whereas I knew I would return time and time again.

This perverse addiction was not caused by the quality of the actual film; it was fuelled by an unslaked desire to see the music itself being played by real musicians on screen. Up until then, rock 'n' roll music, as far as we Irish were concerned, was all sound and no vision. Now, at last, we could see real rock 'n' roll stars in action, belting out their hits as long as we had the price of admission. As far as I was concerned the opening machine gun-like rimshots and accompanying vocal – 'One, two, three o'clock, four o'clock rock' – represented nothing less than the countdown to teenage liberation, and I couldn't get enough of it.

Many years later I was to discover the genesis of the music that so entranced me. I learned how black musicians were unable to play to white audiences because of the deeply segregated nature of American society, and how white musicians, taking advantage of this absence, blended country and western music with rhythm and blues, creating a new musical form which they performed to enthusiastic young white audiences that had been starved of authentic musical excitement for years. Of course, on this side of the Atlantic, all that meant nothing to a young teenager like me. As far as I was concerned, it was simply the rebellious sound that mattered. Mind you, as a slightly chubby, clean-cut twenty-nine year old, clad in plaid with a kiss curl in the middle of his forehead, Bill Haley was the most unlikely leader of a teenage rebellion; and as it turned out, his reign was destined to be short. In that same year of 1956, 'Heartbreak Hotel', a bluesy tale of teenage angst and alienation stormed up the US charts, rewarding its singer, a young white kid from Tupelo, Mississippi with his first number one

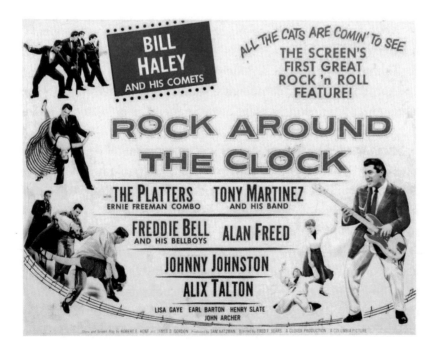

hit. He was called Elvis Presley. Even the name sounded weird. When Scotty Moore, who played guitar with Elvis, first heard it, he said it reminded him of 'a name straight out of science fiction'. As for me in Dublin, Ireland, my initial exposure to that eerie echo-drenched opening line, 'Well since my baby left me', captured me body and soul; and when I saw black-and-white photos of Elvis, with hair quiffed and lip curled, looking mean, moody and magnificent like James Dean or Marlon Brando, it confirmed my belief that this guy was the real deal, a proper teenage rebel.

As a repressed thirteen year old in the grey Ireland of the 1950s, my teenage heart ached to be part of this unbelievably exciting revolt. But what? I'm afraid the only response I could muster was to gather up my meagre savings and head off to the Gramophone Shop, a dark cavernous place sited in Johnston's Court off Grafton Street, which I have to say looked decidedly unpromising. The walls of the shop were brown; in fact the whole place seemed brown, relieved only by black-and-white posters of singers like Count John McCormack and Beniamino Gigli. Without question this was an unlikely haunt for a rock 'n' roll virgin.

Nonetheless, overcoming my nervousness and embarrassment I managed to blurt out, 'Have you got "Heartbreak Hotel" by Elvis Presley?'

To my enormous relief, nobody in the shop laughed or giggled, and the assistant, after rummaging about a bit, handed me a rather large object wrapped in a plain brown paper sleeve. 'Would you like to hear it?' she inquired.

I was startled by her question. I was unaware that if you were considering the purchase of a record you could listen to it before making your decision; in fact, the shop provided several booths for this very purpose. However, the idea completely unnerved me. All I wanted was to hightail it out of the shop.

'No, thanks,' I spluttered, as I struggled to pay for the first record in my collection and, ironically, perhaps the last.

Allow me to explain. With great care I carried home the treasured object, a twelve-inch disc of shiny black shellac, and gingerly placed it on a shelf in my bedroom. Believe it or not, that's all I could do. Like many other Irish families at the time, we didn't have a record player. In my thoughtless pursuit of rebellion I had managed to convert what should have been a noisy exemplar of teenage revolt into a very quiet object of veneration on a shelf in my bedroom. I was like those worshippers who believed that a true relic of some medieval saint – a finger, a thigh bone perhaps, even a pelvis, could connect them in some spiritual way to the greatness of the holy one. I didn't know how long I could maintain this idiotic silent veneration, but fortunately, help was at hand. My grandmother must have got wind of my doleful predicament, because one day on returning home from school, I stumbled across a large venerable wooden contraption in the middle of our living room.

It had been delivered from my grandmother's house. I gently raised the lid, which was circumscribed with rather extravagant moulding. I realized that this elaborate box was an old-fashioned gramophone. Inside was a turntable, a hollow metal arm, a dial to adjust the speed and a small recessed dish containing several sharp metal needles. There was also a loose handle which slotted into a hole on the left-hand side. The front panel was an elaborate venetian blind-like affair controlled by a wooden knob on the right-hand side. Later, I was to learn that when you turned the knob one way the wooden slats opened, releasing full volume; turned the other way, the slats closed and a fairly muffled sound was all that could be heard. Basic but functional: I couldn't wait to give it a go. I rushed to my room and retrieved my one and only record, and, having removed it from its plain brown paper wrapper, carefully placed it on the turntable. I put a new needle on the business end of the metal arm and adjusted the speed dial to 78 revolutions per minute. Shaking with excitement I wound the handle, opened the wooden slats and placed the needle on the now revolving disc. After a few seconds of surface noise, the echo-laden voice of Elvis Presley shattered the silence of my parents' basement flat.

> Well, since my baby left me,
> I found a new place to dwell,
> It's down the end of Lonely Street,
> Called Heartbreak Hotel.

Fantastic! I felt that nothing could stop me now. Without a moment's hesitation I resolved to double the size of my record collection. My second choice, 'Rock Around the Clock', was probably inspired by slight pangs of regret; after all, almost on a whim, I had only just abandoned the Comets for the subversive allure of Elvis Presley. Yet, in spite of all that, I was surprisingly pleased that repeated plays only confirmed my earlier appreciation of the boogie-woogie beat, the slapping double bass and Danny Cedrone's tremulous guitar breaks. In those days, with absolutely no popular music being played on either Irish Radio or the BBC, my generation was forced to get its rock 'n' roll fix by listening to Radio Luxembourg – '208 on the dial!' This unauthorized service was beamed to us after teatime and tended to fade in and out depending on the weather and the signal; nevertheless, most nights in bed, with the covers pulled up and pretending to be asleep, I succumbed to the illicit joys dispensed by the early pioneers of rock 'n' roll. The wayward genius who really grabbed my attention was Richard Wayne Penniman, better known as Little Richard. His first hit, a frenzied vocal called 'Tutti Frutti', was a rousing mix of gospel, jump blues and boogie-woogie piano. On my first hearing I could scarcely believe my ears; but after the second rock 'n' roll film, *The Girl Can't Help It*, was released featuring Little Richard's performance, I had to accept that I also couldn't believe my eyes. What an exotic creature! With his pompadour hairstyle, eye make-up, pencil-thin moustache, baggy trousers and frantic stage behaviour, he was guaranteed to shock the bejaysus out of most parents. I loved him.

'Goodness gracious, great balls of fire' has to be one of the greatest lines in the history of rock 'n' roll, and in 1957, when the southern twang of Jerry Lee Lewis was combined with his piano-pounding rhythms, left hand doing the boogie-woogie but right hand zipping all over the place, a rock classic was born. I knew I had to add this exuberant recording to my expanding collection, but even though I continued to draw great satisfaction from my records it slowly dawned on me that to stretch myself I needed to move beyond listening and begin participating. So, despite having no previous musical training, I made the decision to take up the guitar.

I scrimped and saved until I managed to scrape together the £5 necessary to secure an acoustic Spanish-style guitar. It wasn't much, but it was all I could afford. After getting it home safely I'm embarrassed to admit that my initial engagement with the instrument had more to do with posing than playing. Later, when I eventually got around to trying to coax some music from the thing, my efforts proved singularly inept. I think I might have abandoned the whole notion there and then if it hadn't been for one Lonnie Donegan.

In 1957 he recorded 'Rock Island Line', which in turn launched the short-lived skiffle craze. The Glasgow-born singer had taken an American folk song, first recorded by blues singer Lead Belly in 1930, and with his high-pitched nasal delivery created the perfect vehicle for young impressionable lads to emulate, which we did in droves.

At the time it seemed like everybody was in a skiffle group. All you needed was someone to strum an acoustic guitar, another to scratch away at a washboard and someone else to pluck a homemade bass, easily fashioned from an old tea chest, a broom handle and a length of string. On a personal level I wasn't mad about the skiffle sound, but I wasn't going to ignore an obviously free pass into the world of popular music; and as luck would have it, as I sought to expand my skiffle repertoire I slowly realized that at the root of most songs lay a particular musical structure. For example, if a song was in the key of G, then the accompanying G major chord would be followed first by a C major chord, then a D7 chord, before returning to the G major chord once again, and this harmonic journey would always be completed in twelve bars of music. I had accidentally stumbled on the musical basis of most popular tunes.

Music snobs and cynics tended to dismiss this formula with the disparaging phrase *three-chord trick*, but for a novice like me it represented much more – a liberation of sorts. I now felt ready to take on the world.

Sadly this newly empowered feeling was not to last. By 1958 a new sound came thundering across the Atlantic and skiffle hadn't a chance. 'Rebel Rouser' by Duane Eddy was an echo-drenched mix of twangy electric guitar, screaming saxophone and well-placed southern whoops and hollers. I'd never heard anything quite like it before. The tune, played on the lower strings of the guitar, was richly embellished with electronic tremolo and echo effects. Occasional notes were dramatically bent using a manual tremolo arm. The resultant sound was both resonant and haunting. I was entranced, and I knew one thing for certain: I had to go electric.

Easier said than done, as I was to discover. At that time Dublin music shops had a very disappointing range of electric guitars on offer, usually semi-acoustic models of German manufacture that looked like they might be strummed by some fat geezer wearing lederhosen in a band featuring tubas and accordions. Certainly no sign at all of those elegant guitars that I had seen on film and in photos being played by serious rock 'n' rollers.

All of this window shopping was a waste of fucking time, since even if a suitable instrument was available, I simply hadn't the necessary cash. There was only one possible solution. I would have to make my own electric guitar.

I suppose it was inevitable that I would seek to model my efforts on Duane Eddy's magnificent Gretsch guitar, perhaps in the forlorn

Elgin Road in 2009. This leafy suburb has hardly changed since the 1950s.

hope that when finished it might reproduce that special sound. When it came to drawing up the plans, however, I was at a distinct disadvantage. Having never seen nor held a Gretsch guitar I was forced to sketch out the shapes and contours using black-and-white publicity photos as reference material. In no time at all and by dint of perseverance, I had the basic form of the guitar successfully constructed and prepared to face the awesome task of installing the frets. I say awesome because the job demanded a tolerance of one sixty-fourth of an inch. I must have done something right because the finished guitar for the most part played in tune. Because I was always hopeless at science I realized straight away that I had nothing substantial to contribute to the next phase of the build, the part that would electrify the instrument, but I had a plan. I would approach my friend and neighbour Gerald Burne. I was aware that he harboured no great interest in music, but he was passionate about electronics.

The commodious houses on Elgin Road, a quite leafy thoroughfare in south Dublin, were built originally to house families of senior civil servants working for the British administration in nineteenth-century Ireland, but by the 1940s the British had long gone and a way of life with them; so individual houses became non-viable as single occupancies and ended up being divided into multiple lettings.

My parents rented the basement of No. 14, and the Burne family lived under the roof in the top flat. Even though there were two storeys and five flights of stairs in between, over the years the two families developed a close personal friendship that was both unique and special. Certainly from the very start, Gerald, the elder of two boys, and I became inseparable. We did everything together. As a small kid with curly brown hair, glasses and slightly prominent front teeth, Gerald definitely had the look of a boffin-in-waiting. All that was missing was a miniature white coat. And his temperament only confirmed that initial observation. No matter what question was asked of him, he almost automatically provided a ready answer.

Our first great joint undertaking was aeromodelling. The usual procedure was for each of us to buy a kit of a model aeroplane and then begin separate assemblies in our respective bedrooms. This involved cutting out delicate pieces of balsa wood, sticking them together to create the framework, covering this with fine tissue paper and coating the finished model with cellulose paint, called dope, which did indeed have a curiously intoxicating smell. There was always great excitement when the time to test-fly our new planes arrived. I don't know where it came from, but Gerald usually placed a time-worn brown leather pilot's helmet with goggles on his head and draped a dilapidated adult's leather waistcoat over his shirt and jumper before setting out for nearby Herbert Park, with his latest pride and joy tucked under his arm. I followed quickly behind carrying my handiwork, and the motley crew was completed by his younger brother Geoff who normally found himself press-ganged into carrying all the necessary equipment.

The model aircraft were powered by small noisy diesel engines and flew in a circle controlled by a budding aeronaut at the centre, who, by the use of wires, performed exhilarating aerobatics. However, the danger was that if control was lost, even for a split second, the little plane would plough into the ground with disastrous consequences. Many times we returned home unsure as to whether we could repair the damage or would have to start again with a new model.

I know that there's no explicable connection, but as I developed my interest in aeromodelling, I developed a parallel fascination with puppetry. I was aware that Gerald wasn't that keen, but nevertheless he decided to tag along. We both enjoyed making the puppets and building and painting the scenery, but neglected to spend much time on script-writing or directing; probably because we found that part of the exercise a bit boring. It was only when we inveigled some local kids into parting with threepence each to attend a performance that our naked unpreparedness became obvious. A few minutes after the curtain rose we ran out of things to say and do, and as a result started an unpleasant squabble backstage which quickly turned into a bitter altercation. The show finally descended into chaos after the two puppeteers fell through the scenery onto what was left of the stage. The members of the audience were not amused and rightly demanded their money back.

After that débâcle, my interest in puppetry fizzled out. I was surprised, nonetheless, that our mutual involvement in aeromodelling was also destined to come to a sudden halt. One day Gerald approached me and in grave tones declared, 'Aircraft represent the technology of the past. The future will be determined by rockets.' And then, continuing in hushed tones, he confided that he had encountered a formula that would produce a really powerful rocket propellant. It's worth noting that many years later, the provisional IRA would employ that same formula to demolish Canary Wharf as part of their bombing campaign in England. Our rockets were fashioned from aluminium tubes, packed with Gerald's fuel and then placed on a launch pad built some distance from the house. The back gardens on Elgin Road were divided by six-foot-high stone walls which, in our opinion, were perfect for clambering over and sheltering behind during the countdown to a launch. I have to say I really enjoyed watching the rockets take off with a whoosh and ascend vertically before finally disappearing from sight. On one occasion, however, as we sheltered behind the stone wall, there was a loud bang as a rocket exploded on the launch pad. Gerald immediately let out a great sigh. Initially I assumed it was one of disappointment, but then I realized he was hurt. In his anxiety to see what was going on he had unwittingly exposed himself and had been struck by a piece of shrapnel.

Unbelievably, his shirt was undamaged, but his chest displayed a small perfectly formed indentation on his skin in the shape of the map of Switzerland. He had a glazed look and must have been in some pain, but all he uttered was one word: 'Explosives.' At that moment I realized we were moving on to our next project.

There was a rusty battered old bike abandoned on a scrap heap at the end of the back garden, which Gerald confidently declared perfect for our purposes. Using a hacksaw we cut the frame up into several short lengths, packed them with the formula, crimped the ends and were ready to commence operations. We placed one of the devices on the launch pad, now renamed the detonation zone, lit the fuse and scrambled over the stone wall to await the explosion. It was the loudest bang I had ever heard. The windows in nearby homes rattled and for days afterwards neighbours talked about nothing else but the mystery explosion.

We decided that for our next detonation we would have to seek out a more secure location. We settled on one of the stone archways supporting the bridge that straddled the Dodder River at Ballsbridge. We were correct in calculating that no damage would be caused to either persons or property and that nobody would witness the installation of the device, but failed totally to take into account the acoustics of the situation. The archway, acting like a funnel, channelled the sound of the explosion towards where I was standing which, as it turned out, was far too close. As a result I was rendered stone deaf.

In the aftermath of the explosion and in order to evade suspicion, we decided to mingle with the bewildered burghers of Ballsbridge. I experienced the distinct, if surreal, impression that I had wandered onto the set of a silent movie. People spoke, but there was no hubbub of voices; dogs barked, but no audible yelps emerged; cars passed, but with no rackety engine noise. Everything was entirely mute.

This was not an experience I would care to repeat. After the Ballsbridge incident Gerald opted against any further adventures with ordnance and instead pursued his growing interest in electronics. As for me, I made up my mind that as soon as my hearing returned, I would commit myself to a much quieter pursuit, like rock music.

Naturally it was Gerald's newfound interest in electronics that convinced me he would be the ideal person to solve my electrification problem, and as usual when asked for help his response was quick and to the point: 'Sure, that's simple, all you need are six electromagnets.'

I scratched my head. 'What are they, and how the feck do I get them?'

With growing impatience at my stupidity he countered, 'They're everywhere. They're in every telephone. All you have to do is acquire some phones.'

I immediately speculated that a response to this advice might involve a criminal act. But what the hell – I had to have my electric guitar. To avoid recognition I cycled some distance from my home and with heavy heart vandalized two public telephone kiosks, whose contents provided me with a surplus of electromagnets. I wired six of them together, placed them in a prepared container and then poured hot wax over the lot. When set the unit was stable enough to be installed in position. We were now ready to conduct a test. We plugged the unit into the back of a radio and struck a chord. Nothing could be heard at first, but with some adjustment a sound emerged. But in my heart of hearts, I had to accept that it looked shite and worst of all, sounded absolutely terrible. Gerald was less disappointed with the result; after all, the experiment had worked. But from my point of view I knew it would never be acceptable. I reluctantly saved up and bought a commercially produced pick-up and with some regret consigned our contraption to the scrapheap.

The next phase in the electrification project was the production of an amplifier and, unlike the pick-up fiasco, this proved an unqualified success. By now Gerald Burne had left for England to study electronics but thankfully hadn't forgotten the amplifier issue. In his spare time he beavered away on the construction of what he insisted would be a fabulous guitar amp, and, on his first visit home, surprising us all, he proudly unveiled the product of his hard work: my brand-new amplifier. Without hesitation I plugged in my guitar and with some trepidation, waited for sounds to emerge. It really worked as he promised it would. It was fabulous! Gerald had installed a panel with a series of knobs and switches that controlled both volume and tone, but most exciting of all, there was a knob controlling a tremolo effect. I had not expected this. By turning the knob one way the electronic wobble accelerated, the other and it slowed down. I couldn't believe my luck. At last, after all the tribulations, I had my own electric guitar and amplifier and was primed to perform my chosen music.

This was 1958, and, as if on cue, the first decent rock 'n' roll record produced on this side of the Atlantic was released. It was 'Move It', performed by Cliff Richard and the Drifters, later to be renamed the Shadows. The compelling start featured an echo-laden guitar riff which descended by way of a tumbling glissade into a throbbing note on the lower E string. This was the real deal, and I was ready for active participation. About this time my parents belatedly decided to join the second half of the twentieth century and purchased one of the new-fangled gramophones that could play the seven-inch vinyl records called 45s. I immediately purchased 'Move It' in this brand-new format and, by playing short phrases over and over again, was able to learn the complete guitar part. I felt like a genuine rock star! But, of course, there was a hitch. Up until now I had been alone on my musical journey, however now I required the company of fellow travellers for the next stage of the trip.

CHAPTER 5

Group Therapy

I n 1959, during my penultimate year at school, some friends introduced me to Paul Hennessy, pointing out that he was another rock 'n' roll obsessive. Paul was a happy-go-lucky chap, always smiling, but if he was serious about anything it was music. He even went to guitar lessons. Early on we realized that we both shared a fascination with the guitar music being created by the Shadows, whose instrumental set-up of lead, rhythm and bass guitars and a drum kit followed the original template set by Buddy Holly and the Crickets when they recorded 'That'll Be the Day' in 1957. When Hank Marvin, the lead guitarist, chose as his instrument a Fender Stratocaster, he was following the example set by Buddy Holly. It was Hank Marvin's Stratocaster that helped create the unique and distinctive sound of the Shadows, a sound that we, even as absolute beginners, were determined to emulate.

Right from the start it was obvious that Paul had an excellent sense of rhythm, whereas mine was downright brutal, so by default he became the rhythm guitarist. An added bonus was that my faltering attempts at lead guitar were kept in perfect time by his skilful strumming.

In 1960 the Shadows had a solo number one hit with 'Apache', which we eagerly added to tunes we had already mastered like 'Walk Don't Run' by the Ventures and Bert Weedon's 'Guitar Boogie Shuffle', creating a small repertoire of guitar instrumentals. We spent a great deal of our time rehearsing, probably because we knew for certain that our efforts remained a bit raw for public consumption. Anyhow, during one busy session, Paul suddenly halted and declared, 'Something's missing!'

Perplexed, all I could muster was a meek, 'What?'

Without a shred of irony, he proclaimed, 'Drums!' This pretty obvious contention was followed unexpectedly by a remedial suggestion. 'We should recruit my next-door neighbour, Alan Devlin.'

'Ah, for fuck's sake!' I exploded. 'He's only a kid and anyhow he doesn't play drums!'

Admittedly the first part of my rebuttal was unfair, since Alan was only slightly younger than ourselves, but the second part was the unvarnished truth. On calming down I seriously considered Paul's proposition. Undoubtedly Alan was an extremely talented individual with an inbuilt ability to surmount most challenges. We were hoping that if he accepted our invitation, his next task might be to master the art of percussion. Alan not only accepted our offer but in no time at all developed the necessary skills to accompany our amateur musical exertions.

We were now a real band. A trio!

We felt that this breakthrough deserved a name. I can't remember whose idea it was, but we ended up calling ourselves the Trends.

Some time later I spotted a poster advertising a talent competition to be held in The Barn, a local community hall, and thought it would be a perfect occasion for the first public appearance of the Trends. We three musicians set about rehearsing our programme for the great event, which was due to take place on a Saturday. The qualifying heat was to be run during the afternoon and the final was scheduled for the evening. The Trends sailed through the heat; mind you, the opposition wasn't great – a few singers, an accordionist and someone playing the clarinet badly, all squeaks and whistles. After that we had a few hours to relax before the final. We agreed to meet at half-past seven and when I turned up slightly late, Paul ran up to me with panic written all over his face. 'Where the fuck's Alan?'

I hadn't a clue, but immediately suggested that we split up and conduct a search. I checked out the hall and surrounding area to no avail. Paul headed off to the nearby woods and was appalled to come across our drummer lying on his back encircled by empty cider bottles. With considerable difficulty, he managed to get Alan to his feet; and, having dragged him back to the hall, filled him up with black coffee. Meanwhile I moved the drum kit to the back wall so that if we succeeded in getting our inebriated drummer on stage he wouldn't fall backwards off his stool.

To tell the truth, probably because of the stress and strain of the occasion, I can't remember a thing about our performance, but in spite of everything they gave us first prize: a £5 note.

After the talent competition Alan seemed to tire of music and decided to quit the band. Many years later he became one of Ireland's leading actors, whose career was frequently and tragically undermined by a troublesome personality. Like Brendan Behan before him he was that modern phenomenon, a *celebrity*, who could never resist the temptation to 'act the maggot' in public, often emboldened by a surfeit of alcohol. On one occasion I was in a city centre pub when Alan came in, somewhat the worse for wear, demanding a pint.

'Sorry, Alan, we can't serve you,' asserted the publican. 'And don't show your face around here again until you're sober!'

Alan turned and disappeared out the door, only to return moments later wearing over his head a brown paper bag with torn-out holes for his mouth and eyes. 'Can I have a pint, please?'

It was another neighbour who recommended one of his schoolmates as a replacement for Alan. The potential candidate was Paul Loughlan, a curly blond-headed youth from Phibsboro on the Northside, alien territory to us Southsiders. But we were determined not to allow any geographical prejudices to stand in the way of his future involvement in the band; after all, not only could he play the drums, he had his own kit.

With Paul Loughlan on board things settled down. We began to practise again, and pretty quickly the Trends found themselves being asked to play the odd concert or tennis club hop.

This success, however, was crippled by feelings of doubt that were growing imperceptibly in my mind. Like Paul Hennessy before me, I sensed that something was missing. The answer was, of course, obvious: a bass guitar! But my response to this musical void was anything but normal. I began to fantasize that I could already hear the absent bass part in our music, and it was when I was in the grip of this delusion that I came across an advertisement in the *Evening Herald* stating that the Wolverines Showband were holding auditions for a new bass guitarist. On a whim I decided to apply. Naturally this posed a few problems. I'd never played a bass guitar and I didn't even own an instrument.

With an attitude of 'nothing ventured, nothing gained', I decided to rent a bass guitar for the audition and to chance my arm as far as the playing was concerned. Against all the odds, it must have gone well, because I was offered the job; but this being Ireland, nothing is ever quite that simple. Almost immediately after the audition the band split, and I found myself being offered the same job by the breakaway outfit, now called the Conchords Showband. In spite of any possible reservations I might have had, I decided to accept the invitation: 1960 was coming to a close, I was attending my final year in school, and unbelievably, I'd become a bass guitarist in a showband.

CHAPTER 6

The Showband Show

Perhaps this is as opportune time as any to investigate the Irish showband, a unique phenomenon, idolized and vilified in equal measure. However, as nothing ever takes place in isolation, some amateur sociology might be necessary. The 1950s in Ireland were a grim decade of economic stagnation and catastrophic levels of unemployment, so when Éamon de Valera stepped down as taoiseach in 1957 and was replaced by Seán Lemass, the new government, fearing the real possibility that the blighted state might not survive, reluctantly accepted that radical reform was simply unavoidable.

The failed economic policies of the past, based on notions of self-sufficiency and protectionism, were abandoned and swiftly replaced with the singular objective of encouraging foreign investment in the country. After some time this strategy appeared to bear fruit, to the extent that *Time* magazine published a picture of Seán Lemass on its front cover with the curiously ambiguous headline, 'There's life in the old sod!'

Anyway, with foreign factories springing up all over the country, many Irish people suddenly found that they had a few bob in their pockets, which, after years of forced privation, they were determined to spend on enjoying themselves. However, there was a difficulty: very few places of entertainment where young people could meet seemed to exist. Of course for young men there was always the pub, but young women were unable to join them; at that time, women were refused service in most bars. In the past, Irish people had always gone dancing, but the existing ballrooms were far too few to service the mushrooming demand. A new breed of entrepreneur spotted this potential and began erecting huge barn-like dance halls throughout the land, and the crowds who flocked into them obviously required live entertainment. This is where the showband enters the picture.

It's critically important to appreciate that the showband was unlike the rock group; the latter was in essence a by-product of the recording studio, only performing to live audiences to promote its hit records. The showband was an entirely different phenomenon. As part of the ballroom business, its purpose was both clear and simple. It was there to play live music for the dancing public. This basic fact informs many aspects of the showband story. For example, the showband line-up reflected the composition of the old dance bands that had performed exactly the same function in the past. The rhythm section of drums, piano, guitar and bass was retained and a much pared-down brass section added, usually consisting of trumpet, saxophone and trombone.

The 'show' element, in all probability, referred to the new practice of playing standing up rather than sitting down behind a serried row of music stands. Also many bands took to wearing flashy suits and engaging in what was referred to as 'the steps', a minimal form of choreography.

Irish dancers were discerning in their choice of music. They knew what they liked and, more significantly, what they disliked. They preferred music with an even tempo – less chance of clumsy mistakes with an unfamiliar partner – and certainly they did not like musical surprises; so it follows that they tended to favour well-known tunes. One obvious consequence was a dearth of original material in the showband repertoire, but to draw negative conclusions from the deficiency is, to my mind, a pointless exercise. In the ballroom world showbands who ignored the preferences of the dancing community did so at their peril, and the cruel reality was that dancers were their only public.

Very few people have a good word to say for them now, but I believe showbands played a very positive role in the social and cultural life of the country. In their heyday they entertained multitudes of people and, very significantly, provided well-paid jobs for thousands of musicians. In many ways the showband was the personification of the remarkable social and cultural changes that took place in the course of the 1960s in Ireland. When they toured the length and breadth of a country still struggling to break free from the shackles of failure, they instilled new feelings of hope and confidence by bringing excitement, colour and glamour into the lives of the ordinary people.

The first outfit to become really popular came from Derry City and was called the Clipper Carlton showband. They were swiftly followed by the Royal showband from Waterford; their vocalist was Brendan Boyer, who specialized in lively versions of Elvis Presley numbers. Butch Moore and the Capitol showband were also extremely popular with the newly expanded dancing public.

Ironically, it was further social changes that spelled the end of the showband era. It wasn't the most important issue for the women's movement, but many high-profile women, feeling diminished by being refused service in well-known bars, decided to take a stand. Articles appeared in many newspapers exposing the ridiculousness of the situation. For example some bars, in conceding ground, admitted that they were now willing to serve alcohol to women; but not pints of beer – only half pints – and those at an exorbitant price. With publicity like that, resistance to change collapsed, and finally women were acknowledged to have equal rights of access to the pubs of Ireland.

It's not surprising that women faced with the choice of being herded into draughty ballrooms and lined up on one side to be gaped at by half-drunken eejits on the other, or sitting in a comfortable chair in a pleasant lounge bar having a drink with friends and waiting for some interesting men to turn up selected, in their droves, the lounge bar option. The showband glory days were well and truly over.

When I joined the Conchords I knew feck all about the life of a showband musician. The first detail I learned about my fellow musicians was that they were semi-professionals, a designation inferring that they had day jobs and as a result were extremely careful that their musical commitments did not conflict with their occupational responsibilities. This attitude meant that they were fairly relaxed about rehearsals, did not appreciate having too many engagements – or gigs, as they were called – and certainly none too far from Dublin.

All of this suited me fine because, having left school, I was about to start my architectural studies. I now felt confident that I would be able to successfully juggle my time between music and college. After a few rehearsals and several gigs in small venues that all seemed to go well, we faced our first big challenge: a booking to perform at the Olympic ballroom just off Camden Street in Dublin, a dance hall not to be sneezed at, which even had its own resident orchestra.

When I arrived for the gig, I have to admit I was fucking petrified. This was a totally new experience. Nevertheless I was determined not to make a bollox of it. I calmly put on my band uniform, tuned my bass guitar and apprehensively bided my time. Then, at last, when it was our turn and we were making our way to the stage, a rather thin man, slightly balding and with a determined look on his face, suddenly and unexpectedly stood in front of me and declared, 'This man cannot go on stage – he is not a member of the union.'

My castigator, Jack Flahive, was leader of the resident orchestra and, as I was about to find out, general secretary of the Musicians' Union. I was both shocked and humiliated. I remember thinking to myself at the time, *Fucking hell, is this to be the end of my showband career before it's barely started?*

Meanwhile the band had no choice but to complete the engagement without the benefit of a bass guitarist, while I sat in the wings considering my fate. Later I was persuaded to apply to join the union, but was told I would first have to pass a musical proficiency test. These tests took place on Saturday mornings at the union's headquarters in Gardiner Street.

When I arrived, the entire place seemed infested with spotty youths, all clutching cheap guitars and waiting to be put through their paces.

When it was my turn I entered a basement room and was told to sit down and relax by Paddy Malone, president of the union, a somewhat ample but nonetheless pleasant character. The test was short in duration and required the budding musician to accompany several set pieces of music. Simple enough, you'd think, but I sensed that my efforts were dreadful, and once again questioned whether I had a future as a musician. You can imagine my joy and relief when, a few days later, I received my union card in the post. I was now a member of the Federation of Musicians of Ireland.

Some time later I remember meeting Paddy Malone and, on the spur of the moment, thanked him profusely for helping me pass the test.

'Nonsense,' he replied, and then dolefully added, 'You were the best that day!'

My fellow musicians in the Conchords – Alan on drums, Pascal on piano, Jimmy on saxophone and Christy on trumpet – were all long-standing members of the union and in all probability my union crisis arose because, being considerably older, it simply hadn't dawned on them that I might not be a member.

One custom I noticed at a very early stage was that they frequently referred to themselves as 'heads'. This was a reciprocal term that seasoned musicians used to describe their colleagues. Something else that became quite obvious to me was the existence of a great sense of camaraderie among musicians, a feeling of us against the world, which was continually reinforced by certain bizarre practices. One of those was the use of 'ben lang' or Cockney rhyming slang. Now, since I had spent a considerable part of my youth in various fleapits, I was already aware of this peculiar vernacular through exposure to certain English films: for example, the use of the phrase 'apples and pears' to designate stairs. For Irish 'heads', it became a far more convoluted affair.

One evening as I was playing poker, someone asked, 'Whose Benny is it?'

I was completely bamboozled and had to request an explanation. Benny, it turned out, was the diminutive for Benny McNeil, a well-known Irish trumpet player, which in this case was the rhyming slang for deal – as in, 'Whose deal is it?'

This complicated business was guaranteed to exclude outsiders.

Another form of musicians' language resembled a kind of racetrack tic-tac. I first came across it during a gig, when Pascal, the piano player, turned to me and pointed two fingers downwards in an inverted V gesture. Of course, at the time I hadn't a clue what he was on about; but afterwards he explained that two fingers down indicated that the tune in question was in a key with two flats, namely B flat. This system meant that, even in a very noisy situation, musicians could be informed with a simple gesture of the key of any particular tune. For a band that did a fair amount of busking, this routine proved a godsend.

Apart from myself, the other members of the band had been playing together for quite some time, and as a result had not only gained considerable experience but had also amassed a colossal back catalogue. Consequently, we found we could satisfy most musical requests that came from the dancefloor. We could serve up Dixieland jazz, Latin American music, old-time waltzes, céili music and a lot more besides; but there was one category that proved a major stumbling block, and that was the popular music of the day. At the time, the British beat boom was taking on the world, and everyone was listening to the Beatles and the Rolling Stones – but, sadly, not at our gigs.

I believe the constant turnover of vocalists in our band was an attempt to address this problem. One such vocalist was a chap called Tony; by day a typewriter salesman, at night, Roy Orbison. He did have black hair and dark glasses, but realistically, the resemblance stopped there; however, with a high-pitched voice he did manage to sound a bit like Roy. Naturally, he sang the whole Orbison catalogue but his *pièce de résistance* was 'In Dreams', a song, if attempted by a normal singer, that could result in permanent damage to the larynx. Yet every night, Tony soared effortlessly through the vocal to considerable appreciation. He also played the guitar. His instrument came with an echo unit which, with some ingenuity, he connected to the amplification system. When it was his turn to sing he was able to switch on the unit and instantly convert his voice into a rich, luxuriant, echo-laden affair. When finished, he immediately turned it off, which mean that in comparison the next vocalist sounded as dull as dishwater.

Those of us who performed occasional vocal duties were not too disappointed when Tony decided to move on.

The Conchords were never bound for show-business glory, but we did secure bookings for several prestigious events. One I clearly remember was a twenty-first birthday party organized by a Wicklow family that ran a successful poultry business. Against all the odds, they had managed to get Kenny Ball and his Jazzmen to fly over from London, for just one night, to play at the party. Their record 'Midnight in Moscow' had just become the number one hit in the UK, and they were already booked to appear on British TV the following night. Our role was as the supporting act, so naturally we were first on stage, which, by the way, was in a magnificent marquee – one of many tents, both large and small, that were scattered about the site interspersed by flickering oil lamps.

Our performance that night was greatly enhanced by the presence of our new singer, a young woman from Cabra called Pearl, whose versions of songs like 'Be My Baby' by the Ronettes and 'Will You Still Love Me Tomorrow' by the Shirelles added considerable sparkle to our repertoire. By the time we had come to the end of our session we felt we had acquitted ourselves well and were entitled to relax and enjoy the main act. Unlike other groups whose hit records were often manufactured in recording studios, the Jazzmen were a really good live band, featuring fine musicians, tight playing and excellent arrangements. We appreciated the live versions of their many hits and without question our listening pleasure was greatly enhanced by a generous supply of champagne.

But all good things must come to an end; so, in the early hours of the morning, we packed away our gear and set our course for Dublin. With the van in front, several cars following and myself bringing up the rear, we were making our way through the dark Wicklow hills when suddenly everything came to a shuddering halt. I remember thinking *Shite, not a fucking accident!*

But when I walked up to the front, I was able to make out, illuminated by the headlights of the succeeding car, the curious sight of my fellow musicians busy unloading the equipment from the van, unscrewing the backs of the speakers and revealing a haul of both poultry and bottles of booze, which had obviously been secreted in the course of the gig. This booty was then equally divided between all members of the band, including myself, despite not being in on the actual heist.

I really enjoyed being in the Conchords; I learned so much, and not just about music. But there was one issue that continually rankled, and that was the limiting nature of our repertoire. We just never seemed to get around to playing my kind of music. I longed to encounter some fellow musicians with similar tastes to mine, and together generate the real deal.

You can imagine my excitement when Terry Brady, the drummer with the Chessmen, a young rock 'n' roll outfit, contacted me to say that they were looking for a bass guitarist. Naturally I presumed that I was being headhunted on account of my obvious talent. The truth, which I was to learn later, was of course a little more complicated. At the time, a young attractive Swedish singer called Heidi was in the band, and Noel Pearson, the manager, who later went on to great fame as the producer of hit musicals and the Oscar-winning film *My Left Foot*, insisted that in order to preserve harmony, there were to be absolutely no romantic complications among the members.

However, like most individuals who introduce rules and then personally ignore them, Pearson himself began a liaison with Heidi. Phillip the bass player, who had fancied his own chances, was outraged and immediately quit. At rehearsal the following day, 22 November 1963, Terry Brady announced, somewhat distressed, 'Fucking terrible news – Phillip has left the band!'

Rather nonchalantly, Pearson responded, 'That's nothing. Kennedy has just been shot.'

CHAPTER 7

On the Road

My first rehearsal with the Chessmen went pretty well. I seemed to fit in without too much difficulty, probably because we were all young and dedicated to the music of our generation. The line-up was the typical rock group format: guitars, drums and, in our case, electric keyboards; perfect for playing the various parochial or community halls and sports clubs that were scattered around Dublin.

One such venue where we played fairly regularly was the Matt Talbot Hall in Granby Row, a narrow thoroughfare just behind Parnell Square West. It was owned by the Dominican order who operated a large church nearby on Dominick Street. The hall was named after a so-called holy man, Matt Talbot, a reformed alcoholic who had a penchant for self-mortification; one day on his way to mass, he finally expired just opposite the building which eventually would bear his name.

The dances in the hall were run by Sergeant Big Bill O'Sullivan, who operated strictly incognito – probably due to Garda regulations, which formally prohibited the engagement in private business by members of the force. Noel Pearson developed a special relationship with Sergeant Bill and persuaded him to provide us with a brand-new amplification system in exchange for a series of Saturday-night performances in the hall.

In order to conceal his covert career, the burly cop provided security himself at these dances; usually not a difficult task, since the clientele were mainly working-class teenagers from the north inner city. However, one particular Halloween night when we were playing, his cover was blown wide open. A fight broke out, and despite Big Bill's best efforts, it spread until nearly everyone in the hall was dragged into the fracas.

As was always the case in such contentious situations, we were instructed to keep on playing. However, you can imagine our astonishment when the squawking of Garda communications roared out from our speakers. In despair of restoring order by himself, Sergeant Bill had been forced to call the cops. They were already outside.

The exit door on one side of the hall was opened and then through the main door on the opposite side several guards with snarling dogs on leashes burst in. Within seconds the hall was cleared, leaving several items, like an oddly spinning high-heel shoe, scattered across the dancefloor.

I don't know whether that particular incident curtailed Sergeant Bill's ambitions as an impresario but, to his credit, he provided memorable entertainment for a largely working-class audience in Dublin's inner city. On one unforgettable night in the Matt Talbot Hall, we played support for Dusty Springfield. The fact that the hall was only a small ballroom in working-class Dublin in no way inhibited Dusty from delivering a stunning performance. The appreciative response from the packed hall was amazing.

In a remarkably short time we managed to build up a sizeable support base of screaming teenage girls and even a fan club, started by a girl from Crumlin. We, the members of the band, were thrilled with the enthusiastic response by Dublin's teenagers to our music, but Noel Pearson had his sights set higher; he wanted the band to play on the ballroom circuit where the venues were bigger, the crowds were bigger and the money was definitely bigger.

There was a problem, however. None of the ballrooms would book a rock group. There had to be at least seven musicians plus some brass instruments on stage, or else no deal. Sometimes if a showband was unable to locate a replacement for a sick musician, they would engage in the subterfuge of dressing their driver in a band uniform, sticking an instrument, perhaps a trombone, in his hand and making him stand on stage for the duration of the dance. There was no latitude whatsoever in the implementation of this peculiar convention.

After much discussion, somewhat reluctantly, we elected to enlarge the band by including three additional instruments: trumpet, tenor saxophone and baritone saxophone. Several of us hoped that the new instrumentation might harbour exciting musical possibilities, despite the decision being provoked by our mercenary ambitions towards the ballrooms of Ireland. To the original line-up of Terry Brady on percussion, Willie Halpin on guitar, Alan Dee on keyboards and myself on bass was added Davy Martin on trumpet, Pascal Haverty on tenor sax and John L. Sullivan on baritone.

In rehearsals it quickly became apparent that the new members were talented musicians, particularly Davy Martin, who in the past had played with the RTÉ Symphony Orchestra. Unquestionably, the incorporation of brass riffs and harmonies added greatly to the richness of our performance, and more was to come.

In due course, influenced by the English outfit Sounds Incorporated, we contrived fairly sophisticated rock 'n' roll versions of well-known classical tunes like Rossini's *William Tell Overture* and Von Suppé's *Light Cavalry*. Those arrangements were a joy to play, and a treat to listen to.

As soon as possible, we extended our instrumental playlist with a scorching version of the *Peter Gunn* theme, originally made popular by Duane Eddy. Our interpretation featured Willie harshly twanging out the elemental riff on guitar, closely followed by Pascal abrasively improvising on saxophone.

However, my own favourite was 'Goldfinger', the theme song written by John Barry for the eponymous James Bond movie. Many years before, I had seen the John Barry Seven, featuring the appropriately named Vic Flick on guitar in the Olympic ballroom, and being fiercely impressed, followed John Barry's subsequent career with abiding interest. Ours was an instrumental version fronted by an echo-laden guitar taking the melody line, rather than some meretricious vocalist, while at the same time, the brass section riffed away on those ascending chords always linked to Bond movies.

Because the rhythm section was unchanged, the bulk of our repertoire remained the same; for example, numbers by the Beatles, the Rolling Stones and various other groups, as well as old rock 'n' roll favourites and hit tunes from the current charts. However, we gradually became aware that the new line-up provided a unique opportunity to engage with different and more challenging material. Some of us were fascinated by soul music; especially by the way the vocals were interspersed with staccato bursts emitted by trumpets, trombones and saxophones. We were determined to give it a try.

One of the first soul numbers to successfully make it onto our playlist was 'In the Midnight Hour' by Wilson Pickett, and this was many years before Roddy Doyle dreamed of *The Commitments*.

Certainly, Pearson's hunch paid off as we began to get bookings for ballrooms, spread unevenly across the country. This necessitated the use of a van, and because we couldn't afford to buy a vehicle, we opted to rent one. Pearson arranged for the exclusive use of a Commer minibus, which came with a driver – or, as it turned out, several drivers.

The driver we liked best we called George. Of course, that wasn't his real name. He was christened John or Seán, but Alan decided that with his 'Ronnie' moustache and turned-up coat collar, he was the spitting image of Flash Harry, played by George Cole in the St Trinian's films; hence John became George.

A major disadvantage with the Commer minibus was that the capacity of its tank was insufficient to complete any long-distance journey. Our solution was to instruct the driver to fill a petrol can beforehand, and, as the needle in the fuel gauge teetered towards empty, usually about 50 miles (80 km) from Dublin, pour its contents into the tank, which was normally enough to bring the wretched vehicle home.

Occasionally some of the eejits we had for drivers would neglect this chore, and as a result, in the early hours the minibus would grind to a shuddering halt in the middle of nowhere. As you can imagine, the reaction from seven weary musicians trapped in a tiny tin box until morning, when garages would reopen, was anything but friendly. Abusive terms like 'Gob-shite!', 'Bollix!' and far, far worse would echo around the claustrophobic interior.

As we were soon to learn, playing in the various ballrooms dotted around Ireland turned out to be dramatically different to what we'd become used to in Dublin, where the small venues were often packed with enthusiastic dancers even before we went on stage. In the country, the opposite was the case. Frequently we started playing to an empty hall which, over a period of a few hours, would gradually fill out, initially with women, joined later – but only after pub closing time – by hordes of inebriated men. The women would cluster together on one side of the cavernous ballroom to be ogled by bowsies gathered on the other. Eventually some brave soul would summon up the courage and cross the floor to utter the immortal words, 'Are ya getting up?'

Soon, following this plucky example, practically all the patrons would take to the floor, but sadly pay scant attention to our musical efforts.

The scale of our difficulty became clear when Noel Pearson organized a private audition with Con Hynes, the proprietor of a major chain of ballrooms. This was to take place in Powers Hotel in Kildare Street, which, by the way, Hynes also owned. After giving it our best shot, we joined Mr Hynes to receive his considered opinion.

Looking decidedly unimpressed, he declaimed, 'The hairstyles have to go!' And then, rather curiously, 'Do you not know any black pudding music?'

By this he meant what was then known as 'country and Irish' music.

Con Hynes was not the only impresario to be introduced to the band by Noel Pearson. One day when we were rehearsing in the Mayfair ballroom in Clondalkin the phone rang. It was Pearson, who told us that there was an important American promoter in town who had expressed a wish to hear the band; and, for reasons of convenience, Pearson had suggested that the promoter visit the ballroom himself.

Some time in the afternoon we were alerted by the crunch of tyres on the gravel of the adjoining carpark. It was a chauffeur-driven black limousine, out of which stepped our visitor, a short man dressed in a three-quarter-length black leather coat, wearing sunglasses and smoking a rather large cigar. We were suitably impressed.

We introduced ourselves; he said his name was Barry Gout. Back inside the ballroom we played a few numbers while he paced up and down, puffing on his cigar and listening intently. When we finished he admitted to being impressed, and made clear that he could do something for us.

When he left we couldn't believe our luck, yet we were unsure of his intentions. To our surprise he turned up at our next gig and afterwards recommended that, even though the music was superb, our presentation could do with an overhaul. With that in mind, he booked us into Burtons the tailors on the corner of Dame Street and ordered new suits for each and every one of us.

By this stage we had become quite friendly with Barry, and began to socialize with him at meals he hosted in some of Dublin's best restaurants. During one of these suppers he confessed that he really liked Dublin and had decided to move his operation to offices he had just leased in Dame Street, opposite the Olympia Theatre. At the end of the evening he took Willie and me aside and quietly inquired if we would give him a hand setting up his new premises.

The next day, at the appointed hour, we discovered that he had already engaged the services of Switzers, a leading department store, to look after the interior design aspect of the project, so really all we had to do was move various pieces of furniture around and install a fairly sophisticated hi-fi system. While doing this I couldn't help but notice framed photos of famous artists already hanging about the place. One featured Cliff Richard with a signed dedication: 'Good luck Barry, Cliff.' I also spotted Tom Jones, Dusty Springfield and several others.

When we were finished, Barry gave us a £10 cheque each. We both attempted to decline the offer, but he was not for turning. You can imagine my astonishment when, a week or so later, my bank called to inform me that the cheque had bounced. I couldn't believe it at first, but the dud cheque was only the curtain raiser. A few nights later, when we were getting ready to go on stage in the Kingsway ballroom, the bailiffs burst into our dressing room and literally stripped the brand-new suits off our backs. All of Barry Gout's fraudulent purchases were in the process of being returned to their rightful owners. As it turned out, he hadn't a bob to his name. It was all a bizarre confidence trick. Reflecting on our absurd experience I came to the conclusion that Barry Gout suffered from a very unusual psychological condition, and if there isn't a name for it, I can supply one: the Santa Claus complex.

Eventually he was brought to court and sentenced to six months in Mountjoy Prison for fraud. Noel Pearson was the only one who paid him a visit, and reported back that the prisoner seemed quite at home behind bars. Barry's only request was for Noel to bring a packet of mints on his next visit.

When Barry Gout was finally released, he walked through the front gates of the prison, strolled along the North Circular Road, on to Dorset Street, down North Frederick Street and into O'Connell Street where, without breaking his stride, he checked himself into a penthouse suite in the Gresham Hotel. He only lasted a day or two in such luxury before the police were called and he found himself in court again. This time, however, the judge placed him in the custody of a garda with specific instructions to bring him to the docks and place him on the next boat bound for England, which was most fitting, because that was where he was from. He wasn't even American.

After all the excitement of the Barry Gout affair we had no choice but to settle back into the normality of life on the road, with mixed fortunes when it came to the quality of our designated drivers. There was one who singularly irritated us. We dubbed him Paddy the Snarge. For those innocents who are unaware, a snarge is a man with a predilection for sniffing ladies' bicycle saddles.

One dark winter night, travelling back from Cork, we came upon a diversion between Monasterevin and Kildare, imposed because the main road was flooded. It was a windy secondary road and as we bumped along with me in the front passenger seat, I happened to spot a rather severe bend in the road ahead; at the same time, glancing across, I realized that Paddy the Snarge was fast asleep, probably dreaming of a cycle park full of ladies' bikes.

My useless response was to yell, 'Watch out, we're not going to make it!' before the minibus crunched into a hedge on the curve of the bend.

Sitting in front I was privileged to witness, floodlit by the headlights, the amazing sight of drum cases, having broken loose from the roof rack, bouncing down the field below us, scattering in all directions a herd of cows that had been resting in the dark.

Without thinking, I decided it was time to abandon the crashed vehicle, so opening the passenger door I stepped into fresh air and tumbled in the darkness to the ground below. It was only then I realized just how lucky we had been. The front section of the van was hovering over a six-foot drop, held in that precarious position by a tangled mass of twigs and branches.

*

As semi-professional musicians, several of us were finding it harder to juggle our daytime obligations with the increasing demands of life on the road. In my own case this pressure coincided with a growing disillusion with my architectural studies, so when the band decided to turn professional in 1964, I had no real problem in abandoning the academic life to become a full-time professional musician.

We quickly discovered that a major bone of contention, familiar to all professional bands, was the holy season of Lent. Irish Catholic bishops discouraged the holding of dances during this period, so to avoid forty days and forty nights of starvation, Irish professional musicians had little choice but to emigrate temporarily. Luckily, across the water, English Catholic bishops apparently didn't maintain the same prejudice, so there was lots of work to be had in the many Irish dance halls dispersed across Britain.

For our first season playing away, Pearson managed to secure several weeks of bookings across London in dance halls belonging to the Irish promoter Bill Fuller. Part of the deal was the provision of transport, which turned out to be a large decrepit coach with a top speed of about 20 miles (30 km) per hour. To some extent this was just about acceptable, since we believed that all our engagements were in London; but, as we were to learn, promoters frequently change their minds. Without warning, Bill Fuller decided to rearrange our schedule by adding a night in Manchester halfway through the tour.

We were despondent. We couldn't possibly drive from London to Manchester and back in the snail-like coach. We realized we had to find an alternative means of transport. Eventually, Pearson managed to rent a Bedford van which could travel faster, but practically speaking was far too small to accommodate seven musicians, one driver and all the instruments. Nevertheless, amid a chorus of moans and groans and packed like sardines in a tin can, we reluctantly set off on the long journey to Manchester.

Pearson agreed to do the driving so that at least the musicians would not be totally exhausted by the experience. After six hours of extreme discomfort we finally arrived at Plymouth Grove in Manchester, the address of the Astoria Ballroom. We had just enough time to set up the gear, grab a quick meal, have a wash, put on our band uniforms and get on stage. Unexpectedly, the night was a great success. The Manchester Irish seemed to like us, so after packing away the gear, we elected to have one celebratory drink at the bar before the unwelcome return journey. However, to our dismay we realized that Noel, who was supposed to drive back to London, had been unable to resist the temptation of the bar during the dance. Obviously he couldn't get behind the wheel; so I sighed resignedly. 'Ah fuck it, I'll drive.'

Clearly the mileage for the return journey was the same, but it felt much longer. We finally reached London just in time for morning rush hour traffic. I distinctly remember stopping at a red light on the corner of Leicester Square and Tottenham Court Road, only to hear a heart-stopping shriek. A drowsy Alan had just forcefully become aware of one of Pascal's abnormal sleeping habits: from time to time he slept, zombie-like, with both his eyes wide open. Faced with this terrifying apparition, Alan, half-asleep himself, screamed and began to lash out in all directions. Within seconds the rest of the band degenerated into a brawling mass, and I found myself catapulted out the door by a flying guitar case only to land beside a pair of big shiny black boots. As I scanned vertically it became apparent that they belonged to a very tall London policeman, who, rather patronizingly, questioned, 'Irish, are we, sir?'

By this stage, calmness had returned and all were sitting rather sheepishly in their places. This prompted a jaded response from the policeman: 'Well, now you have a green light, sir, perhaps you had better be off.'

The final chapter in the story of the Bedford happened when Pearson was tasked with its return. In truth, the little van had taken far too much punishment on the Manchester trip, because it finally gave up the ghost within sight of the rental company. Refusing to be daunted, however, we took full advantage of a slight incline and free-wheeled the rest of the way to deliver the van before beating a hasty retreat.

The next Lent, Pearson concluded another deal with Bill Fuller. This time it was for a residency of several weeks in Manchester's Astoria Ballroom.

Noel decided that we would travel from Ireland by boat with the van, avoiding any possible repeat of the last Lenten transport fiasco. Willie and I opted to travel the short journey from Liverpool to

Manchester by train. We had just settled in when a strange character entered our carriage and, placing his case on his lap, began playing cards by himself. He struck up a conversation with another passenger, which resulted in them playing Find the Lady. As I expected, because I had seen a similar operation back home, the other passenger began to win some serious money.

This provoked Willie's interest to the extent that he asked if he could join in. I tried explaining that it was a con, but he simply wouldn't listen. Having won his first few flutters he began to bet more heavily, and then at that point his luck seemed to change. Soon, having lost all his own money, he turned to me and borrowed all I had. Of course he lost that as well. For the last bet there was a lot of money at stake but

Playing my Fender bass in a newspaper photograph.

Willie was left with nothing to wager. It was then that I noticed him glancing up at the overhead rack where we'd placed our instruments. My heart sank. *Jesus, he's going to bet his fuckin' guitar.*

Quickly I intervened and handed him my overcoat. 'Bet that!'

Which he did, and, of course, lost.

Rather disconsolately we watched the cardsharp and his accomplice depart from the carriage with all our money and my overcoat. I've heard of someone losing their shirt on a bet, but losing someone else's overcoat is a twist too far.

The residency at the Astoria turned out to be a statement of fact, for there was ample accommodation for musicians above the actual ballroom. This meant that after the dance we could indulge ourselves with a few drinks before going upstairs to bed. I don't know if it was caused by the drink, but it was above the ballroom that another aspect of Pascal's nocturnal behaviour became evident. He was a sleepwalker. After one or two rambles when the lads woke him up and put him back to bed, someone suggested that it might raise a laugh if he was left to get on with his sleepwalking. So, the next time it happened, he was steered through the fire escape door, down the emergency stairs and out on to Plymouth Grove where he continued to ramble along until one of the lads, feeling guilty, decided to wake him up.

A bewildered Pascal, dressed only in his pyjamas, came to not in bed, but on a main street in Manchester, a hundred yards or so from the Astoria Ballroom. He was furious. We promised never to repeat such behaviour.

Back in Ireland we found ourselves playing many more venues in the North, probably because Pearson had done a deal with a guy from Belfast called Shultz, who preferred anonymity on account of his day job with the BBC – an institution that took a dim view of moonlighting.

You didn't need a university degree in sociology to recognize that the North was a different place, and that the difference literally began at the border. Every southern band had to stop at a customs post and get a carnet, which listed every instrument and piece of equipment, officially stamped before continuing their journey. Normally this was a simple rubber-stamping affair, but occasionally, a grumpy official would insist on checking a particular item. This nearly always resulted in every instrument and piece of equipment being laid out on the road beside the van, because the item requested had been packed first and of course came out last.

Another issue of concern was the anthem, or rather the anthems. Which to play? Obviously if we were playing in St Mary's Hall or the local Orange Hall the choice wasn't difficult, but if we arrived at a venue where we were, as yet, unsure of the tribal geography, then it became a problem.

One time we arrived quite late to our first ever engagement in Dungiven in Co. Derry, and I innocently inquired, 'Do we play "The Queen" at the end of the dance?'

The curt response: 'Play that and ye'll all be feckin' shot!'

The promoters of a new ballroom in Limavady, also in Co. Derry, which we were booked to open together with the Bachelors, a successful vocal trio, came up with a novel proposal. In the dressing room was posted a notice suggesting that instead of 'The Queen' or 'The Soldier's Song' the band should play 'The Londonderry Air' or, as it was popularly known, 'Danny Boy'. To our amazement, when we did as advised, everyone in the ballroom stood to attention.

Romano's, a public ballroom on Queen Street in Belfast, was one Northern venue where we had succeeded in building up a considerable following; and one night, after a well-received performance, a group of girls bunched around the bandstand enthusiastically inquired, 'When are you back again in Belfast?'

I replied, 'We're back next week.'

'Oh great, where?'

Unwittingly, I answered, 'The Astor,' which, by the way, was another public ballroom in the Smithfield area.

Crestfallen, they declared, 'Oh, we can't go there, it's a Taig hall!'

For the first time it dawned on us that our Belfast fan base was predominantly Protestant. Unfortunately we were to discover that there was a far more sinister aspect to such sectarianism.

Pascal had a cousin, Fonsie, who lived on the Falls Road, and he came to nearly every dance that the Chessmen played in the Belfast area. On one occasion, however, he turned up in a terrible state. He had a black eye, several stitches and was bruised all over. Shocked, we asked him what had happened. To us his explanation seemed extraordinary. He confessed that it had been his own fault, that he should have known better. A few nights before he had gone to a film in Belfast city centre and while strolling home through the Village, a loyalist district, he was tempted to treat himself to a fish supper. In the chip shop several of the patrons figured out that he was a Catholic, so they dragged him outside and beat the crap out of him. This happened years before the outbreak of the so-called 'Troubles'.

✳

One frequently repeated critique of showbands was their perceived failure to innovate, or to create original material. In most cases this was an accurate assessment, but there were a few bands that attempted to challenge the stereotype. Certainly, both in our repertoire and in our recordings, the Chessmen tried to perform as much original material as possible. For example, having an excellent brass section allowed the band to take on music and taxing arrangements that most other bands wouldn't have touched with a barge pole, and, in Alan, we had a songwriter who turned out enough original material to ensure that each of our recordings could feature one of his compositions.

Our first record, 'Fightin', was both written and sung by Alan and told the story of a ballroom brawl. I never asked, but assumed it was inspired by the crazy Halloween night in the Matt Talbot Hall. It had a chunky Chuck Berry-like riff augmented by brass, and featured a strident guitar solo by Willie. I always felt that, at least in Ireland, it was a record before its time.

'There's Nothing to It' was the B side of our second single; again it was written and sung by Alan. To my delight, it started out with my solo bass line skipping happily along before being joined by the rest of the rhythm section. It also featured a short but melodious trumpet solo by Davy Martin. A few years ago I saw the movie *Rat* starring Pete Postlethwaite, and heard 'There's Nothing to It' on the soundtrack.

Unquestionably it was the experience of playing in Irish ballrooms across Britain, and being moved by the plight of many emigrants who were forced by economic circumstances to leave the land of their birth, that compelled Alan to write 'Michael Murphy's Boy':

> I can't get a decent job
> To bring me in a few bob
> I'm just one of a mob
> An' filled with discontent
> The bit I've had's been spent
> Or lost, or drunk or lent.
> But I won't go, I won't go,
> I'll give it one more try.
> My name is Patrick Joseph
> I'm Michael Murphy's boy.

It was a ballad, influenced by the songs of Dominic Behan, and provided us with our first big hit.

In those days, recording was a fairly primitive affair; multitracking, overdubbing and the like were no more than the imaginings of a technological fantasist. I don't know where Pearson got the information, but one day he announced that recording on film soundtrack produced a far better sonic result, so he booked us into Ardmore Film Studios to record 'Michael Murphy's Boy'.

We set up in a small space that doubled as a preview theatre and began recording. After a few hours we received a visit from the studio people. They informed us that the film in production was *The Spy Who Came in from the Cold* and, because the producers wanted to view some rushes, asked if it would be possible for us to make the space available for half an hour. Since we were ready to take a break anyway, we said yes. Several of us were standing outside when a black limousine silently slid to a halt. The chauffeur strode back and opened the passenger door. We beheld Richard Burton, the star of the film, and his wife Elizabeth Taylor, arrayed in a three-quarter-length fur coat, step out and make their way into the preview theatre. After thirty minutes they emerged and Burton thanked us personally for being so obliging, before he and Liz were driven away to their penthouse suite in the Gresham Hotel.

In the mid-1960s, at first imperceptibly, a new local variant of an American style of music, namely 'country and Irish', began to win the hearts and minds of the dancing public, especially in rural Ireland. To my mind it was nothing more than maudlin, sentimental slobber, often badly executed – but my opinion was decidedly a minority point of view. To survive professionally we had little choice but to include it in our repertoire. Con Hynes would have been proud – at last the Chessmen were playing loads of black pudding music.

One night, after a gig in the west of Ireland, having performed hardly a single rock 'n' roll tune, I found myself feeling utterly disheartened. After all, it was the desire to play such music that had prompted me to become a musician in the first place. I ruminated; so much for the young man's hedonistic dream of sex, drugs and rock 'n' roll. In Ireland it turned out to be nothing but pints, fags and the odd knee-trembler at the rear of some ballroom in the back of beyond. I realized that I had come to the end of the road. There and then I decided to quit.

CHAPTER 8

The Interview

When 1966, the fiftieth anniversary of the Easter Rising, came around, the Irish government of the day was determined to make the most of it. Many members of Fianna Fáil, the party in power, regarded themselves as the true inheritors of the legacy of 1916, a sentiment certainly reinforced by the fact that the founder of their party, Éamon de Valera, a survivor of the Rising, the War of Independence and the Civil War, was now the president of the country. Not quite the whole country, of course; the majority in the six north-eastern counties, in spite of Fianna Fáil's pledge to end partition, steadfastly resolved to remain British.

Naturally this obvious embarrassment did not form part of the government's extensive commemorative programme, which included a major TV series, a colossal pageant with a cast of thousands in Croke Park and military ceremonials including a massive parade in Dublin on Easter Sunday that involved the army, the navy and the air force and all the equipment they could muster. I remember thinking that this display would not have been out of place in Red Square.

The controlling narrative of the whole affair was what I would term a narrow-gauge nationalist one, designed in the main to ask no questions and to reflect well on both the government and the state. For example, there was no space whatsoever to honour the significant role played by women in the Rising, probably due to a sense of guilt over the disgraceful treatment of women by the independent state established in 1922; and certainly there was no examination at all of the social and cultural ambitions of these brave men and women who took up arms against the greatest empire in the world in 1916.

I have to concede that it wasn't until many years later that I began to develop such critical ideas about history and politics. At the time, the government's best efforts almost passed me by: my mind was pre-occupied with more personal concerns. I had just abandoned music, something that had monopolized my life up until then, and to make matters worse I had no idea in the wide world what to do next.

However, I have one piece of advice for the unwary: when you retire from something, stay retired. After several months of musical inactivity I foolishly agreed to play for just one night with a well-known group, the Chosen Few, whose bass player was indisposed. Their vocalist and keyboard player was a young handsome lad with a cheeky smile called Fran O'Toole. A decade later he was to be brutally murdered with two other members of the Miami showband which he had joined in an ambush staged by loyalist paramilitaries.

From my point of view, the gig with the Chosen Few was a disas-ter. I struggled for most of the night with aching fingers due to my lack of practice and, not knowing most of their programme, I found myself forced to busk along rather aimlessly. Afterwards, in order to avoid the temptation of further embarrassment, I decided to sell my guitar. Brush Shiels, the leader of Skid Row, another popular group, must have heard of my predicament and quickly made me an offer of forty quid. I accepted.

Philip Lynott was a member of his band, but right from the start, Shiels did not share his musical tastes. Eventually it came to a head. 'I had to tell him he had to go,' says Shiels. 'It's like being the manager of a football team – you've been great for us up till now, but—'

Lynott was crushed, but to soften the blow Shiels offered to teach him the bass, so Philip Lynott left Skid Row with the promise of music lessons and my Fender bass under his arm. My musical career may not have been crowned with international success, but my instrument, by virtue of being photographed in the hands of the young Phil Lynott, gained world renown.

For me, however, there was no going back.

*

It was a period of real uncertainty. However, I decided to bide my time, and hope that something interesting might turn up. I was able to fund my indolence with savings made while working as a musician; the Irish showband musician was, comparatively speaking, pretty well paid. I discovered this myself during a previous trip to England when the Chessmen were engaged to play for a week at the Astoria in Manchester.

We had one night off, so the drummer Terry Brady and I decided to make the short rail trip to Liverpool and drop into the Cavern Club, already celebrated as the place where the Beatles started playing in public. On the night in question there were several groups on the bill,

Towers Pub in the 1960s with Betty, Tim Goulding, Orphan Annie and others.

and one of them had a record in the British top twenty. After they had finished their spot, I got talking to the singer and praised their efforts.

'Thanks, mate.'

'Do you mind me asking, what's the money like?'

'Ten pounds.'

'That's not much.'

'Well, it's all we were prepared to pay.'

'You mean *you* pay?'

'Well, yes.'

So while an English group with a hit record paid £10 for the privilege of playing in the Cavern Club in Liverpool, the Chessmen were being paid £250 a night to entertain dancers in an Irish ballroom in Manchester.

Back in Dublin, I'd continued my career as a young successful showband musician, rather immodestly sporting a shiny flash car with several shiny flash suits to match. On nights off I used to frequent the No. 5 Club, Dublin's version of the Cavern Club. It was smaller and even more dingy, and was similarly housed in a cellar. The fare on offer in the Harcourt Street premises was simple enough: rock 'n' roll music, dancing, fizzy orange drinks and potato crisps, but it proved to be a magnet for those young Dubliners who saw themselves as the cutting edge of the music and fashion scene in the 1960s.

On one of my first visits, I spotted a vivacious young woman who was not only a brilliant dancer but a 'dedicated follower of fashion'. Her clothes were inspired by the latest creations from London's Carnaby Street, her blonde hair was close-cropped like Jean Seberg's in Jean Luc Godard's *Á Bout de Souffle* and her eyes were suitably sooted up like Dusty Springfield's. I was smitten.

After some discreet inquiries I discovered that her name was Betty Carabini and that she was just sixteen years old. It took me ages to pluck up the courage to ask her to dance – probably due to the fact that I was a brutal dancer. Anyhow, when I finally managed to ask, I was delighted to find myself accepted as a dancing partner. In no time at all we graduated to other simple pleasures like going to the cinema or having a jar in a pub.

At that time, my pub of choice was Toners in Merrion Row, the kind of licensed premises that my father called a 'spit and sawdust' bar. By the time I became a regular customer there was no sawdust on the floor and apparently no spitting, but little else had changed. My memory is of being enveloped in a cosy, warm, dark brown space with shimmers of light reflected from old advertising mirrors. The convivial mood was further enhanced by the genial owner of the premises, Joe Toner, a bald man who had a rather round face and wore glasses and a habitual smile. Mr Toner lived above the shop with his father, his two sisters and an enormous English sheepdog called Woopsie.

Toners was an agreeable bohemian watering hole, especially for the younger generation. The older literary heavyweights like Brendan Behan, Patrick Kavanagh, Brian O'Nolan and Anthony Cronin rarely strayed far from the pubs located around Grafton Street, like McDaids and The Bailey. Even a partial listing of some of those I met in Toners gives an indication as to why an evening spent there was not an evening wasted.

An early friend was Tim Goulding, already working as an artist and looking the part with his long dark hair and mandarin moustache. His blond curly-haired friend Tim Booth was working in advertising and also making some art. The two Tims together with their friend Ivan Pawle later formed the psychedelic folk band Dr Strangely Strange, which developed quite a cult following. Another mutual friend was Patricia Mohan, the tenant of a property not too far from Toners at 55 Lower Mount Street, which she generously made available to those who missed the last bus home, or worse still, who hadn't a place to go after the pub had closed. The place became affectionately known as the Orphanage, and Patricia was nicknamed Orphan Annie. The Orphanage not only provided shelter for waifs and strays, but also hosted many extraordinary parties and was a port of call for diverse international visitors.

A good few of the pub regulars had Trinity College connections and one of those was Norman Steele. He taught in the philosophy department but, one day, he abandoned academia to raise pigs in West Cork. His wife Veronica, on noticing that the local farmers were producing a surplus of milk, decided to rectify the situation by making cheese from the waste product. Her creation, Milleens, led the way in developing the successful international profile of Irish artisan cheese.

Dave Robinson, an old school acquaintance, occasionally drifted into Toners sporting a rather spectacular afro hairdo. At the time he was working as a photographer, but eventually abandoned the camera and took up band management instead. He moved to London and founded Stiff Records, the independent record company.

I first made Philip Lynott's acquaintance when he was a vocalist in a group called the Black Eagles. He was just fifteen at the time. Typically, showbands had to play four to five hours at a dance, so sometimes, in order to ease the load, they would hire a local group to play the first hour or so. Philip was raised by his grandmother in Crumlin, a Dublin working-class suburb; the rest of the band also came from Crumlin, as did our manager, Noel Pearson, so I guess it was inevitable that the Black Eagles would support the Chessmen whenever we played in Dublin.

Philip was always proud of his Crumlin roots. He later said, 'When I'm in England, I say I'm from Ireland. When I'm in Ireland, I say I'm from Dublin. When I'm in Dublin, I say I'm from Crumlin.'

Philip began to wander into Toners in the mid-1960s, and quickly struck up a friendship with Tim Booth and Ivan Pawle. He also frequented the Orphanage, where he encountered a mutual friend who gloried in the name Annie Christmas. Tim Booth recalls that she was a great vivacious big-built woman, who took Philip under her wing. In part-homage to that experience, Philip called his first band Orphanage. This was a few years before he started Thin Lizzy and became Ireland's first international rock star.

Even though most of the friends I made in Toners were of the younger generation, there were many notable exceptions. I have a clear memory of an enthralling evening in the snug with Stephen and Kathleen Behan. At the time they were both of an advanced age, but still as sharp as a knife. Kathleen Behan was an extraordinary woman who presided over a brilliant and controversial Irish family which included Brendan, at that time the most celebrated post-war Irish author and playwright, Dominic, singer and songwriter and Brian, a writer and radical trade unionist. Her first husband, Jack Furlong, and her brother Peadar Kearney were active during Easter Week, 1916. Peadar wrote the Irish national anthem, 'The Soldier's Song'. Kathleen herself had a great store of Irish rebel songs and ballads. She was always on the side of the underdog and was instinctively patriotic. 'I was born a Fenian and hope to die a Fenian,' she once declared. Jack Furlong died in the great flu epidemic in 1918; Stephen Behan, Kathleen's second husband, was a painter and decorator and an active republican. They were married for just two months when Stephen was arrested. It was 1922 and Ireland was in a state of civil war. The experience that night in Toners snug was a rare privilege.

By 1967, even though I was officially unemployed, my regular trips to Toners and the No. 5 Club did not abate, but became more frequent due to the obvious fact that I no longer worked nights. All of this was rendered feasible by my diminishing savings, but I was well aware that this idyllic situation could not last indefinitely. Nevertheless, I remained convinced that I'd get a break. And one night in Toners something did turn up, but not exactly what I expected. On the evening in question, I was on my own in the pub, Betty having just left Dublin to visit her mother who had moved with her family to Manchester. I was sitting with some cronies in the centre section when a commotion suddenly broke out in the front of the pub. Someone peeped through the dividing partition doors and announced that Micheal Farrell, the artist, had just come back from New York and was celebrating his return. As it happened, I was already familiar with his work; I had seen his last exhibition in the Dawson Gallery in 1966. It featured several large hard-edge abstract canvases that reflected his growing interest in Celtic imagery. He called the series *Thourables Wake*, which, according to Cyril Barrett, the philosopher and critic, 'had nothing to do with the mourning of one Thourable, but referred to the coils of smoke which follow in the wake of a censer or thurible'. Barrett noted that Farrell was not a great one for spelling, due to his admitted dyslexia; this, in turn, was probably the cause of the misspelling of his own first name.

The pictures on display were both powerful and assured and exhibited a real understanding of the properties of the new acrylic paint, which had just become widely available. At the time I remember thinking that we hadn't seen anything quite like it before in Irish painting.

Farrell had returned to Dublin to execute a major commission for the Bank of Ireland and one reason for his presence in Toners that night was to find someone who might be willing to assist him. Tim Goulding was the first person to be asked, but for personal reasons he declined. Tim then approached me and offered to introduce me to Micheal. On learning of a potential assistant, Micheal burst through the partition doors, furiously puffing away on one of his evil-smelling French cigarettes.

My first impression was of a tall, slightly ruffled individual with straight dark hair combed to the side creating a sort of quiff, which threw into shadow his dark brown piercing eyes. He also had an engaging smile, which was capable of disarming even the most persistent adversary. However, without question, his most striking feature was a prominent nose, which his mother believed came from her aristocratic Spanish ancestors. Micheal, for his part, suspected that Jewish blood had a role to play. (As it turned out, mother and son were wrong on both counts.) Even then, the Farrell nose exhibited some wear and tear, but it would suffer many more indignities in the years to come.

The interview, if you could call it that, was brusque, brief and to the point.

'Can you draw a fuckin' straight line?'

I mumbled something in the affirmative.

'OK, well, here's the fuckin' deal – I'll pay you a fiver a week and all the bloody drink you can take.'

Since what was being offered seemed at the very least interesting, and since interesting work was what I had in mind, I muttered my acceptance.

'Great, and now that the deal is done, let's have a bloody drink!'

Over the course of a few pints it was decided that I would start work the following morning by driving to Saintbury, a house on Killiney Hill, where Micheal had very recently taken up residence.

Some travel writers have suggested that Killiney Bay rivals the Bay of Naples for its magnificent situation; but although you could just about glimpse the sea through the trees surrounding the property, Saintbury was anything but magnificent. It was a large run-down house, a damp mansion with no heating, a suspect sewage system and an overgrown tennis court. Micheal chuckled, 'If you looked out the kitchen window there were fuckin' rats as big a' hares, and they weren't playing tennis!'

Dusty old stuffed heads of wild animals decorated the front hall. The house also had a large decrepit ballroom, which Micheal had hoped to convert into a studio to paint the commissioned pictures; but it proved to be too small and he was forced to make other plans. The house had unquestionably seen better days, and for Micheal and his family it proved to be totally inappropriate. But as I was to realize later, it was a typical gesture. He simply couldn't resist the temptation to live in a mansion. And a rent of just a fiver a week probably indicated a far more practical motive. Micheal rented the property from Maureen O'Sullivan, the Hollywood film actress who famously starred as Jane opposite Johnny Weissmuller in the hugely popular *Tarzan the Ape Man* movie.

My arrival at Saintbury coincided with breakfast, when I met Micheal's wife Pat and their son Seamus for the first time. They appeared somewhat undermined by the strain of living in such a dilapidated home; Micheal, on the other hand, was buzzing about the place, cooking food and talking excitedly about the work ahead. He explained that because the ballroom wouldn't work as a studio he had as an alternative found a space in Ardmore Film Studios in Bray. A huge canvas woven on a gigantic loom in Belgium had already been shipped to Bray and stretched by film technicians on an enormous frame made from scaffolding bars. The stretched canvas was large enough to accommodate the two paintings, each measuring 6 x 4 metres (20 x 14 ft), side by side. All that remained to be done was to prime this massive piece of cloth.

With a glint in his eye, Micheal called on me to finish my breakfast. 'We have to prime a canvas the size of a fuckin' tennis court today!'

When we arrived at our space in Ardmore we were greeted by two large scaffolding towers standing to attention in front of the huge stretched canvas and, on the ground, I could see tools and materials carefully laid out. All the paint, including the primer or gesso, was the best-quality American acrylic, which Micheal had brought back from New York in large plastic buckets. This was the very first lesson I learned from Micheal. 'Always use the best materials. If you use shite it will always come back and bite you on the arse!'

He handed me a bucket of gesso with a large paint roller and tray, and told me to climb up the tower and get painting. The plan was that we would begin at either end, and work our way across to meet in the middle, all the while moving the towers, which were equipped with specialized wheels. This was painting on an industrial scale, and we completed the first coat by lunchtime. It was exhausting work, so when Micheal suggested that we seek some refreshment while waiting for the paint to dry, I raised no objection. Ardmore, of course, was first and foremost a film studio and, at the time, was being used for the production of *The Lion in Winter* starring Peter O'Toole and Katharine Hepburn. I can't remember if it was during that liquid lunch in the studio bar that Micheal first encountered Peter O'Toole, but meet him he assuredly did, and they were to become firm drinking buddies. Naturally I tagged along, eager to fulfil the second condition of my verbal contract with Micheal. After that lengthy lunch break we returned to apply the second primer coat, and with considerable exertion the work was finally complete. It was only then that Micheal decided to call it a day.

Even at that early stage, I had developed a basic routine. I would leave my parents' flat in Ballsbridge at about 5.30a.m., drive to Killiney, pick up Micheal and then on to Bray, where the two of us would be ready to start work at around seven in the morning.

Having primed the large canvas, the next task was to mark out the designs for the two paintings. Micheal suggested that we use the tried and trusted squares method. An accurate sketch is divided into squares and a canvas of the final dimension is marked out in a similar number of squares. Obviously, because of the large size of the proposed painting, the squares on the canvas were much bigger than those on the sketch. But it was possible, by carefully observing the design contained within a small square on the sketch, to replicate the same design on a larger scale within one of the bigger squares on the primed canvas. Sounds simple? My arse!

It took days for Farrell and myself, scrambling up and down the towers, stretching lengths of string, dropping plumb lines, using metal rules, setsquares, a large compass and dozens of pencils and rubbers and expending a hell of a lot of sweat and tears, to get the job done. I was by now familiar with Micheal's idea for the commission, which involved painting two large mural-sized canvases to be installed on either side of the banking hall in the bank's headquarters in College Green.

In compositional terms, however, a major problem was caused by a series of columns deployed along the central axis of the space, which would obscure any complete view of either painting. Micheal's solution was to propose a diagonal series of intertwining circles for one painting and a diagonal series of interlocking triangles for the other. As a result, the compositions would slowly unfold as the viewer walked through the colonnade. In Micheal's design the circles and triangles would be blue and green respectively, and would float on a background of grey clouds. I couldn't wait to start painting. The plan was to begin with the background, but before we applied a brushstroke of paint Micheal insisted that the drawn circles and triangles be covered over carefully with masking tape, a task that proved both tedious and tiresome. 'We must have used twenty miles of fuckin' masking tape,' Micheal later confessed.

Finally, we were ready to commence painting. Micheal first mixed several shades of grey, and with one brush loaded with a dark colour he created a cloud-like shape on the canvas. Very quickly, with another brush, he painted a lighter shade abutting the darker form and began to soften and blend the still wet edges of the two shades together. For this job he used brushes called badger softeners. My role in all of this was to spray a light mist of water over the canvas, ensuring that the water-based acrylic didn't dry too quickly, while assiduously avoiding the application of too much spray, which might have caused the paint to run. I didn't find this easy.

After some time, obviously feeling rather knackered, Micheal suggested we exchange roles. I have to admit the painting was even more taxing than the spraying, but I really appreciated the challenge, especially the blending of the paint with the badger brushes. Between us we continued to share the workload until, eventually, the background was completed.

Exhausted, we stripped off the masking tape and stood back to admire our handiwork.

'Well, fuck me!' whooped Micheal. 'That deserves a pint or two.'

The following day he set about painting dark grey shadows, which, in his imagination, were cast by the circles and triangles onto the lighter grey cloudscape. In realistic terms this was somewhat illogical, but graphically speaking it proved to be rather elegant. When James White, the director of the National Gallery, saw the finished pictures, he praised Micheal's exceptional ability 'to devise visual harmony in difficult surroundings. Geometry freed the necessity to represent visible reality'.

Up until then, everything in the composition was monochrome: many shades of grey. But now the time had come to introduce colour. Micheal began by mixing two buckets of paint, one blue, one green, carefully matching them to the colours on his original sketches; but before any painting could begin he insisted that we prepare the canvas. I knew what that meant. 'We'll have to mask out everything except the circles and triangles to make sure we don't make a bollix of applying the paint. It has to dry out smooth and flat and not fuckin' streaky!'

So once again we embarked on the numbing task of sticking miles of masking tape to the surface of the two paintings. To some extent, one rewarding aspect of using masking tape is that once the boring bit is done, several coats of paint can be applied easily and evenly. Another very special moment comes when the masking is stripped away to reveal, for the first time, the latest passage of work.

We had now been working on the pictures for just over a month and there remained only one aspect of the commission to complete, which was painting the light grey lines that bordered both the circles and triangles. Because the lines around the circles had to be painted by hand, Micheal took on that task, which he performed with great dexterity using a sable brush like a practised sign writer. I was to execute the straight lines bordering the triangles because masking tape could be used and, by that stage, I had become quite skilled in its application.

By the end of the fifth week we had finally finished the commission and took enormous satisfaction in rolling back the scaffolding towers to reveal, in all their splendour, two of the largest pictures ever painted by an Irish artist in the course of the twentieth century.

Despite sceptical opinion, I remain convinced that fate plays a significant role in determining the life choices of any individual. If I hadn't met Micheal Farrell that particular night in Toners, I'm pretty sure my own life might have drifted in an entirely different direction.

It was only many years later, when I looked back on those few weeks with Micheal in 1967, that I fully appreciated the radical impact they had on my life. In practical terms I learned so much that even though almost fifty years have passed, I still draw on that short but very special experience.

One example immediately springs to mind. Badger brushes remain an essential part of my practice, regularly used to apply glazes and blend colours, which in turn create a particular look that many people immediately associate with my work. Catherine Marshall, the art historian and critic, correctly observed that my brief spell with Micheal Farrell 'was the only art training he ever received'.

Naturally all the time that we were working together we were chatting away, and ultimately I learned a great deal about Micheal's attitudes to life, art and the Irish art scene. I admired the fact that unlike many Irish writers and artists who sat around in various bars talking about art but not making any, Micheal, even though he himself had a prodigious lust for life, never wavered in his commitment to his craft or to his capacity for hard work.

In spite of having to labour virtually non-stop, sometimes for over twelve hours a day, there were a few social occasions when we could let off some steam. This was when I first witnessed Micheal's 'extrovert devil-may-care attitude to his social behaviour' as described by his brother David. He would seek attention by swearing profusely and laughing raucously. He had an irreverent sense of humour and seemed to think it was hilarious to introduce me as 'the banjo plucker', his assistant. More remarkable was his name for Sir Basil Goulding, one of

Ireland's leading art collectors and, as a director of the National Bank of Ireland, probably responsible for getting Micheal the commission in the first place.

Basil's fortune came from the fertilizer industry, which led Micheal to christen him 'Sir Basil Manure'. Neither Basil, myself nor many others took great exception to being on the receiving end of his mordant wit, so he simply carried on regardless. In the memorable words of his friend, Brian O'Doherty, the writer and artist, Micheal was 'a walking opera'.

Having been totally immersed in the world of Micheal Farrell's art for five weeks, I decided that I might have a go myself; but in spite of my recent experience, I still had the problem of not knowing how to paint, never mind the more serious issue of what to paint. I decided to go back to basics.

I'd always known how to make things; after all, I had made puppets, model airplanes, even an electric guitar. So, in the same bedroom where I had fashioned those objects many years before, I began to construct two 3D art pieces using shaped aluminium sprayed with brightly co-loured cellulose paint. The first was an abstracted female form called *Torso*. The second featured a bell that rang when a button was pressed. It was titled *Pinball* after the machines in amusement arcades. Both were largely influenced by pop art, particularly its English variant. Ciaran Carty, the writer and critic, once wrote that, 'They looked more like fairground things than something off the assembly line in Detroit.'

Even though I was fairly happy with the results, in the grand scheme of things I remained decidedly uncertain as to my future plans. Obviously a radical change was required. On the spur of the moment, I decided, like many young Irish people before me, to travel to London – if not to seek my fortune, then perhaps to find enlightenment.

Pinball, metal construction, 61cm x 46cm, 1967.

CHAPTER 9

A False Start

On my first day in London I fell on my feet. I literally bumped into several lads who studied architecture with me in Dublin and had emigrated after qualification. They were the proud tenants of a small property at 7 Reese Mews, South Kensington, and they offered me, rent-free, a small spare room.

South Kensington was one of swinging London's trendiest neighbourhoods; while living there, I often caught sight of photographers, models, rock stars in the restaurants and bars of the locality. However it wasn't until much later that I learned of our most famous neighbour, when the entire contents of 9 Reese Mews were removed and transplanted, in all their cluttered glory, to the Hugh Lane Gallery in Dublin. Francis Bacon's studio is now an essential destination for anyone wishing to study the life and work of the great artist.

One of the first places I explored was the nearby Victoria and Albert Museum, a repository of astonishing sculpture, furniture and ceramics – and so much else. I spent several days wandering about the place until eventually I became bored of being on my own. I felt I needed company, so I wrote to Betty, who was still with her mother in Manchester, asking her to join me in London. By return of post Betty accepted my invitation and promised she would travel by train to London the following weekend. After meeting her at Euston, we made our way to the mews in South Kensington where she was slightly taken aback to discover that she would be sharing the place with a bunch of Dublin males. Tactically, I had neglected to mention that not insignificant detail in my letter. However, she didn't flare up and justifiably reject the situation out of hand. She simply went into our small room and began to tidy it up. Perhaps growing up with three brothers and two sisters in an equally small house in Dublin had prepared her for the necessary compromises involved in such communal living. Although she was very young, just seventeen, Betty proved to be an expert when dealing with complicated domestic arrangements: like working out an acceptable rota for activities such as washing and basic cooking. In this I was hopeless, whether through lack of experience or laziness.

From the start, our days in London were spent indulging my preferences – for example, visiting museums and art galleries; yet I soon noticed that Betty had begun to develop a curiosity in such matters herself. This development ushered in many lively discussions about various artists and exhibitions, which demonstrated clearly to me that she could recognize a good picture when she saw one; conversely, she seemed to have an innate ability to immediately spot a sham.

Our time was not taken up entirely by cultural pursuits. We decided to treat ourselves to a bit of shopping, or, in our case, window-shopping. We took ourselves off to the famous Carnaby Street, which turned out to be a rather narrow walkway behind Regent Street lined with colourful boutiques. I can't remember whether Betty bought anything on that first visit, but I certainly recall a foolhardy purchase of mine: a pair of pink jeans. I quickly discovered that even then, they were a bit outré for swinging London. On their first outing, walking past a building site, I was greeted by a barrage of wolf whistles. This mortification resulted in them being consigned to my suitcase, never to appear again.

We were less than a month in London when Micheal Farrell contacted me to say that he and Pat were coming over from Dublin the following week, and would like to invite us to a party in their old flat in Holland Park. He suggested we meet beforehand in a pub called the Prince of Wales. When we arrived, the place was jammed with noisy friends and old neighbours, so conversation proved difficult; I just about managed to introduce Betty to Micheal and Pat. After a few hours, the crowd began to drift from the pub and walk the short distance to the flat where the party was just starting. Here real conversation was possible, and Micheal took the opportunity to introduce me to acquaintances from the London art scene. These included his very good friend, the artist Patrick Caulfield, whose spare but elegant paintings had always impressed me. The English critic Marco Livingstone once wrote that Patrick Caulfield 'developed an art of consistent richness and force by using the utmost economy of means and reference material that is often debased and in questionable taste'.

Micheal had gleaned from Betty that as a child, she had been an Irish dancing champion, so, much to her embarrassment, he kept insisting that she give a demonstration. Eventually, more to keep him quiet than anything else, she agreed, and, even though she hadn't performed for many years, the partygoers generously applauded her efforts. She performed a slip jig that nowadays would be familiar to anyone who has seen *Riverdance*.

It was early in the morning when we returned by taxi to Kensington, totally exhausted.

✷

A rugby supporter from the Bunch of Grapes, a pub that we frequented, suggested we accompany him to the London Irish rugby club's grounds one Saturday afternoon, to see a match and guzzle a few pints. Upon arriving we bought some drinks and lined up on a grassy verge to watch the match. Some time later, bored with the football on offer, I began to look around, hoping to come across something more interesting than the scrappy sporting contest itself. My eyes settled on a mundane object discarded on the sodden grass. It was an old cigarette carton flattened by the trampling of many feet. I remember thinking, *Now this could be interesting.*

At the time, I was aware of the influential American art critic, Clement Greenberg, and his theory that a painting was simply a flat two-dimensional surface. He insisted that any attempt to depict the illusion of a third dimension was ultimately dishonest. Looking at the flattened cigarette carton I remember thinking that this was once a three-dimensional object that had now been transformed into a two-dimensional one, and wondering whether it could be an interesting concept for a painting.

At that moment I heard the shrill blast of the final whistle and completely forgot my train of thought, but I did remember to put the flattened carton in my pocket for future reference. By this stage, my meagre funds had almost run out and the attractions of London had begun to recede, so, sitting down with Betty one evening in the Bunch of Grapes, we began to discuss our options.

1. We would return to Dublin;
2. We would get married;
3. I would become an artist.

The first was easy. We just had to buy the tickets. Number two was possible, but not in the immediate future. We would have to wait until at least May the following year, when Betty would be eighteen and therefore legally entitled to get married. As for resolution number three, we realized that such a madcap idea was hopelessly ambitious and would take a long time to fulfil.

CHAPTER 10

The Emigrant Returns

It must have ended one of the shortest periods of exile in Irish social history when I left London and returned to Dublin. But I was a changed man. I now knew precisely what I wanted to do and was chomping at the bit to get started.

Because Betty hadn't yet met my parents, we decided, in order to avoid scandalizing them – especially my sensitive Catholic mother – to revert diplomatically to our pre-London living arrangements. Betty moved back to her north inner-city family home in Broadstone, and I returned to my parents' flat in Ballsbridge. Nevertheless, in spite of our geographical separation, we continued to meet regularly and to formulate plans for the future. Almost immediately we agreed that a meeting between Betty and my parents had to be organized, so with some trepidation, I arranged for her to come to my parents' flat. When we arrived the atmosphere was tense, but I needn't have worried about my father; he instantly took to Betty. My mother's response was predictably more reticent. In my opinion, this was due not to any obvious clash of personalities, but rather to a quiet sense of personal disappointment that her son, in whom she had so much invested, was now going to marry a working-class girl from Dublin's inner city. We, for our part, having successfully if awkwardly surmounted our first hurdle, set about investigating what to do next. After all, as a young couple, we had no illusions about our situation. We were beset by very real difficulties.

We had no money.

We had no income.

We had no home.

Thankfully, the accommodation issue was quickly resolved. Betty's mother, who had kept up the tenancy, insisted that we move into the family home; and, although Betty was initially resistant, hoping to start a new life in a new place, she finally consented to her mother's generous offer. As for money and a steady income, since my only marketable skills were vaguely architectural, I started looking for work as a draughtsman. After failing many embarrassing interviews, I was relieved to be offered a job with an engineering firm to start work as soon as I returned from my honeymoon.

At this point I received a rather curious call from Micheal Farrell, informing me that the film people from Ardmore had been impressed by our work and were prepared to offer us jobs as scene painters. Micheal, ever alert to an opportunity, accepted and went on to create scenic backdrops for films like *Dracula Has Risen from the Grave* in 1968 and *The Country Dance* in 1969. But I turned down the offer, feeling inhibited by a new sense of responsibility.

Even though Betty and I were unbelievers, we reluctantly agreed to get married in St Mary's Roman Catholic Church, Haddington Road, close to my parents' flat, to avoid the possibility of my mother succumbing to a real or imagined heart attack. In those days, before a wedding could take place, the names and addresses of the intended couple were read out from the pulpit. However, in our case, the priest agreed with some irritation to dispense with the practice.

In the weeks before the wedding, for reasons of convenience, Betty had moved in with Paula Rockett, a mutual friend, who was living with her aunt and cousins in the top flat of 14 Elgin Road, where I also happened to live. We tried to explain that having the same addresses was entirely innocent, but I don't believe the reverend clergyman was entirely convinced.

For the ceremony itself, Betty nominated Paula Rockett as brides-maid and asked her older brother Gerard to give her away. I couldn't resist soliciting Micheal Farrell to act as best man. For years afterwards, he claimed he was asked because he was the only one of my friends with a suit.

For me, the mass was desperately confusing, since the last mass I had attended was conducted in Latin. After the Second Vatican Council, the ceremony was now performed in English. Nevertheless, when, with some relief, I heard the phrase, 'Go, the mass is ended,' we filed out of the church to be greeted not only by family and friends but also by a whole contingent from Toners. A small group of family and friends

On our wedding day, 1 July 1968.

went to a nearby hotel for the wedding breakfast. It was then that I met Betty's mother and her two sisters for the first time: they had come over from Manchester for the wedding. The honeymoon was necessarily short, just a few days in the west of Ireland, on account of the fact that I had to start work the following Monday.

The job was with George Milner and Sons, a company supplying aluminium windows to most of the new office blocks shooting up all around the city.

On my first day, a colleague sidled up and whispered, 'I suppose you'll be joining the union?'

And even though the thought hadn't occurred to me, I muttered, 'Well, yes.'

Within a few months we found ourselves on strike over a staffing issue. The employers had suspended three colleagues, who were department heads, and replaced them with their own three sons. We immediately went on strike. As we picketed the factory I was hugely encouraged by the action of other trade unionists. They simply refused to pass our official picket line. In response, Milner's went to the High Court and were granted an interim injunction against picketing. We appealed that decision and won. The original court order was quashed and the workers were reinstated; but it was a pyrrhic victory. On our first day back we were greeted with new and more difficult working conditions imposed without any consultation. I could see the way things were going and I decided to get out.

Nevertheless, even though my trade union career was brief, that experience of the necessarily constant struggle for equality and justice has remained with me ever since.

*

Obviously with no weekly income, Betty and I were back in the grip of poverty; but once again, fate intervened, this time in the unexpected form of Noel Pearson, ever the impresario. He had recently taken over the management of the Betty Whelan model agency and needed letterheads and brochures in a hurry. He called me and asked if I would design them. Even though I had no previous experience of graphic design, I accepted the commission and bluffed my way through the process. Thankfully the results were reasonably successful and led to the opening up of a modest income stream as a freelance designer.

During my time in Milner's I had still been determined to advance what was, at the time, my non-existent artistic career; so I decided to submit my two pop constructions to the annual show organized by the Irish Exhibition of Living Art, which was first established in 1943 to display those radical artists who found themselves excluded from the Royal Hibernian Academy's summer exhibition which was the most important forum for artists in Ireland at the time. Due to the quantity of submissions it was considered almost impossible for a young unknown artist to gain entry to the Living Art show, so you can imagine my astonishment when I learned that my two pieces had been accepted. Better still, they were singled out for praise by the critic from the *Evening Press*: 'The first moment of contact with the Living Art was promising. Robert Ballagh's *Torso* attracts with its two aluminium bowls with blue painted buttons suggesting eyes and breasts.'

And critical praise was not the only outcome. When that huge trawl of contemporary art, the ROSC exhibition, washed up on Irish shores, I found myself invited to the official opening.

ROSC was the brainchild of the eminent Irish architect Michael Scott. In early 1964, recuperating after a heart attack in the south of France with artists Louis le Brocquy and Anne Madden, the germ of an idea began to form. On his return to Ireland he travelled west to meet James Johnson Sweeney, then director of the Museum of Fine Arts in Houston, Texas and formerly director of the Solomon R. Guggenheim Museum in New York, at Sweeney's Irish home in Westport, Co. Mayo.

Together they discussed and finally consolidated the concept of an exhibition featuring the work of fifty contemporary artists chosen by an international jury chaired by Sweeney, which would only include art made in the previous four years.

Of course, by the time I got to see the exhibition in the main hall of the Royal Dublin Society, all that preparatory work had been done. Initially what impressed people most was not so much the art itself, but the installation of the exhibition designed by the Irish artist Patrick Scott. International critics described it in terms such as 'arresting, exciting, dazzling, marvellous, sensational, stupendous'. For myself, sifting through the works on display, I came across for the first time examples of the new American pop art. The fields of bright acrylic primary colours, the razor-sharp outlines, the hopelessly ironic content in the paintings of Roy Lichtenstein and Robert Indiana overwhelmed me. To my youthful eyes, everything else in the exhibition seemed dreadfully dull. But what was even more exciting was the realization that, with some ingenuity, I might be able to produce something just as impressive by following their example.

Even though the ROSC exhibition was deemed a great success, it was not without controversy. In making their original selection, the international jury – consisting of James Johnson Sweeney, Willem Sandberg and Jean Leymarie – included Micheal Farrell as the only Irish representative. When the members of the local organizing committee heard of this, they were not happy. They felt there were other Irish artists more deserving of inclusion and pressed for their selection. The international jury stood firm; so Michael Scott, unhappy that his favourites had not been chosen, introduced a rule that *no* contemporary Irish artist would be selected. As you would expect, the omission of any Irish artist proved a controversial decision. Sweeney invited Micheal Farrell for tea in the Shelbourne Hotel, where he explained why he could not after all represent Ireland in the show. Micheal was hugely disappointed, and even though he always denied it, I believe that the ROSC fiasco influenced his decision to leave Ireland for good in September 1971.

In our small terraced house in Broadstone, meanwhile, I set up a drawing board in the kitchen and, buoyed up by the positive response to my pop constructions, I began to plan my next assault on the Irish art scene. I knew, in my heart of hearts, that this undertaking would have to involve the act of painting – something I had avoided so far; but now, thanks to my musings on the rugby touchline in London, I felt I had, at the very least, some notion of what to paint. I began by collecting various packages, unfolding them and laying them out flat on my drawing board. Contemplating the result, I began to appreciate that American pop artists, in celebrating consumer culture, invariably chose ubiquitous corporate brands as their subject matter – an obvious example being the Campbell's soup can paintings by Andy Warhol. I had something different in mind.

For example, in choosing a pink and powder-blue candy-striped HB ice cream packet, I knew full well that it would be recognized immediately by any Irish person who grew up in the 1950s. At that time, during hot summer days, we kids would go to our local shop and impatiently watch as the candy-striped wrapper was folded back to expose a block of pure white ice cream, which was then cut into thin slices and offered to us, with a wafer on either side, for the sum of two pence. Another choice I made was a box of matches manufactured by an Irish company, Maguire and Paterson, and marketed under the curious title The Friendly Match.

On my small drawing board I set about creating accurate scale drawings for the prospective paintings in order to clarify my intentions. I planned to paint broken black lines to represent the folds, which were, in every aspect, invisible on the flattened cartons. Also, I had no intention of reproducing the original logos or lettering; instead I decided to replace them with bands of appropriate colour. In addition, I designed a painting of a huge razor blade, an object so flat, with no depth whatsoever, that together with the proposed package paintings, paid due deference to Greenberg's theory of flatness and the integrity of the two-dimensional surface.

At the time I remember speculating, *All I have to do now is paint the damn things!*

So, in a small upstairs back bedroom, drawing directly on my experience with Micheal Farrell, I stretched canvas, marked out the design and, with masking tape and acrylic paint, completed each of several paintings to a standard that I considered acceptable.

The next task was to find a place to exhibit them. Dublin in the 1960s had only two commercial galleries, the Dawson Gallery and the Hendriks Gallery, both fully committed to a stable of established artists; as a result, unproven young painters found it extremely difficult to

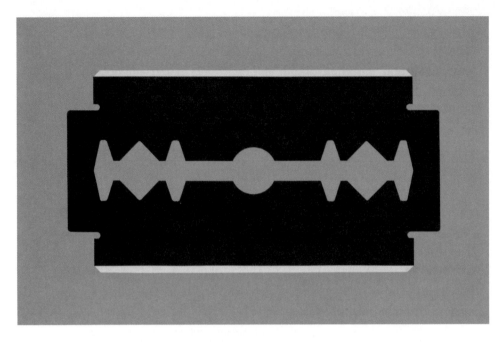

Razor Blade, 189cm x 189cm, 1968, Collection of the Arts Council of Ireland.

exhibit their work. Luckily, early in 1968, fate intervened when Brown Thomas, the fashionable department store, decided to open a gallery in its Grafton Street outlet. Amanda Douglas, a young Trinity College graduate, was placed in charge; and her first exhibition in February, entitled Young Irish Artists, was opened by Sir Basil Goulding. It featured the work of ten artists, many of whom were veterans of Toners, including myself and Tim Booth. The critic Anthony Butler wrote that 'Robert Ballagh's classical pop pictures mingle elegant restraint with posterish brashness, thus creating significant tensions,' and Raymond Gallagher noted that, 'Robert Ballagh's work shows an ability to be amusing and serious at the same time. His *Matchbox* and *Ice Cream* are excellent examples of pop art, showing objects deeply embedded in the collective unconscious in a surprisingly new and artistic way.'

However, far more exciting than any review was my discovery that *Ice Cream* had been bought privately, and that the Arts Council of Ireland had acquired *Razor Blade*.

The latter purchase, by the way, caused a minor controversy when Quidnunc, an *Irish Times* columnist, snorted, 'I would very much like to know on what grounds the dear old Arts Council flogged one hundred and thirty quid of your money (and mine) on a Robert Ballagh representation of a safety razor blade… I begin to wonder if the tail is wagging the Arts Council dog.'

As far as I was concerned, I didn't give a damn. With my first sales under my belt and an endorsement by the Arts Council, I was more determined than ever to press on with what now looked like an art career.

But what to do next?

Still obsessed with the theory of the flat surface, slowly a memory of the maps that I loved to draw in school floated into my thoughts. What could be flatter? Once again installing my drawing board on the kitchen table, I prepared designs for what I hoped would be an exciting new series of paintings, this time featuring map imagery.

At the outset I decided that rather than depicting recognizable geographical patterns, I would draw shapes that were purely abstract. On the other hand, by including straight lines I also hoped to draw attention to arbitrary political boundaries, often imposed on the landscape contrary to the interests of local people.

When I began painting the new map pictures, I noticed that no matter how carefully I applied the masking tape, the paint occasionally crept under the tape, leaving a messy edge. To counteract this, I decided to paint a thin black line over the place where two colours joined in order to hide any imperfection. This not only worked perfectly, but to my delight it imparted an entirely new and more polished look to my paintings. Pleased with the results, this time I felt confident in submitting a diamond-shaped map painting to the Irish Exhibition of Living Art. My confidence was rewarded when it was accepted and awarded a prize.

At the time, I recollect declaring, 'It can't get much better than this!'

But I was wrong.

Overleaf: Map painting, 1968.

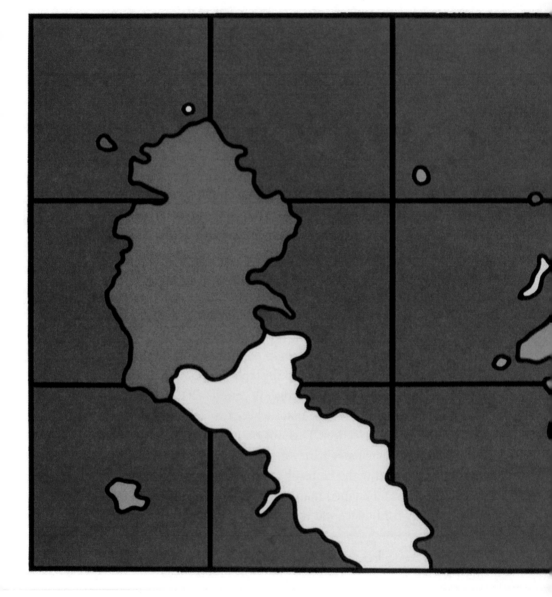

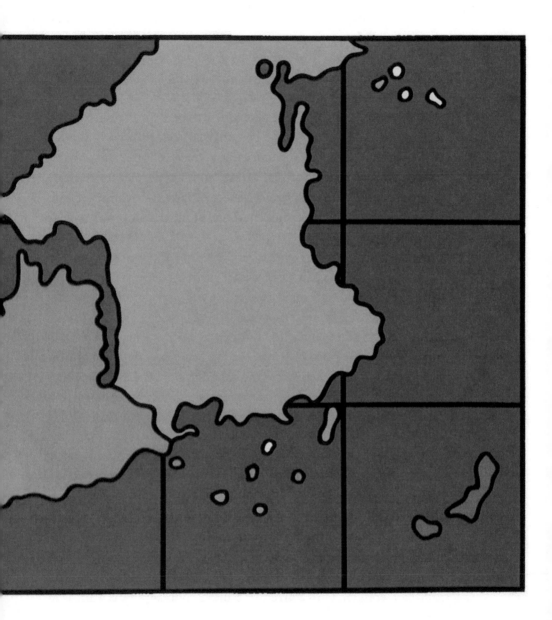

*

On 24 September something far more significant happened: my daughter was born. It was earlier in the year, after Betty realized she was pregnant, that we decided I would be present at the birth. At the time, this was unusual and even frowned upon in Irish hospitals, so we were surprised when her gynaecologist agreed to our request.

In the months before the estimated birth date we attended several pre-natal classes, which to be perfectly honest, I found hideously embarrassing, being the only male in a roomful of pregnant females. Finally, however, nature took its course and Betty went into labour.

After arriving at the Rotunda Maternity Hospital, while Betty was being examined by the medical staff one of the nurses took me aside and quietly recommended that, like a real man, I should take myself to Conway's pub across the road, have a few pints and wait for someone to come and inform me when it was all over. Of course, having already committed myself to being at the birth, I was having none of this. But nature did not make it easy, especially for Betty. Her labour went on and on, and to add to our difficulties there was a shortage of beds that night, so she was placed on a trolley in a corridor. By midnight the nursing staff had got so used to me hanging about the place that they kitted me out in scrubs and made me an unofficial medical orderly. I ended up not only pushing Betty about the corridor but also pushing other women in and out of the delivery room.

Eventually, the waiting could go on no longer. I was told that they had decided on a forceps delivery and that I couldn't be present in such an emergency. Both dejected and worried, I found a nearby chair and prepared to wait once again. In no time at all, however, a nurse appeared and informed me that the delivery had been a success, and that both mother and daughter were fine. We decided to name our beautiful new black-haired daughter after an actress we both admired, Audrey Hepburn, who starred in a movie opposite Burt Lancaster playing an 'Injun half-breed' called Rachel.

Hence her name was Rachel.

CHAPTER 11

Fresh Shoots

I t was probably my prize-winning map painting that prompted Basil
Goulding to ask me to come to his office to discuss a commission.
Goulding's, the family business, were building a large office block
on the banks of the Grand Canal and Basil had already commissioned
Micheal Farrell, Barrie Cooke and Anne Madden to produce large
works for the building.

Basil had three big spaces on the third floor in mind for me, hinting
that a map theme might be appropriate. I accepted the commission
and set about creating accurate and well-finished sketches. When Basil
saw them he was impressed, and suggested that I start work straight
away. I replied that I'd love to, but there was a problem. I explained
that the finished pictures would be larger than those painted by Micheal
Farrell for the National Bank, so there wasn't a hope in hell that I could
paint them in a small studio measuring just 3.5 x 1.8 metres (12 x 6 ft).

'Leave it to me,' replied Basil. 'I'll get back to you.'

Basil agreed with the builders that when the finishing-out stage
was reached, I could come on to what would still be a building site
and paint the murals.

So every morning I arrived at the same time as the plasterers, the electricians, the painters and the carpenters, went to the third floor and got stuck in. Instead of creating three enormous single canvases, I opted to divide each one up into individual smaller pieces, which I later assembled together in grid format to make one large picture. Once again my chosen medium was acrylic paint on canvas.

When the three murals were finally completed, I remember feeling reasonably satisfied with my work. Basil seemed delighted, and wrote in a letter of thanks:

> You got the deep blue satisfyingly deep and right; and the weight of the grid-lines; and, with immense discrimination, the colour of the land masses… Altogether I find myself extremely complimented and very proud of my good judgement in feeling sure of your prowess… I shall be finding myself excuses to visit people working in the Ballagh area, and will probably be mooning about there of an evening after they have gone.

By then I had become quite friendly with Basil. Physically he was a small, slim man and obviously quite fit. He skied fearlessly and as a young man had played squash for Ireland. He had grey hair with a slight curl, bright eyes and an impish smile, which often reflected a truly eccentric personality. The shareholders of the Bank of Ireland were to learn of this when on one occasion the chairman of the board arrived at their annual general meeting on a pair of rollerskates, which he duly handed to the doorman. 'Park these, please.'

One day I had a call from Heather Welsh, Basil's private secretary, inviting Betty and myself to a formal dinner at Dargle Cottage, his attractive home on the banks of the Dargle River in Enniskerry, Co. Wicklow.

Of course I accepted, but the invitation sparked considerable panic. What would I wear? I didn't own a dinner suit. The problem was partially solved by brushing up the dark blue suit I wore for my wedding and the purchase of a bow tie. I almost passed muster. Betty, on the other hand, had no such problems, as she already had several fashionable items in her wardrobe.

The other guests were various captains of industry and commerce, together with their wives. To our complete surprise, after we had eaten dinner the women stood up and announced that they were 'withdrawing'. To the obvious discomfiture of the representatives of Ireland's nouveau riche, Betty didn't budge. One spluttered something about her being perhaps more comfortable with the ladies in the drawing room. Betty politely replied that no, she was fine and was rather looking forward to sampling one of Basil's Cuban cigars. Basil alone was unfazed by this breach of etiquette and remarked later that the conversation, the brandy and the cigars seemed much improved by the presence of female company.

Basil was always quietly subversive in whatever sphere he operated. In financial circles there was a feeling that Goulding's, as a company, was in some difficulty and required immediate new investment. In an attempt to resolve the situation Basil negotiated a beneficial deal with Con Smith, a successful businessman. Tragically, however, Smith was killed in an Aer Lingus plane crash near London. A replacement arrangement was rapidly put in place and Basil signed a deal with rising entrepreneurs Tony O'Reilly, Vincent Ferguson and Nicholas Leonard.

At the time, I was attending regular meetings of the Contemporary Irish Arts Society, an organization established by Basil to raise funds, purchase artworks and then donate them to public institutions. The main beneficiary was the Municipal Art Gallery in Dublin – effectively the country's major museum of modern art, which, in those days, received no purchase funding whatsoever.

Basil had asked me to join the committee, which already included such notables as James White, director of the National Gallery, the artist Cecil King and Gordon Lambert, a businessman and art patron.

After one particular meeting, when news of the Goulding's deal was in the air, Gordon Lambert quietly confided to me, 'Well, there goes business morality in Ireland!'

I remember being shocked, because I construed the remark to be sectarian; that he was suggesting that Catholics were now taking over from Protestants.

However, just a few years after Tony O'Reilly and his colleagues became involved in the affairs of Goulding's, the production of fertilizer had ceased completely in Ireland and the work force had been reduced from 2,000 to less than twenty. I then came to realize that Gordon Lambert's comment was not about religion but about propriety.

When I met Tony O'Reilly myself I experienced a modest example of that attitude.

'How are things in the art world?' he casually inquired.

I should have replied, 'Fine,' but instead I embarked on a rambling diatribe about how difficult it was to make a living from art in Ireland.

'Listen,' he said, 'I have the answer to your problems.'

I pinned my ears back, expecting to hear some significant and creative business wisdom.

'You have two solutions,' he said. 'You can either increase your prices, or increase your productivity.'

Feeling slightly deflated I remember thinking, *Does he seriously believe that the marketing of art is the same as the marketing of a can of beans?*

As a young man O'Reilly had been a surprising choice to take over from Lt. General Michael J. Costello as chief of the Irish Sugar Company, but this appointment proved to be only a stepping stone in his personal advancement. He left Ireland to become head of the Heinz food company in Pittsburgh.

I will never forget another formal evening at Basil's summer house, a stunning steel and glass structure designed by architect Ronnie Tallon to cantilever over the Dargle River in the verdant grounds of Basil's home in Co. Wicklow.

When we arrived we noticed that there was already a line of ministerial Mercedes cars parked outside the summer house, and inside the house we could see that most of the other guests were either businessmen or politicians. We noticed not only Tony O'Reilly and his friend and business associate Jim McCarthy, but also the Labour Party ministers Justin Keating and Conor Cruise O'Brien. Basil bounded up to greet us, wearing a huge green stuffed frog on his shoulder.

Feeling slightly uneasy, I asked, 'What are we doing here?'

He grinned mischievously at us and said, 'When I was going through the invitation list with Heather, I suddenly realized that I would have nobody to talk to!'

The meal itself was pleasant enough, and afterwards small groups gathered to engage in the usual after-dinner chat. I found myself with a group of businessmen who were discussing the upcoming 1974 British general election. All seemed to believe that the Conservative Party would win, and even though it would have been wise of me to keep my mouth shut, I blurted out, 'I think Labour will win.'

'Nonsense,' snorted Tony O'Reilly. 'I bet you a case of champagne that the Tories will win.'

Slightly embarrassed, I confessed that since I could hardly afford a snipe of champagne, never mind a whole case, I would have to decline the bet.

At that point one of Basil's very good friends, Sir Valentine Duncan, chief executive of Rio Tinto Zinc, one of the biggest companies in the world, intervened. 'I'll make you a wager that you can honour. If the Tories win you will give me a painting, but if the Labour Party wins I will visit your studio and buy a painting.'

I immediately agreed and we shook hands on the deal.

As it happened, the Labour Party did win the election, and shortly afterwards I received a letter from Sir Valentine congratulating me and promising that on his next visit to Dublin he would happily discharge his obligation.

As I didn't hear more from him, even after Labour returned to power, I made discreet inquiries with Basil.

'Oh, didn't you hear? Valentine died.'

I should have accepted O'Reilly's bet. This ended my only venture into political gambling.

✶

It was only later that I began to decipher what the whole evening at Basil's was about. A coalition government in Ireland had been formed between the conservative Fine Gael Party and the Labour Party, and since Labour members for several years beforehand had been declaring that the 1970s would be socialist, it seemed only natural for the business community to discover if they were really serious about socialism. Hence the presence of several Labour ministers at the dinner. I remember reflecting how many major decisions that have the potential to affect the lives of citizens are made not in parliament, but at private gatherings between businessmen and politicians.

Basil Goulding was an exceptional individual, not just as a businessman but also as a serious patron of the arts; especially in his understanding of the needs of struggling young artists. His wit and wisdom were unconventional, to say the least, and nowhere better expressed than in the following catalogue note, written in 1974:

> I should like to write well about Robert Ballagh and his work. I mean both. But what does 'well' mean?
>
> As to an artist it often enough means psychocraptically: as to his works circumbollocally. Those foreseen, I must unsuccessfully avoid them. Actually he's a frightfully good type and his works are smashing.
>
> Intermediately let me tell that he's nearly unique in Ireland in developing a mind wide trawl to catch world tide humanitudes; and in serving them then with either a neo-Lancelotic derring-do (when he espouses rectitudes or wrongtitudes) or, by turns, a cold nosed analisation. In this exhibition we feel a satisfied tepidation of the latter. I seem to have dealt, unusually, with first things first. But one has to ask how so notable a secondary quality as dexterity crept into the piece. Was it great aptitude that spawned the conceptual caviar? Or was it that that called up this. Perhaps we can cosily define an egg as a good idea for breeding chickens: which is, obviously, not original.
>
> But in case there be a danger of these thoughts of mine imputing patronage or diminution – 'good show, young'un' – may I be seen now to draw myself to my full depth and declare Robert's work to be about foremost in

the slender category of Irish work which is professionally fully fledged; which is recognitive of modes and mentalities and miens of our present ether; which formulates and invests them to painterly punch; which is relievingly un-constipated and nudgedly ironical; which… er… conveys

Some years previously in 1969, I had received a letter from Amanda Douglas inviting me to stage a one-person show in the Brown Thomas Gallery. Naturally I accepted, but saw it as a real challenge. Up until then my work had been essentially formalist in nature. I had made paintings that merely asked questions about the role of painting itself. It was now time, I felt, to move on, to make art that might address some of the key issues of the day.

By marrying my hard-edge acrylic painting technique to a simple figurative approach, I hoped to create paintings that commented on social and political issues, like the Vietnam War, the struggle for civil rights in the United States and the campaign for civil rights in the North of Ireland.

My approach was to select key photographs, reduce them to silhou-ette form and then use the graphic results to create multiple repetitive imagery. In painting the resulting designs I employed a grey palette to reflect the media representation of reality, since both newspapers and television were black-and-white at the time. However, for dramatic effect, I also introduced occasional passages of bright acrylic colour.

Dr Conor Cruise O'Brien opened the exhibition on 15 July 1969. It was not unusual then to find O'Brien associating himself with the radical left. In his opening address he asserted, 'Here are the symbolic disasters of our time; here too is that efficient impersonality of the modern media, which brings us visually so close to the terrible event, while at the same time insulating us from it in feeling. Man in the past has mastered forces, which on any obvious calculation ought to have mastered him. The forces, which he now must master, if he is not to destroy himself, are in himself and in the society which he has made and is making. The struggle of self-adaption for survival is not only reflected but is actually going on in the world of art and here before our eyes, in the first exhibition of an exceptionally gifted, thoughtful young artist, Robert Ballagh.'

Cruise O'Brien's positive judgement, to my great relief, was replicated in most reviews of the show. The critic from the *Evening Press* remarked that, 'He has robbed cinema of style and technique and moulded them to the static frame and silent wall. It is not too much to say that he has succeeded in making this transmutation with something not short of genius.' And the *Irish Independent* commented that, 'His draughtsmanship is notable, extremely accurate and precise, and he uses brilliant acrylic colours against dark grey-toned backgrounds to produce sharp electric images. His starting point is often a news

Marchers, acrylic on canvas, 152cm x 152cm, 1969.

photograph, as in the painting based on the famous photograph of some years ago of a self-immolating Buddhist monk in flames. Of this, he makes a three-frame image, one in grey flat tones, the second with beautifully painted orange and yellow flames, and the third a darker-toned grey image again. It conveys the swift horror of the death of the monk with great power.'

While working on the paintings for the Brown Thomas exhibition I received an invitation from the artist Cecil King for Betty and myself to visit his flat in Baggot Street for some afternoon tea.

Cecil, a short, stocky, slightly balding man, who quite honestly looked more like a businessman than an artist, not only managed to paint elegant minimal abstract pictures but also found time to serve on several committees charged with the promotion of the visual arts. It was when he was cutting a slice from a delicious-looking chocolate cake that he sprang the surprise. He said that he had been appointed commissioner for the Paris Biennale, and that I had been selected to represent Ireland in the painting section. I was shaken: to represent one's country. I remember thinking, *My father did this many years ago in sport, now I'm doing it in art!*

We were breathless at the thought of travelling to Paris for the exhibition, in the Museum of Modern Art on Avenue Président Wilson.

When we eventually arrived, we discovered that not only was the scale of the exhibition enormous, with the participation of artists from all over the world, but the installation itself was downright chaotic. On our return, I wrote to a friend:

> It was a real horse-trading affair. People kept robbing the best places to hang their work. Cecil King grabbed a good spot for me and made me stand there for hours while he collected my paintings and hung them. Then I had to stand there for hours more to make sure nobody whipped them down.

Nevertheless it was an unbelievable experience, seeing my three paintings holding their own in such international company.

*

In 1969 the Irish Exhibition of Living Art had a problem. Normally the annual show was held in the College of Art in Kildare Street but their space was no longer available. Politicians in Leinster House next door had evicted the art college and claimed the vacant space for themselves. The Living Art committee was forced to either cancel the show or seek an alternative venue. Their decision was to open the exhibition in the Crawford Art Gallery in Cork on 21 August, and later transfer it to Belfast.

The weekend before, however, the sectarian time-bomb that had been ticking away persistently for years in the North of Ireland finally exploded. CS gas was fired by the Royal Ulster Constabulary on Catholic youths in Derry. Protestant mobs followed the police unhindered into Catholic areas in the North and viciously attacked the people and their houses. Taoiseach Jack Lynch called for the introduction of a UN peace force. British Minister James Callaghan ordered in the Prince of Wales's Own Regiment to take up security duty. Things would never be the same again.

Meanwhile a special train had been chartered to ferry artists and art patrons from Dublin to Cork for the opening of the Living Art exhibition. Betty and I were on board and in spite of the Northern conflagration being news headlines, to my shame I hadn't given it much thought. I had other things on my mind; I had just been told that I had won a major award in the exhibition. However, such apathy was about to be challenged during the prize-giving ceremony.

Micheal Farrell, who had won first prize, declared when he stepped up to receive his award, 'I wish to put myself on the side of right in relation to the things that are going on in the North of Ireland. Art is above politics but not humanity. As an artist and a man I have never used my work for any political end. I am so moved by wrong and know what is right and with regard to the horrific happenings in the north of this island, I will in the future not allow my work to go north until that state has achieved the basic fundamentals of a decent society.'

Of course Micheal's intervention put all artists in the exhibition on the spot.

Ultimately, nine other artists, including me, refused to show their work in Belfast. All the withdrawn works were subsequently exhibited under the title *Art and Conscience* at 43 Kildare Street. The premises had been made available by a newly formed 'citizens' committee', itself funded by a secretive operation that would eventually lead to the sacking of Charles J. Haughey and Neil Blaney, two ministers in Jack Lynch's government, for allegedly importing arms for use in the North of Ireland. They were both subsequently cleared by the controversial 'Arms Trial'.

A press statement was issued on behalf of the artists: 'We withdrew these pictures because they were to be shown at a Stormont sponsored Arts Council gallery. We felt that this regime had to be denied any semblance of credibility and cultural responsibility.' The statement was signed by Robert Ballagh, Michael Bulfin, Elizabeth Carabini, Robin Costelloe, Gerard Dillon, Micheal Farrell, John Kelly, Evin Nolan, Nano Reid and Darine Vanson.

For the record, one of the artists involved was Betty, who under her maiden name had submitted a hard-edge abstract painting entitled *At Sixes or Sevens*, which resembled the op art paintings of artists like Bridget Riley and Victor Vasarely, as part of a dare conjured up by several artists' wives. Growing weary of their respective husbands' constant claims to artistic greatness, they decided, since they joked that they could probably do as well themselves, to create several pictures and submit them to the Living Art exhibition. Ultimately, Betty was the only one to follow through on the dare, and her work was accepted.

∗

Some time after withdrawing my painting from the Living Art exhibition in Belfast I faced a dilemma. I was chosen to represent Ireland in an exhibition, *Celtic Triangle*, organized by the Arts Councils of Ireland, Northern Ireland, Scotland and Wales. They planned for the exhibition to visit Cardiff, Edinburgh, Dublin and finally Belfast. Should I continue with the boycott or should I try to paint something that might comment on the developing situation in the North?

After much soul-searching I chose the latter option. That, however, was the easy part. All my initial efforts came to nought. In desperation I turned to history. How did artists in the past deal with the pressing issues of their day?

After considering many examples of historic artistic engagement I eventually selected three paintings that seemed to suit my purpose. Eugene Delacroix's *Liberty Leading the People* rhymed with Northern realities where nationalists in Belfast and Derry had erected barricades to protect their homes from loyalist mobs. Jacques-Louis David painted *The Intervention of the Sabine Women* in protest against internecine violence after the French Revolution. It seemed to me that his gesture was relevant to the sectarian violence in the North. And finally, Francisco Goya's painting *The Third of May* 1808 in which French soldiers shoot Spanish patriots seemed appropriate, recognizing that the initial welcome by nationalists for British troops on Northern streets had inevitably turned hostile. Picasso had already adapted *The Third of May* to comment on the Korean War, but had considerably altered Goya's composition. I felt sure that it represented something of an artistic crime to interfere with the actual structure of the chosen masterpieces so, in order to make the intended content of the pictures available to a contemporary audience, I opted instead to paint hard-edge pop art versions of the originals.

I was pleased with the results, but the immediate general response was both uncomprehending and hostile. 'Cartoonish send-up of famous paintings,' ridiculed the *Irish Times*, while the *Scotsman* scoffed that 'Robert Ballagh, presumably in some kind of revolt, reduces masterpieces by Goya, Delacroix and Poussin (sic) to the basic terms found in comic strip procedures.'

Even in Belfast there was misunderstanding. Brian Ferran, a native of Derry and the Northern Arts Council's exhibition officer, decided to hang *Liberty on the Barricades*, my version of the Delacroix, in the gallery window in Bedford Street just behind City Hall, hoping, perhaps, for some kind of political reaction. Ultimately, there was only one complaint and that was from a loyalist councillor who strenuously objected to the display of naked breasts by the Arts Council.

Even so, gradually, the true meaning of the paintings began to gain acceptance. In his definitive study, *Goya and His Critics*, Nigel Glendinning placed an image of my version of *The Third of May* alongside Picasso's, commenting that in my painting there was a striking parallel 'between the presence of French troops on Spanish soil in 1808 and English troops in Ireland in the 1970s'.

*

Robin Walker, the respected architect and my former tutor, was designing a restaurant building for the new University College Dublin campus at Belfield, just outside the city, when he approached me about creating abstract patterns for the large moveable screens that were to be an essential feature in the finished building. I always admired Robin Walker's minimal yet elegant approach to architecture so I had no hesitation in responding positively. My brief was to prepare scale drawings, write out a specification document and then supervise the professional decorators charged with doing the actual painting.

My original intention was to use standard opaque colour to paint the design onto the screens, but when I saw the attractive surface of Douglas fir plywood I felt I had to alter my plans. Instead of covering over the plywood with paint, I opted to specify transparent polyurethane stains to allow the grain of the wood to shine through. At the workshop where the screens were to be painted, I was met by a tradesman in white overalls, clutching several pages of my specification document. He scratched his head and inquired, 'Do you really want me to do it this way?'

Recognizing that I had drawn up the specifications to suit someone of my limited competence and not an experienced painter and decorator I mumbled, 'Well, if you can manage…'

'No trouble,' was the confident reply.

He immediately took to the task and quickly demonstrated his considerable skills. Even though I realized that my role as supervisor had become redundant, I continued to return each day simply to watch him work. I picked up the kind of intuitive skills that you never learn from books. They have to be passed on. They're all in the bend of the wrist, the slant of a hand. You have to see it being done before you can do it yourself. At the time, in the context of my own work, I was beset by the problem of trying to paint the illusion of wood grain. In conversation one day I explained my problem. The craftsman's instant reply was, 'You need to use a scumble technique. We use it to paint false grain on doors.'

He then proceeded to give me a demonstration. Mixing an opaque brown oil colour with a transparent glaze medium he was able to replicate, with a few brushstrokes, an almost exact representation of wood grain.

My next question: 'What about marbling?'

Moveable screens in the University College Dublin restaurant building.

His response was, 'The trick is to paint several oil colours wet into wet, blending them together to create a cloudy effect. Then you dip a seagull's feather into diluted oil colour and drag it across the painted surface.' Thus, he explained, you can simulate the striation of marble. This was followed by another practical demonstration. Needless to say, the screens were completed to perfection and Robin Walker seemed to agree.

The original brief was to create a brightly coloured abstract pattern that would visually connect all the screens no matter which way they were arranged. Responding to this challenge I typeset the word REVOLUTION in large bold capital letters on paper and then proceeded to cut up the paper into small abstract pieces which formed the basis of the design. My unlikely fancy was that some day, by complete chance, the twelve screens would be rearranged in such a manner that the original word would suddenly reappear for all to see.

Sadly, this was not to be. Some time later the university maintenance staff mistakenly painted over the screens as part of a renovation project; so the designs were effaced, never to return.

✳

David Hendriks was a middle-class Jamaican who first came to Dublin in the 1950s to study at Trinity; after college, because he liked the place so much, he stayed and opened his first gallery in 1956. He developed an enviable reputation for showing important contemporary art. He was a tall slim man, with a tanned complexion, always immaculately dressed and invariably encircled by a wisp of smoke curling from a delicately held cigarette: the personification of elegance. David first put a few pieces of mine in a group show, but then in 1970, offered me my own solo exhibition in his gallery.

Little did he realize, in making the offer, how challenging that exhibition would be. At the time, I was questioning why the notion

Overleaf: *The Third of May after Goya*, acrylic on canvas, 183cm x 244cm, 1970, Dublin City Gallery, The Hugh Lane.

of supposed 'good' taste played such a crucial role in alienating the majority from any meaningful participation in the fine arts. Accordingly, I set out to create an exhibition that would threaten the very idea of 'good' taste. I systematically set out to introduce low art materials into a high art setting. I used dyed nylon fur, false leopard skin and quilted plastic as framing devices for magnified images of liquorice allsorts, dolly mixtures and iced caramels, all painted in lurid colours.

Basil Goulding welcomed the show as 'a cold nose up the arse' and in the *Irish Times,* Brian Fallon suggested that 'the show is laden with satirical implications… and what saves this show is the sheer skill and flair with which it is executed.' However, Dorothy Walker, even though she praised the work, correctly observed 'that I cannot imagine anyone wanting to buy them'.

The show was not a commercial success, but, in spite of the challenge it had posed, David stood by me.

Although I had served with Gordon Lambert on the Contemporary Irish Art Society committee, it wasn't until I became involved with the Hendriks gallery that I really got to know him. Not only was he a silent partner in the gallery, he was also David's partner in life, but nobody spoke openly about gay relationships in those days. It wasn't until after 1993, when homosexuality was decriminalized in Ireland, that many gay people began to feel comfortable publicly expressing their sexuality.

As chief executive of the huge biscuit empire that included Jacob's and Boland's, Gordon Lambert occupied a key position in Irish industry but, like Basil Goulding, he had also developed a keen interest in the arts; he had not only built a significant personal collection but also served on many important art boards and committees. His customary conservative appearance, neatly turned out in a business suit, always seemed slightly at odds with his passion for avant-garde art.

In my own case I was struck by how familiar he seemed to me. This, of course, was because of his family background. The Lamberts, like the Ballaghs, were south Dublin middle-class Protestants who possessed

Gordon Lambert, acrylic and silkscreen on canvas, 180cm x 190cm, 1971,
The Irish Museum of Modern Art.

a well-mannered demeanour and a passion for sport. Like my father, Gordon's brother Ham played cricket for Ireland.

One day in the gallery, Gordon approached me with a proposal to paint his portrait. I was completely taken by surprise; in the course of my short career, I had never once considered engaging in portraiture. Yet I knew I had to accept the challenge, since Gordon was such an important collector. I decided to create a full-size likeness on three individual canvases stacked vertically. I depicted him in a dark grey business suit with a green tie but, in order to stress the importance of art in his life, I portrayed him holding a large abstract painting. Gordon himself owned a tapestry based on the original abstract painting *Homage to the Square* by Josef Albers, which hung in the Municipal Gallery in Parnell Square. To draw attention to the significance of collecting and owning art, I decided to make the hands gripping the edges of the canvas three dimensional, so I persuaded the sculptor Brian King to make a casting from my own hands.

The final task, however, was the one I was dreading: painting the face. I knew that I simply didn't have the necessary skills. What to do? Once again American pop art came to the rescue. I remembered that Andy Warhol had created portraits of celebrities like Marilyn Monroe and Elvis Presley using silkscreened photographs, so I said to myself, *If it's good enough for Andy, it's good enough for me.* I obtained a photo of Gordon, had a stencil made and, with sepia-coloured ink, silk-screened the image onto the canvas. The portrait was complete.

*

I now felt, having staged two solo exhibitions, won several awards, completed several important commissions and represented Ireland on two occasions, that it was about time I tested international waters; and since New York was the acknowledged centre of the modern art scene, where better to start?

By a complete coincidence, the week before my departure I happened to bump into James Johnson Sweeney on Grafton Street, whom I had briefly met at ROSC. On hearing that I planned to visit New York, he obligingly said, 'Here's my phone number – look me up!'

So once I was settled in Manhattan, I phoned him and he instantly responded, 'Will we meet in my club or in the apartment?'

'It's up to you,' I stuttered.

'Well, then come to the apartment.'

At the appointed hour I turned up at 80 East End Avenue to be greeted by a fancily dressed doorman. He ushered me into the elevator, which finally came to rest on the top floor. When the doors opened, Sweeney was standing straight in front of me and, with a genial smile, welcomed me into the penthouse apartment. He directed me to a table and some chairs and it was then that I noticed a bottle of vodka and two glasses, and knew that this was not going to be a short visit.

James Johnson Sweeney was a short, thickset man, usually dressed in a three-piece suit, and looking for all the world like a colonial diplomat. His thinning hair was grey and he sported a bristly moustache on his upper lip, but his most obvious facial feature, a bulbous nose, was spectacularly pinker than the rest of his face.

The Sweeney fortune was originally made in the nineteenth century through the selling of lace imported from Ireland, but when the supply of Irish lace became insufficient to service the demand they resorted to importing replica lace from China. It was hawked around the United States by travelling salesmen who, ironically, were themselves Irish travellers who had emigrated to the southern states.

James was introduced to art by his mother on their travels in Europe. He received a Bachelor of Arts degree from Georgetown University and he studied art and literature at Cambridge, the Sorbonne and Siena. As he was born with the century itself, on my visit he was seventy-one years of age and, for the record, I was twenty-eight.

Sweeney was incredibly proud of his Irish heritage; I clearly remember him taking immense pleasure in describing how his father walked to school in Co. Donegal in his bare feet. As we were sitting on chairs and beside a table that resembled Mies van der Rohe's Barcelona furniture, I couldn't resist commenting on how much I appreciated the design. He told me that these very chairs were the originals designed by Mies for his pavilion at the Barcelona World's Fair in 1929, and that when the fair was over he purchased them. He also pointed out that when Mies came to the States in 1935, not being certified and therefore unable to practise, he borrowed them back and gave them to a furniture manufacturer to copy so that he could make a living.

With the sun slowly setting and as the city lights began to sparkle, the view from the penthouse across the East River became quite spectacular.

'What a sight,' I marvelled.

Quite casually he responded, 'Fernand always loved that view.'

Somewhat shamefully, I asked, 'Fernand who?'

'Fernand Léger, of course.'

I was astonished: Léger was one of my favourite early modern painters.

We chatted for hours, mainly about Ireland, but also about art and about how difficult it was for a young artist to make a breakthrough.

Iced Caramels, acrylic on canvas, 1970, Dublin City Gallery, The Hugh Lane.

He promised to help me in any way he could. Eventually it was time to call it a day, or, in our case, more appropriately, a night.

True to his promise, Sweeney arranged for me to meet several art dealers. I dutifully called into their respective galleries and showed them slides of my work. Some were interested, some not, but the one that made the greatest impression, as far as I was concerned, was an individual called Ivan Karp. He had been the manager of the Leo Castelli Gallery and had looked after the early careers of Andy Warhol and Roy Lichtenstein, among others; but, being ambitious, had decided to strike out on his own and establish his own space, distinguished by the unlikely name of the OK Harris Gallery.

I arrived at the downtown gallery at the agreed time and was told to go straight into Mr Karp's office by his secretary. When I opened the door, there he was, looking like a stereotypical Hollywood producer, revolving on a swivel chair, chomping on a huge cigar and holding forth on the phone with the kind of accent in which New York is pronounced 'Noo Yoik'.

He signalled for me to sit down. I did what I was told and began looking around the rather large office. I immediately noticed that the walls were crammed with stunning examples of the latest trend in painting, sharp-focus realism in which, even though they were hand painted, all resembled blown-up photographs.

Finishing his call, he turned to me. 'I'll be with you in a moment; first I have to see an Irish guy.'

What was he expecting? Someone with red curly hair and freckles, perhaps?

I timidly retaliated, 'I'm Irish.'

'You don't look Irish to me. Never mind. Let's look at your stuff – you've got two minutes!' he snapped.

I nervously tumbled my slides onto his desk. Popping one of those magnifying lenses that jewellers use into his eye, he began scrutinizing the slides, one by one. After about twelve, he put the slides down, removed the magnifying glass, looked straight at me and somewhat incredulously inquired, 'Are you sure you're from Ireland?' followed quickly by, 'These are too good – no art ever came out of that bog.'

I was stung into silence. He carried on with the rest of the slides and finally put one aside and kept tapping it. 'This is the one.'

I was taken aback, because it wasn't even part of my original selection. It was a small gouache sketch in monochrome of a group of people depicted in silhouette, looking at some of my paintings in a gallery setting.

'You could really get something out of this.'

He then informed me that he wasn't taking on any new artists, but he was prepared to pass on some useful names for me to contact. I said thanks and left – quietly noting that I'd had more than two minutes.

∗

After the New York trip I arrived back in Dublin buzzing with excitement to advance some of my new ideas. But once again there was a problem: the perennial one of having no studio space. The small back bedroom studio had reverted to its original function; it had become my baby daughter Rachel's bedroom.

In the end, it was an old friend from Toners, the artist Frank Lee Cooper, who rescued me. At the time, he was renting a studio on the top floor of a building in Parliament Street near City Hall, and, feeling that it was large enough to accommodate two artists, suggested that we share both the space and the rent. I jumped at the offer, even though the facilities were primitive, with no electricity and shared toilets; but on the positive side, there was ample space and excellent natural light. These conditions had obviously been acceptable to several previous tenants, like the artists Patrick Collins, Arthur Armstrong and David Hone.

In less than no time I found myself, fully installed in the new studio, making preparations for my next exhibition, scheduled for the following year in the Hendriks Gallery. I decided to follow up on Ivan Karp's advice and develop the concept of pictures of people looking at modern paintings.

First of all, taking advantage of the new studio space, I opted to paint the pictures on a scale in which the figures would be life-size; and because they were looking at pictures, they would be depicted from the rear. Nevertheless, being practical and critically aware of the seven flights of stairs in the building, I reverted to the practice, previously employed in the Gouldings murals, of constructing a large picture by joining together several smaller canvases in a grid format. Secondly, I decided that to contrast with the figurative elements, I would only include versions of paintings by famous abstract painters. Once again, the bulk of the work was completed with acrylic paint, but occasionally – in the case of difficult passages, like painting the texture of hair – I used the oil paint scumble technique.

It took several trips to deliver all the individual canvases to the Hendriks Gallery and then, like an enormous jigsaw, they had to be joined together. Finally, a way had to be construed to display the damn things. They were huge. Having staggered around the gallery for hours trying to place them, David and I and Joe Cullen, the gallery framer, had almost given up when we were joined by Ronnie Tallon, the architect. After considerable discussion we decided to bypass the eighteenth-century architecture, namely the fireplace and Georgian windows, and create a completely independent installation in the front room of the gallery. I have to say it looked wonderful, an opinion that was obviously shared by both the Arts Council and the Bank of Ireland who, between them, bought the entire installation.

However, once again, several notices were hostile. Bruce Arnold in the *Irish Independent* predicted that the Arts Council would 'in five years or so, feel a certain prickle of embarrassment that they had been so rash', and Brian Fallon in the *Irish Times* wouldn't 'take bets on all this in ten years' time, let alone fifty. Ballagh is almost too much a child of his time'.

But did I care? I had just had my first sell-out show, and thanks to the New York visit, a gallery on Madison Avenue had offered me an exhibition. Certainly no one was more surprised than I by my rapid rise in the Irish contemporary art scene, especially since I felt no more

Overleaf: Exhibition in the Hendriks Gallery, 1972.

talented than many others of my generation; however a casual remark by the painter Cecil King cast some light on my preferment. We were in Paris for the Biennale in 1969 when he mischievously quipped, 'You know Robert, we all thought that you were a Protestant.' As I hadn't a clue what he was on about I didn't respond and pushed the matter to the back of my mind, where it steadfastly remained until much later, when it resurfaced with unexpected clarity after I came across a description of a particular dinner in 1980 by Homan Potterton, then Director of the National Gallery of Ireland. The big art event in Dublin that summer was ROSC 80, staged together with an ancillary exhibition 'Chinese paintings from the Sackler Collection'. Arthur Sackler was a major American art philanthropist and a dinner in his honour was held in the Burlington Hotel. The guests, about eighteen in number, were drawn from the Irish contemporary art world. After dinner, following several speakers, the historian and ROSC committee member Anne Crookshank got to her feet. She was always a tremendously amusing speaker with her piercingly exaggerated voice rising in decibels only to be interspersed by peals of her own laughter. 'We are so pleased to welcome you to Ireland, Dr Sackler,' she trilled, 'so pleased indeed. You see we are such a very small band of enthusiasts here, who are passionate about bringing art and particularly contemporary art to the people, and tonight we welcome you to our (pause) bosoms.' Vibrating vigorously with laughter she continued, 'And nearly all of us enthusiasts are in this room; you are meeting the crème de la crème.' More laughter. 'And do you know what it is about us, Dr. Sackler?' The distinguished guest appeared puzzled. 'The thing about us – and I'll go around the table one by one – is that we are nearly all… (long pause)… Protestants.' She then pointed out the collector Gordon Lambert, the painters Patrick Scott and Cecil King, the sculptor Deborah Brown, the architect Robin Walker and the Director of the National Gallery of Ireland, Homan Potterton. Certainly, in the small cosy Irish art scene fondly described by Professor Crookshank on that night it was not a major disadvantage to be of the Protestant persuasion.

CHAPTER 12

Winter in Ronda

The winter of 1977 must have been a fairly dismal one, because when it finally came to an end I clearly remember boring the arse off anyone who would listen to my threats of never tolerating the damp, the cold and above all the greyness of another fecking Irish winter. Of course nobody paid a blind bit of notice; that is, until one spring evening, when an old friend dropped into our house for a drink and a bite to eat. I first met Cyril Barrett in the 1960s when he came to Dublin to organize a ground-breaking exhibition in the David Hendriks Gallery, which featured works by the leading proponents of the new op and kinetic movements – the likes of which we insular Irish had never seen before.

Cyril was a most unlikely curator, as they like to call them nowadays. As an ordained Jesuit, his true vocation was as a man of the cloth, and his regular day job involved lecturing in philosophy at Warwick University; nonetheless he still managed to find time to write about and promote contemporary art, and it's worth noting that he was an early and enthusiastic champion of the English artist Bridget Riley at a time when her work was relatively unappreciated. Cyril cut a tall, gangly figure with a slight stoop, some sort of back problem I think, and was invariably togged out in time-worn priestly garb with a light dusting of dandruff on his shoulders. His thinning dark hair was oiled and combed back, presumably in the same style he had followed unthinkingly for decades. He loved good conversation, particularly if lubricated with good wine, and whenever he finally completed a well-argued point he would triumphantly transfix you with an expression that could only be described as a cross between a grin and a grimace. I always enjoyed his erudite yet good-humoured company, and made sure to meet him whenever he visited Dublin.

On that particular evening I had barely begun wittering on about my winter of discontent when he unexpectedly cut through me in mid-sentence with, 'Would you fancy spending next winter in the south of Spain?'

Without even considering the consequences, I heard myself mumbling my agreement.

His response was both curt and intriguing. 'Good. Well, leave it to me.'

No more was said that evening about our putative Spanish adventure, which suited us fine, because, to be honest, both Betty and I were quite apprehensive about Spain due to our only previous experience in the land of Generalissimo Franco.

In 1968, as a belated honeymoon, we booked a cheap package deal to the resort of Sitges, just south of Barcelona; it was progressing quite agreeably until one evening in the bar of our modest hotel, I foolishly raised the topic of Spanish politics. Our previously loquacious barman immediately shut tight as a clam and an uneasy silence descended like a dark cloud over the drinkers. The next day, when there was nobody else around, the barman whispered to us, in conspiratorial tones, that in any gathering there were always spies and informants who would gladly report malcontents to the Guardia Civil; and as a result, jobs could be lost, or worse. Nevertheless, in spite of this sinister undercurrent, we were determined to enjoy the sunshine and the clear sea during the day and the good cheap wine in the evenings.

After a few days, we felt an obligation to visit the great city of Barcelona. We took the short train journey from Sitges, and as we walked from the station we were startled by a strange hissing sound. At first we couldn't account for the sibilation but then, to our amazement, we realized that it emanated from a bunch of old crones, dressed from head to toe in black, looking for all the world like the witches so dramatically depicted in Goya's great etchings *Los Caprichos*. It slowly dawned on us that the cause of the commotion was Betty's dress. The spectacle of her mini-skirt was morally repugnant to these self-appointed moral guardians. We hurried past only to be confronted at the next corner by a similar coven that elected to add torrents of spittle to their armament of abuse. By now Betty had had enough; we decided to beat a hasty retreat to our hotel in Sitges and, understandably, at the end of our short holiday, vowed never again to set foot in Spain.

Our resolve was weakened when Cyril Barrett told us that his friends Harry and Elma Thubron, who owned a cottage in the south of Spain, were prepared to make it available to us for the sum of £5 a week. Any further resistance collapsed when a Spanish friend assured us that, ever since Franco relinquished power, the political and cultural environment had become much more open. Like many other male artists, Harry Thubron left business matters to his wife, so it was Elma who wrote to us providing enough information to get to their cottage outside Ronda in the province of Malaga, and further advice about organizing our lives once we were there.

We decided, because we hadn't much money, to drive in our Ford Escort estate to the south of Spain. We told the school that the children (our second child Bruce was born in 1974) would be absent for several months, and set off, taking the ferry from Rosslare in Wexford to Le Havre in France. We planned to stop with Micheal Farrell and his family in Paris.

Micheal advised me to head for Porte de Versailles but, as the landscape changed from urban to rural, I gradually realized we were going in the wrong direction. I pulled up, parked the car, and managed to stop a motorist. He told me I was travelling to Versailles, not Porte de Versailles; I should turn around and, after about 12 miles (20 km), I would come upon Porte de Versailles. I thanked him profusely, but as I watched his rear lights fade into the gathering gloom, I realized that

I had left my car keys on the roof of his car. Holy fuck! What to do?

In my panic I had parked our car in front of a garage with a roller shutter, which slowly began to rise. I rushed over to explain what had happened to its owner who, understandably, was expecting to drive out.

He proclaimed, '*Pas de problème*,' and, snatching tools from the garage, climbed into our Ford Escort, cut some wires, installed a switch and declared the car ready to go. It was then I realized that he was a trained mechanic. But there remained another problem: the petrol cap, which also required a key.

Again, '*Pas de problème.*'

He drilled out the lock, removed the existing cap and gave me a plain rubber one in its place. I couldn't thank him enough; yet, in spite of my best efforts, he absolutely refused any payment and simply wished us a heartfelt '*Bon voyage.*'

I interpreted his help and generosity as a positive omen for the long journey ahead. As far as I could judge, Micheal seemed to have settled well in Paris. He was fortunate that, with the help of a friend, he had secured a tenancy in La Ruche, which has a long history of housing distinguished artists such as Picasso, Soutine and Matisse. It was originally designed by Gustave Eiffel for the Exposition Universelle (Great Exhibition) of 1900 and, because of its octagonal plan, each studio or apartment was shaped like a wedge of cheese. The Farrell family, consisting of Micheal, Pat and their three boys, Seamus, Liam and Malachy, were allocated an extra wedge, yet in spite of that, the space was rather cramped. Micheal was also allowed to use a small shed in the grounds, which he converted into a studio. Conveniently located across the road from La Ruche was a small bistro, Café Dantzig, which Micheal frequented with increasing regularity. For Micheal the many bars, bistros and cafés in Paris became an essential part of his life; not just for the wine and beer but also for the *craic* and camaraderie. Café Triste and Café de Flore also featured in several of his more memorable paintings. Among his many firm friends in Paris were the Dutch artist Mark Brusse and the brilliant lithographer Jacques de Champfleury. Nevertheless, in spite of his successful acclimatization in Paris, I always felt that a certain part of his being remained firmly attached to Ireland.

After a few pleasant days, we began the long journey south. In France we chose to use the national roads rather than motorways, and the small family pensions and restaurants we found on these roads suited both our taste and our pocket.

However, this practice was to change in Spain. It was evening as we approached Burgos, south west of the Basque Country, and all of us were exhausted and starving. On the outskirts of the city I spotted a utilitarian building with a large carpark and a sign, HOSTAL, blinking in the diminishing light. I decided to give it a try. Yes, they did have a room and yes, they could feed us. Without hesitation, I signed us in. In the morning, as we emerged for breakfast, we realized that most of our fellow guests were truck drivers, so, acknowledging their superior

Harry and Elma Thubron's cottage outside Ronda in southern Spain.

knowledge of the road, decided that similar accommodation would suit us perfectly for the rest of the journey. There was one disadvantage, however, and that was their peripheral location, which made any exploration of the nearby town or city extremely awkward.

I intended to make sure this wouldn't happen once we reached Madrid. I was determined to visit the Prado Museum at all costs. I was well aware that the Prado, having one of the greatest art collections in the world, would require days, if not weeks of exploration, so having just a few hours, I reluctantly limited myself to the Spanish masters, especially Francisco Goya and Diego Velázquez.

Goya, without doubt, was a truly humane artist and the Prado holds most of his major works, including the challenging dark paintings, but it was his *The Third of May* 1808, which had played such a significant role in my early career, that I was most anxious to see. When I stood in front of the enormous canvas I can only say I was humbled by the immense power and emotional intensity of the picture, and, once again, learned that no matter how effectively a reproduction can represent the form, the colour and the tone of a picture, it can never deliver its true essence.

Some say that Velázquez is a painter's painter and, if that means he knew how to skilfully manipulate paint, then what I saw of his work in the Prado certainly confirmed that opinion. But, of course, he's much more than that. And if proof is required, it's to be found in his masterpiece *Las Meninas*.

I had previously seen it only in reproduction, and I was overwhelmed by its sheer scale, coming upon it in its high-ceilinged room in the Prado, standing 3.5 metres (12 ft) tall in its huge black frame. On the surface it seems a fairly simple idea, a painting within a painting in which Velázquez is glimpsed behind a huge canvas, probably painting a portrait of the king and queen of Spain. But the more you look, the more you become aware of its many complex and subtle layers of meaning. In spite of the cerebral efforts of writers, historians and philosophers to decipher this truly enigmatic painting, it has never fully given up its secrets and probably never will. As I recollect what captivated me most on that occasion was the actual mood of the piece;

its interior darkness giving way to a unique luminosity that focuses our attention on the various characters who inhabit this extraordinary canvas. I had never felt that way about a picture before. And, to my amazement I also noticed that the closer I got to the surface of the canvas its incredible veracity began to dissolve into a maze of seemingly abstract brushstrokes. Yet, at the same time, I was amazed at how those skilfully applied dabs of oil paint managed to disclose the very sense of the picture's subject matter.

Within a few days we found ourselves near Ronda and, following the excellent directions provided by Elma Thubron, took the road to Seville. After about four miles we left the road and began negotiating what was little more than a track; and after the most bone-shaking experience of our lives, we arrived at our destination: a tiny cottage beside a stream, in a valley below the historic town of Ronda. I parked the car and walked about a quarter of a mile to a neighbouring farm to get the keys. On my return we let ourselves into a tiny traditional house with a red tiled roof, one small living room, a bedroom, a kitchen and a toilet. There was a small modern extension, which was obviously Harry's studio, but it immediately became the children's bedroom. As there was no running water I returned to the farm, which had a traditional circular well, and drew water by means of a rope and a bucket. Easier said than done. When you drop the bucket into the inky depths you have to make sure it hits the water at the right angle so it will fill up. If you fail it will simply float on the surface. Initially I was feckin' hopeless; and though I slowly improved, I never became an expert.

On that first day, I eventually staggered back with two extremely heavy containers of cold, clear spring water and was able to fill the cistern above the toilet, much to the relief of those who were patiently waiting to use it. It was also at that point that I appreciated why the cottage was sited so close to the stream. Because there was no electricity, Elma had warned us to avail ourselves of the daylight and to make sure that the oil lamps were working. So, again on that first day, I filled the lamps with paraffin and checked the wicks to be certain that when night came there would be light. Elma had also told us, because we were up high in the mountains and it could get quite cold at night, to be sure we had sufficient firewood to keep a fire going. With that in mind, I set off with the children along the banks of the nearby Guadalevin River to collect driftwood and fallen branches or anything else that might burn; I found that old shoes and sandals made excellent combustible material. The kitchen hob was powered by a gas cylinder, or *bombona* as the locals called it, and there was a full one there on our arrival. So as night fell, we lit the oil lamps, set the fire and made some tea before retiring to bed, totally exhausted.

A few days later we were inside the cottage when we heard someone call out, 'Hello, is there anyone at home?' – spoken not just in English but with a proper home counties English accent. A tanned handsome woman with shoulder-length auburn hair and a slightly mischievous smile was standing outside in the sunshine, leaning against an old Renault 4. 'We're neighbours, we live just down the valley. We heard you were coming to stay at Elma's.'

We introduced ourselves. She announced that she was Hilly and asked if we would join her later for a bite to eat in the pub across the way. This surprised me, because I hadn't noticed a pub myself, but when we met at the agreed time, I understood why. Essentially the pub was the front room of a family home and the menu consisted of whatever the family were eating that night.

In the course of the meal Hilly told us she was married to a Scotsman, Alastair Boyd, who was away in London, and that they had a young son, Jaime, who during the week stayed with a family in Ronda in order to attend school, but came home for the weekends. She suggested that when Alastair returned we would all meet up for lunch or a picnic.

Unfortunately, we had need of Hilly even before then. The rocky track from the main road to the cottage proved too much for the Ford Escort, and it finally collapsed. Hilly drove me to a garage in Ronda where I attempted to explain the problem. The garage man said they would come the next morning. As I suspected, the left rear suspension was broken. He explained that they would have to tow it to the garage in Ronda to fix it.

'Fine,' I said. 'When will it be ready?'

'*Mañana*,' came the immediate reply.

I must admit I was sceptical, but when Hilly brought me back the next afternoon it stood there as good as new. I asked where they got the spare part.

The garage man smiled. 'No, no, we made it ourselves,' he said, and pointed to a forge at the back of the garage.

When I was presented with the bill I couldn't believe how cheap it was. That improvised repaired suspension not only carried us back to Ireland but was still working perfectly when I sold the car years later. Automation and globalization seem to have put paid to all that skill and craft.

*

True to her word, when Alastair returned from London Hilly hosted a lunch at their farm, a short drive away that nevertheless involved crossing a rail track and fording a small stream. Alastair was a tall, well-groomed man; I thought he had an aristocratic bearing, without actually realizing the truth of my description. As I was to learn, Alastair was in fact Lord Kilmarnock, apparently the black sheep of an aristocratic family, who had gone to Spain years before and had chosen to stay. He was delightful company and entertained us with stories of his early days in Spain, travelling on horseback along the many trails that once linked the important places in Andalusia. Alastair wrote a book about those experiences, *The Road from Ronda*, and he presented us with a treasured signed and dedicated copy. I can't remember if it was during that lunch or on a later occasion that Alastair explained the main reason behind his frequent trips to London. The attendance fees paid by the House of Lords provided a much-appreciated stream of ready money, but to obtain it Alastair had to be present at Westminster.

One evening when we were in El Puente, the makeshift bar close to our cottage, Alastair informed us that he was off again to London the following week; taking me aside, he whispered, 'Look after Hilly while I'm away.'

I promised, 'Of course we will.'

Betty decided that in spite of our primitive kitchen conditions she would cook a special dinner for Hilly. It turned out to be a great success, lubricated with not a little wine and brandy. That night Hilly revealed that she had been married to the author Kingsley Amis, but, apart from a slight hint that he had been a bit of a shit, she didn't go into much detail. Later I was to learn that on one occasion, at a dinner party hosted by Kingsley and Hilly, he disappeared with each of the women at table one by one. She also mentioned, I think with some pride, that their son Martin was making quite a name for himself as a writer.

That evening Hilly, in her own words feeling 'slightly squiffy', wobbled to her Renault 4 and got in.

Faintly concerned I mumbled, 'Will you be all right?'

'I'll be fine,' she said, and the car bumped and swayed into the night.

The next morning, when she failed to turn up on time for an arranged shopping trip, we were slightly more worried. Eventually she arrived, looking a bit bedraggled; she had a sticking plaster on her

Betty, Rachel and Bruce about to swim in an irrigation tank.

forehead and the Renault appeared to have a few more dints. Hilly confessed that on her return journey the night before, she had driven into a ditch, which forced her to abandon the car and walk the rest of the way home. In the morning she had prevailed upon a neighbour with a tractor to drag the car out of the ditch and, as she put it, 'Here I am – right as rain!'

Going shopping with Hilly in Ronda was a real treat. We invariably began in the Mercado Municipal, the city market. The entrance, off the Plaza de España, was a small dark space with a wonderful aroma of spices and the occasional loitering gypsy selling songbirds impaled on a metal ring. Past the darkness it opened out into the market itself, a spacious ramshackle affair with a rickety glass roof and a fantastic array of stalls selling fruit, vegetables, meat and fish; far more varieties than we were familiar with. Piles of quince, figs, custard fruit, swordfish, sea urchin, razor clam, lamprey, wild boar, hare, partridge and quail were laid out in profusion. Since Hilly knew many of the stallholders, we usually returned to the cottage laden with provisions. Sadly that market no longer exists; because of its prime location, it was torn down and replaced by a luxury hotel.

Inevitably we would finish the shopping expedition with a few beers and some tapas in a favourite bar before wobbling back a little unsteadily to the *campo* or, as we say in English, the countryside.

Ronda's setting is unforgettable, spectacularly perched across a vertiginous rocky cleft, 120 metres deep, which divides the town. A narrow bridge, completed in 1793, connects both sides. It is an awesome example of eighteenth-century engineering, the road surface supported by three arches, one of which rises from the floor of the gorge. The footpath on the bridge delivers a spectacular view across the river valley far below, encircled by a distant mountain range. The building of the bridge spanned more than four decades and local folklore relates that its architect, Martín de Aldehuela, fell to his death while trying to engrave the completion date on the bridge. Its name, the Puente Nuevo, the new bridge, might seem odd until you learn that the town's other two bridges, the Puente Árabe and the Puente Romano, both date back to the time of the Moors. In Ernest Hemingway's *For Whom the Bell Tolls*, he recounts how, at the start of the Spanish Civil War, the 'fascists' of a small town were rounded up and thrown over a cliff. This episode was based on events in Ronda. La Ciudad, or old town, on the southern side of the Tajo gorge, is almost completely unspoiled, with a maze of narrow streets leading into small squares with many beautiful buildings. The orange-tree-lined Plaza Duquesa de Parcent with a small park and fountain provides a quiet oasis. On its northern end, the Iglesia de Santa Maria La Mayor stands on the site of Muslim Ronda's main mosque. Just inside the entrance is an arch, covered with Arabic inscriptions, which was the mosque's *mihrab* (towards which worshippers would pray, as it was the part closest to Mecca).

The Palacio de Mondragón is one of the finest buildings in the old town, although when we were in Ronda in 1978, it was completely closed up. Fortunately for us, Alastair had lived there in the 1960s when he operated a language school; as a result, he was able to gain access and show us around the magnificent building. It was originally constructed for Abomelic, ruler of Ronda in 1314 and was subsequently home to a succession of Moorish governors until the siege of Ronda in 1485 ended Arabic rule. It was converted into a Mudéjar Renaissance mansion named after the knight Melchor de Mondragón whose coat of arms is above the main entrance. The ground floor has three courtyards, but only the patio preserves an Islamic character with its rich tiling and arches; another leads into a formal garden running to the edge of the cliff. After our unique visit in 1978, Alastair quietly confided that he had sold his interest in the palace for just £6,000 sterling.

Across the Tajo lies the Mercadillo, or commercial centre, with offices, shops, bars and restaurants, but it also boasts the oldest and largest bullring in Spain, a magnificent building constructed in the eighteenth century. The rules of bullfighting were allegedly first established in Ronda, and a native, Pedro Romero Martínez, born in 1754, is credited as the father of modern bullfighting. Every year in September, they stage a fiesta where the culture of bullfighting, as portrayed in the paintings and etchings of Francisco Goya, is replicated. Ronda has always drawn artists looking for an authentic version of Spain, like Victor Hugo, Orson Welles, Ernest Hemingway, Rainer Maria

Rilke and the painter David Bomberg. Welles requested that his ashes be scattered on the farm of Antonio Ordóñez, Ronda's most famous torero, just north of the town.

✳

In spite of being responsible for the near demise of Hilly, we decided, since Alastair was still in London, to organize another dinner party and hope for the best. Obviously Hilly was thinking ahead, because she arrived on her horse, Jaguar. I have to say the horse's fierce name perplexed me at the time considering she was such a gentle creature. But perhaps the Spanish word for mare, *yegua*, sounding not unlike 'jaguar', was the explanation. Anyhow, I suggested that Hilly put Jaguar into the tiny field with some bushes and a few scrawny trees that adjoined the cottage. We then sat down to enjoy a meal on a table that had been dragged outside. In spite of only having a rudimentary gas hob at her disposal, Betty managed, with considerable ingenuity, to cook a delicious paella. After dinner we went inside and drank brandy in front of a blazing fire.

It was then that Hilly amazed us once again. She disclosed that her maiden name was Bardwell and that she was related to the poet Leland Bardwell. We both knew Leland, who was very much part of Dublin's literary scene. When I was an architectural student I happened to choose McDaids in Harry Street, just off Grafton Street, as a watering hole. Even though it was a small and rather dingy establishment, it suited me fine. In the words of the poet Anthony Crown 'it has an extraordinary high ceiling and high, almost gothic, windows in the front wall with stained glass borders. The general effect is church-like or tomb-like, according to mood.' As it turned out there were older and far more notable drinkers who also frequented the place. The poet Patrick Kavanagh, the playwright Brendan Behan and the novelist and essayist Brian O'Nolan, one of whose pseudonyms was Flann O'Brien, regularly held court there, though not necessarily at the same time; there were certain antagonisms at play. This small bohemian group, together with writers such as Anthony Cronin and

Benedict Kiely, represented the dying embers of a literary set that was censored, marginalized and generally impoverished, yet still managed to fan the flames of resistance to the intellectual torpor that reigned in the Ireland of the 1950s.

They were often joined by the next generation of poets and writers that included Michael Hartnett, Pearse Hutchinson and Hayden Murphy. However, not all regulars in McDaids were of a literary bent. For example, I recall, with considerable affection, the accomplished portrait painter Eddie McGuire, with his often genial but occasionally explosive personality, as well as the small but impish American artist Charlie Brady who, in spite of a lifetime in Ireland, never lost his New York accent. But in November 1972 this convivial set-up was damaged beyond repair. McDaids was put up for sale. The barman Paddy O'Brien, who was much respected by the clientele, attempted to purchase it; but, sadly, he was unsuccessful. As a result he decamped to nearby South William Street to tend the bar for the publican Tommy Smith who had just purchased Grogan's pub. Like seagulls following a trawler, practically the entire McDaids crowd followed Paddy O'Brien to Grogan's and it was there that I struck up friendships with many writers and artists.

Leland Bardwell was a true bohemian. She was born in India in 1922, the daughter of Mary Collis and Pat Hone. Her father was a railway engineer and came from a family that included two distinguished painters, Nathaniel Hone the Elder and Nathaniel Hone the Younger, plus the stained glass artist Evie Hone. While the Hones had produced misfits and several dissolute characters, Leland outdid them all in her capacity for rebellious freedom. When her family returned to Ireland she attended Alexandra College in Dublin but left at sixteen when an unplanned pregnancy led her to England. In 1948 she married the poet Michael Bardwell and had twins, Billy and Anna. While in London she was a regular in the bohemian world of Soho and met many artists and writers, like Anthony Cronin and Francis Bacon. Leland moved back to Dublin in the late 1950s where she met Fintan McLachlan, whom she described as 'the most beautiful young man I had ever seen'. They had three sons, Nicholas, Edward and John.

Leaving Dublin in 1986 she occupied the gate lodge at the Tyrone Guthrie Centre at Annaghmakerrig, Co. Monaghan before finally settling in the 1990s on the coast of Co. Sligo. Her ramshackle lifestyle outraged conventional Irish prudishness but provided the inspiration for her poetry, plays and autobiographical novels.

Finally that night, when it was time to go home, we all gathered at the flimsy gate to the field, only to discover that the bloody horse had opened it and gone walkabout. I know a horse represents a very big needle but, unfortunately, the analogy with the haystack held true: this needle was jet black and we were searching on a night that was as dark as pitch. After about an hour, stumbling about in the inky gloom, at last I came across her, calmly standing by the river close to the cottage. She must have heard our shouts and cries and not bothered her arse to respond. I persuaded her back to the cottage, so a delighted but tired Hilly could mount her and direct her to safely amble their way home.

When we originally informed the principal of our children's school of our proposed Spanish adventure, she admitted that inevitably they would fall behind in their schooling, but the experience of a different country and its culture would provide adequate compensation. This analysis was to be challenged when I met the headmaster from a small rural primary school, sited not a quarter of a mile from Elma's cottage. He said he would be delighted to have Rachel and Bruce in his class. Foolishly, I said we would ask the children first. Naturally and like a shot, they declined the offer of going to school in Spain. This rejection represented a salutary lesson in how over-reliance on democracy doesn't always succeed when it comes to raising children. Yet, in spite of avoiding any formal schooling, our kids managed to pick up a modest Spanish vocabulary from playing with the local children.

Also, in the course of their short spell in Andalusia, the children learned to appreciate how much hard work is called for when you don't have access to the basic services that many of us take for granted, like water and electricity.

I'm not sure of the lasting benefits of horse-riding, but certainly the children had plenty of opportunities to master that skill on Hilly's amiable Jaguar. Another surprising achievement was learning to swim, considering we were high up in the mountains and far from the sea. However, we noticed that the local farmers had constructed large concrete tanks to contain water for irrigation, and we realized that even though they were rather inelegant, they made perfect swimming pools.

When we first decided to spend the winter of 1978 in the south of Spain I convinced myself that a totally different environment would inspire me to create some new and exciting pictures. Sadly, it didn't work out like that. For a start, on most days, I spent so much time and energy engaged in simple domestic chores that I found there was little left for creativity. Even worse, when I did find time to go sketching and painting with watercolours, I found that not only were the results pathetic and uninspiring, but I felt slightly ridiculous. At that early stage in my career I may have been unsure of what kind of artist I was but, after my experience sketching in the Spanish countryside, I certainly knew what I wasn't. I put away the art materials, never to appear again until I was back in Dublin. Luckily for me, I had thrown a copy of *Ulysses* into my suitcase and started to reread it. James Joyce succeeded in making a statement of universal significance by dealing honestly with his own experience and by concentrating on things he knew intimately. I decided that I would be guided by his example.

Eventually, running out of time and money, we acknowledged with considerable regret that we would have to curtail our Andalusian idyll. So, bidding farewell to our newfound friends, we embarked on the long journey home.

Many years later I learned that Alastair and Hilly had returned to London to care for Kingsley Amis, who had become unwell: an intriguing, if elderly, *ménage à trois*.

By then I knew quite a lot about Hilly's life story. Hilary Ann Bardwell was born in 1928 in Kingston-upon-Thames, the youngest daughter of an official in the Ministry of Agriculture. She repeatedly ran away from Bedales School before finally enrolling in the Ruskin School of Art in Oxford. Kingsley was a persistent philanderer and his refusal to break off his affair with the novelist Elizabeth Jane Howard effectively ended their marriage in 1963. In 1967 Hilly married Shackleton Bailey and accompanied him to the US, where he was a professor in the University of Michigan. However, while on holiday in southern Spain in 1970, Hilly decided not to return to America but instead remain in Ronda where she had met Alastair Boyd. In 1972 their son James or 'Jaime' was born, and in 1977 she divorced Shackleton and married Alastair.

Because of her kind and caring nature, after Kingsley's marriage to Howard broke up in 1981, Hilly made the remarkable yet selfless decision to return to London with Alastair and look after the lonely old curmudgeon. The arrangement was that Hilly and Alastair ran the house while Kingsley continued writing and paid most of the bills. Martin Amis wrote movingly of how his mother cared for his cantankerous father in his final illness: 'You reminded him of love, Mum. You were the peach.'

Sir Kingsley Amis died in 1995, Lord Alastair Kilmarnock in 2009 and Lady Hilary Kilmarnock in 2010. She was a remarkable woman.

*

Back in my Dublin studio I struggled to turn the thoughts and feelings stimulated by the Spanish experience into an image that might capture some of what had happened during our winter in Ronda. Ultimately, the theme I chose was a variation on *Number* 3 which I painted in 1977, where, instead of posing the family outside the urban setting depicted in the Dublin painting, I placed everyone in front of the sun-dappled cottage in Ronda. I had toyed with including the yellow Ford Escort, since it had taken us to Ronda and back, but eventually decided that its incorporation would be wrong.

In order to simulate a sensation of southern heat, I used a transparent glaze for the shadows cast by the vine leaves. I tested all the blues

Overleaf: *Winter in Ronda*, oil on canvas, 183cm x 244cm, 1979, The Central Bank of Ireland.

I had at my disposal: ultramarine, cobalt, and found them all unsatisfactory. Then I came across a battered old tube that I had never used before – 'Antwerp Blue' – and to my surprise, the results were perfect. It was then that I remembered where I had obtained that particular tube of oil paint. When the politicians shut down the art college in Kildare Street, Truman's, the nearby art store, was forced to close due to loss of custom, whereupon Denis, an old friend and one of the staff, gave me a bag of art materials that was about to be thrown out. And that bag contained the tube of Antwerp Blue.

Undoubtedly the major visual art experience of the Spanish adventure was our visit to the Prado Museum and the opportunity to see *Las Meninas* by Diego Velázquez for the first time. Accordingly, I decided to incorporate several references to the masterpiece in my own painting. Unlike Velázquez, who places himself behind a huge canvas, I sit on a chair in the shade, reading a book with a reproduction of *Las Meninas* on the cover. *Las Meninas* translates as 'ladies-in-waiting' and Betty, to her great annoyance, finds herself in a similar supporting role. A pile of books, including *Ulysses*, are on the ground. Through the open door a mirror, which in the painting by Velázquez provides a glimpse of Philip IV and Mariana, the king and queen of Spain, now reflects my image photographing the scene. Rachel, in a bikini, echoes the pose of the little princess La Infanta Margarita Theresa, and Bruce pokes at a lizard rather than teasing the king's dog, as the male dwarf Nicolasito Pertusato does in the original picture.

Winter in Ronda not only pays homage to one of the greatest paintings in the world, it also embodies a warm personal memory of a truly special experience and some great friends.

CHAPTER 13

Adventures in the Art Trade

O n a previous visit to New York I had made contact with
Richard Lerner, from the Lerner-Heller Gallery on Madison
Avenue. He seemed very interested in my work and even came
to my studio in Dublin to view work in progress. Shortly afterwards,
he offered me an exhibition featuring my *People Looking at Paintings*
series, so I began to work fast and after several months successfully
completed the required number of pieces. It was only then that I
received the disheartening news that the show had been cancelled.
He gave no explanation, but I was left with a load of paintings and
nowhere to show them. Cecil King and Oliver Dowling, the exhibitions officer with the Arts Council, came up with an ingenious plan,
something that I myself would never have considered. They suggested
that I travel to Switzerland and attend the Basel art fair, where I would
be able to make contact with art galleries and hopefully provoke some
new interest in my work.

Betty and I went to the bank and withdrew most of our savings to
finance the trip. Nearly all the money went on an excursion air ticket;
much of the rest covered a season ticket for the fair and a week's bed

and breakfast accommodation, which left just about enough to buy one meal a day. On the first morning I began by surveying the scene, trying to single out galleries that might be interested in my work; and after a lunch of sausage and chips I summoned up the courage to walk into some and sound them out. Not one of them would speak to me. The second day, much the same: no interest whatsoever. I began to realize that these people were, above all, art dealers; they were there to deal, to sell, to make a profit, not to waste their time gazing at the efforts of a young unknown artist. By lunchtime on Wednesday I was in despair, after three days of traipsing about the place and not one real conversation with a fellow human being. I would have gone straight home, but of course I couldn't. The excursion ticket obliged me to stay the full week. On Thursday, more out of a sense of grim duty than anything else, I returned to the fair and once again began to trudge about the profusion of galleries, laid out in serried ranks of booths and stalls, when, to my intense relief, a Parisian dealer from the Galerie des Quatre Mouvements said, '*Oui*, I will look at your paintings.'

I prepared to take out my slides. He put up his hand and politely said, 'First I must make a phone call.'

So I stood in front to his desk for five, for ten, for fifteen minutes, until, with growing exasperation, I was about to tell him exactly what he could do with his gallery, when he put the phone down and announced, 'Now, let's look at your slides.'

He examined them carefully and began to divide them into two piles. After some time he pointed to the pile containing six slides. 'We are prepared to buy these. How much?'

In a state of shock, I quoted Irish prices, which, of course, were much lower than those in Europe.

He responded, 'Fine, but naturally we expect a 50 per cent reduction.'

I must have looked aghast because he suggested that I go away, reflect for about a half hour, and then come back with a decision. On my return, I drew attention to the fact that the paintings were in Dublin.

'No problem. We will pay for the transport.'

That clinched it. I accepted the arrangement and pocketed £2,500. Walking away from the Galerie de Quatre Mouvements, I spotted for the first time Aktionsgalerie, a small Swiss gallery displaying interesting realist portraits that were laminated with mirrors and finished with decorative vintage frames. As I examined them, the gallery owner approached me. He was lanky with dark curly hair and looked more like a student than an art dealer. He introduced himself as Rudolf Jäggli and began to discuss the portraits, which he said were the work of his wife, Margrit. I believe that originally he saw me as a potential customer, but then quickly realized I was an artist.

'What kind of work do you do?'

'As it happens,' I replied, 'I have some slides that I can show you.'

He looked at the slides and almost immediately judged them 'very interesting', and proceeded to offer me an exhibition in his gallery in Bern. Of course I accepted, and straight away we shook hands on the deal.

I took the next day off to see the sights of Basel, and was fortunate to see Hans Holbein's masterpiece *The Dead Christ*, a truly awesome painting. Most people are familiar with Holbein's naturalistic portraits of the aristocratic Tudors, but this particular painting is an entirely different proposition. Unlike the usual reverential portrayals of the Passion of Christ, the artist has created an accurate representation of a dead human being whose wounds show clear evidence of torture. Holbein depicted Christ's cadaver in a brutally realistic manner. In 1980 I was influenced by this extraordinary picture when I created the cover for *On the Blanket*, Tim Pat Coogan's book about the protests by prisoners in the H Blocks.

I couldn't wait to get back to Dublin and tell Betty the good news. As the date for the Swiss exhibition approached, we examined all the options and came to the conclusion that, strictly from a financial point of view, the best way for us to travel to Bern was by train. Betty's sister Marie came from Manchester to look after Rachel, and we set off, carrying bundles of paintings between us, to catch the boat for England. Then, like emigrants of old, laden with their precious belongings, we travelled by train from Holyhead to London, where we took the boat and train to Paris, all the while clutching our valuable cargo. At least the pictures were those constructed

from several small canvases joined together, so we were just about able to carry the entire exhibition in an accumulation of bundles. When we arrived at the Gare du Nord, Swiss Railways unexpectedly insisted that it was not possible to take the paintings on board the train; instead they would have to be consigned to the freight car. To tell the truth, we were relieved, since we were exhausted after dragging the damn things across one bloody border after another.

Everything went swimmingly until the train stopped at the border between France and Switzerland. Then, with considerable dismay, I caught sight of the paintings being unloaded and deposited on the platform before the train itself pulled out and we watched the stack of canvases disappear from view.

To calm myself I mumbled to Betty, 'Don't worry, the Swiss are in charge.'

And when Rudolf Jäggli met us at the station and was informed of the problem, he voiced a similar confidence: 'Don't worry, they'll probably be on the next train.'

So we waited for the next train and the one after, until there were no trains left.

Rudolf was soothing: 'Don't worry, we'll come back in the morning.'

In the meantime he suggested that we go to his place to unpack and to rest. To save money we had already agreed to stay with Rudolf, or Rudi as he liked to be called, and his wife Margrit, in their cottage in the countryside outside Bern. Margrit welcomed us into their home, where we discovered that we were not just staying in a Swiss cottage, we were lodging in a zoo. The Jägglis were the proud owners of twenty-seven fennecs (Sahara desert foxes), two ocelots and a monkey. Thankfully all were caged except for the male ocelot.

Early on, Rudi casually remarked, 'Don't expose your back or shoulders if he's above you – he's inclined to pounce.'

I didn't need to hear that. When I entered the toilet for the first time and spied two eyes staring down at me from the top of a wardrobe –

Joseph Sheridan Le Fanu, oil on canvas, 1975, The Arts Council of Ireland.

apparently a favourite lair – the consequence was instant constipation.

After breakfast we headed back to the station to await the pictures, but again they did not come. Nobody seemed to have a clue where they were. Finally Rudi contacted Margrit's uncle who was a senior official with Swiss Railways, and thanks to his intervention the pictures were located; but they weren't delivered to the gallery until the morning before the actual opening. It took the rest of that day to join all the pictures together and finally hang the show.

The opening itself turned out to be an anticlimax. Only three guests turned up. There was a celebrity concert that night in Bern; anybody interested in culture was there, and obviously not in the gallery to see the work of an obscure Irish artist. As some consolation, when we returned to the Jäggli home, a bottle of champagne was opened and we sat down to raise a toast. As it was deemed a special occasion, Margrit released the monkey which, bizarrely, lavished me with attention. A little later, however, when Betty touched me affectionately, the monkey jumped up and bit her on the arm.

Margrit explained, 'Oh, she can be quite jealous of other females.'

It was not the most triumphant night: not a picture sold, and a biting, jealous monkey.

When Rudi finally took us to the station to catch the Paris train he began to apologize for the lack of sales, only to be interrupted by Betty who exclaimed, 'Last night I had a dream and in it you sold all the paintings.'

At that we all shook hands and waved goodbye.

A few days after we arrived back in Dublin we received a telegram. Just a few words: 'Betty's dream came true. R. Jäggli.'

In a subsequent letter Rudi explained what had happened. Isy Brachot, one of Belgium's leading dealers, was travelling from Zurich to Brussels and was forced to change trains in Bern. Having a few hours to kill, he decided to take a stroll and wandered into Rudolf Jäggli's gallery. He decided, there and then, to buy the whole show. Shortly afterwards, Isy Brachot himself wrote a letter inviting me to stage an exhibition in his Brussels gallery.

We'd had enough of trains so we decided to drive to Brussels, a decision reinforced by the fact that Betty was pregnant. After Rachel was born, we had hoped for another child but sadly nothing happened. The doctor we consulted seemed to think there was an obstetric problem so we gave up hope, and then, years later, to our amazement, Betty became pregnant again.

On our arrival in Brussels we discovered that the Galerie Isy Brachot was located in an attractive shopping district. There was exhibition space on the ground floor with street frontage, and more at first-floor level. Above that there was a photographic studio that recorded every painting shown in the gallery and consequently was able to provide prints to magazines and newspapers. The hanging was done by trained gallery staff and supervised by a man named Maurice. He was short and tidy with a neat moustache, and was clad in a brown overall with *Galerie Isy Brachot* embroidered on the pocket. My work was installed on the first floor; the ground floor was given over to an exhibition by the surrealist painters René Magritte and Paul Delvaux. When we arrived at the opening, Maurice greeted us at the door with the news that thirteen paintings had already been sold; yet when we looked around the exhibition there wasn't a red spot in sight. On closer examination, however, I saw tiny brass plaques engraved with the word *vendu* discreetly hanging from the paintings that had been sold.

Towards the end of the evening a young man came up and said that his mother had bought a small picture and that she would like to invite us for lunch. We accepted and drove to the address he'd given us on the agreed day. The house was a beautiful detached family residence in an attractive neighbourhood, and when we were shown into the living room we saw a Chagall over the fireplace and a Matisse hanging on the opposite wall. However, it was the presence of five paintings by René Magritte, in an alcove, that really caught my eye. I had always been captivated by Magritte's paintings but had only seen them in reproduction, and certainly the ones I was now looking at were new to me, as they had never been reproduced in books.

'Ah, but *cher* René did them specially for us,' explained our hostess, Madame Oshinsky. It turned out that Magritte and his wife Georgette had been close friends of the Oshinskys and had occasionally attended soirées at the Oshinsky home, and even though Magritte himself had died in 1967 they had continued the practice of holding evening parties.

'We're meeting this Saturday – you must come.'

At the dinner table I was placed between the Belgian poet Louis Scutenaire and his wife Irène. He was a bald man with a genial expression, and despite translation difficulties we struck up an immediate rapport. He confessed that he and Magritte shared a passion for the Gothic novel, and in particular for the Anglo-Irish writer Joseph Sheridan Le Fanu, author of that weird novella about a female vampire, *Carmilla*. Another favourite writer of his was also Irish, Charles Maturin, with his strange, digressive novel *Melmoth the Wanderer* about a man who has sold his soul to the Devil in exchange for a long life. There was something about those Anglo-Irish melancholics that appealed to both Magritte and Scutenaire and their surreal fascination with expressing the unconscious mind and its dark impulses. According to Suzi Gablik in her book *Magritte*, 'The artist suffered the "bizarre affliction" which was at once the source of all his ills and all his melancholic progress: *ennui*.'

Scutenaire had written the first proper biography of Magritte and had organized a major retrospective at the Pompidou Centre in Paris. 'You must visit my home and see my Magrittes,' he suggested.

There was also a university professor at the table who, at that point, chipped in and invited us to come and see *his* Magritte. I quietly noted to myself that his collection was in the singular. Naturally we took them up on their respective offers.

It was the professor himself who opened his hall door, and as I looked past his shoulder, I gasped; there it was, in all its glory: *The Empire of Light*, a magnificent oil painting by Magritte. Its lower half depicts a streetscape by night, illuminated by a single lamplight, while the top half discloses the contradiction of a beautifully blue daytime sky: an astonishing image, reproduced all over the world in postcard and poster formats.

The Scutenaire home was in a modest middle-class terrace, but inside it was crammed from floor to ceiling with work by Magritte. Scutenaire had thirty-five original oil paintings, hundreds of sketches and drawings, plus other fascinating material. In hushed tones he asked if we would like to see Magritte's pornographic pictures, which had never been displayed in public. Of course, we replied. These turned out to be drawings that I would describe as rude rather than pornographic.

We spent hours examining and discussing his collection. It was a rare privilege. Scutenaire was a somewhat unusual host; he insisted we all have a beer, but because of his pride in Belgium's wide variety of beers, no two guests were allowed to sample the same brand.

At some stage Betty began rolling a cigarette.

'Would you roll one for me?' he asked.

When she gave it to him, he sniffed it and popped it in his mouth.

'Do you want a light?'

'No, no,' he replied, and slowly ate it.

I remained in contact with him for many years, exchanging letters on an infrequent basis, his in French, mine in English. His handwriting was precise and always in green ink.

Not long after my exhibition in Belgium the Arts Council commissioned me to paint a portrait of Le Fanu, who had lived in the building they occupied on Merrion Square. On completion, I sent a photo to Scutenaire. His reply was brief, and again written in green: 'Le Fanu would be pleased.'

*

We returned to Dublin buoyed up by our Belgian experience. To have had another sell-out exhibition was more than I could possibly have hoped for, and the immersion in the world of Magritte was something I will never forget.

I adored Magritte's approach to painting, the way he employed conventional means to express radical ideas. Suzi Gablik wrote that 'René Magritte liked to refuse the name of artist, saying that he was a man who thought and who communicated his thought through the means of painting.' Magritte himself observed that 'if the spectator finds that my paintings are a kind of defiance of *common sense*, he realises something' and recalled that 'someone once asked me what

GALERIE

ISY
BRACHOT

AVENUE LOUISE 62A

1050 BRUXELLES

TELEPHONE : 511.05.25

ROBERT BALLAGH

8 NOVEMBRE
14 DECEMBRE 1974

the relationship was between my life and my art. I couldn't really think of any, except that life obliges me to do something, so I paint. But I am not concerned with "pure poetry" nor "pure painting". It is rather pointless to put one's hopes in a dogmatic point of view, since it is the power of enchantment that matters.'

Obviously Isy Brachot was more than pleased with the outcome, because in double-quick time, he offered me a return exhibition after an interval of only eighteen months. Isy Brachot was always well turned out, attired in a beautifully tailored suit, shirt and tie, and, as I learned when I received his first letter, he gloried in the title M. Isy Brachot III. His gallery occupied a complete building on the fashionable Avenue Louise and boasted facilities that were certainly new to us. On the ground floor, apart from the main gallery, there was a small intimate space, furnished with a gilded easel and a sumptuous couch where any client who expressed an interest in a particular canvas could relax and view the work privately while sipping a glass of champagne. Another unusual gallery practice was revealed when I was hanging my exhibition on the first floor and, for some reason, entered M. Brachot's office. He was observing a battery of TV monitors on his desk. I imagined that this was some security exercise, but then it dawned on me that he was studying the people who were wandering about the gallery. If a special client spent a considerable time looking at a certain picture, M. Brachot would approach them with the added advantage of knowing that they already had an interest in the work.

When I started working for the second Brachot exhibition I was acutely aware that I simply couldn't paint any more pictures in the exact same manner. Over a dozen exhibitions featuring the *People Looking at Paintings* series had been held in various locations around Europe in the previous few years. On the other hand, I knew that Isy Brachot wanted more pictures of people looking at paintings. So, persevering with the theme, I decided to drop the grid format and instead create individual canvases; and, because I had now developed a certain facility

Catalogue cover for my exhibition in Galerie Isy Brachot.

with oil paint, to turn a few of the people around and paint their faces either in conversation with their fellow subjects or looking straight out from the canvas.

I thought the new paintings turned out quite well, but when we arrived in Brussels and delivered them to the gallery, Monsieur Brachot was not of the same opinion.

'They're completely different,' he complained.

'Well, it's the same theme,' I garbled, with some embarrassment.

'That's not the point,' he snapped. 'I wanted exactly the same style.'

Of course the exhibition went ahead; but as if to prove his point, less than half the pictures sold. It was to be my last outing with Galerie Isy Brachot.

The disappointing experience, however, taught me a valuable lesson about the art business. Commercial success for the artist and of course for the art professional is frequently predicated on the creation of a recognizable style or brand that, hopefully, will attract some market response. The next imperative, in the context of actual market demand, is the ability to service that demand. If you examine the careers of many of the most commercially successful artists today you will find that they all conform to some version of that particular practice. For myself, I knew I would die of artistic boredom if I were to keep repeating myself in perpetuity. I was at a crossroads.

CHAPTER 14

Fit to Print

W hen I made the decision to become an artist I never, for a moment, thought about the financial implications of such a choice. But it didn't take long to find out just how impossible it was for a young artist to make a living from painting and selling pictures in Ireland.

Clearly there were reasons for this; one being both obvious and unfortunately, immutable – the size of the Irish population. In any society, only a tiny proportion of people are interested in buying pictures, or can afford them, which means that in the case of Ireland, art lovers have always been few and far between. But many civilized societies supplement private patronage with state support for the arts. Sadly in Ireland that form of assistance has been nugatory. Even today, in terms of state investment in the arts, Ireland ranks at the bottom of the European Union countries, where the average spend is 0.6 per cent of gross national product. Ireland devotes 0.1 per cent of its gross national product to arts and culture. Tragically there has been very little improvement in the situation since Sir Thomas Bodkin issued his scathing report in 1950, which indicated that no other country in Western Europe cared less or gave less for the cultivation of the arts than Ireland. However, none of this weighed heavily on my mind when, in 1969, after my first solo exhibition, I made the quixotic decision to become a full-time artist by abandoning my job as a draughtsman, which at least provided a weekly wage. I was now able to concentrate fully on painting but, as I was soon to discover, that freedom came at a price.

Even though my exhibition was well received and I had been selected to represent Ireland at the Paris Biennale, I found I was earning practically nothing. I knew this couldn't go on. I would have to find another way of earning enough to live. Other young artists had the option of a teaching job but this was not available to me; I had no qualifications.

It was a chance encounter with an old school friend that suggested a possible solution. He was running a small printing firm and asked if I would complete some finished artwork for him. Although I hadn't a clue what he was talking about, I immediately volunteered. He explained that what he needed was someone to mock up and design leaflets, posters and business cards. I quickly discovered that the only qualification for the job was the ability to be both neat and exact and not necessarily the possession of a soaring artistic talent.

Thankfully, in time I became reasonably proficient and was able to obtain enough work to supplement the meagre return from my artistic endeavours. I readily admit that most of the jobbing work I did for printers would never have won awards, so you can imagine my pleasure when the Department of Posts and Telegraphs contacted me in 1973 and invited me to design a stamp to commemorate the centenary of the World Meteorological Organization. This commission would, I felt, allow me to design something of more significance.

As I had never designed a stamp before, the department arranged a meeting with the stamping branch of the Revenue Commissioners, who produced security material like motor tax discs, social welfare stamps and postage stamps for the government on an old photogravure machine in Dublin Castle.

The staff were very helpful and explained how designing for the photogravure machine would be quite different from what I was used to, namely designing for the off-set litho machines favoured by most

commercial printers. With photogravure, the designer had to take into account that just four colours could be printed by the machine; and since one colour was usually reserved for typography, this left only three colours to exploit. The satisfactory reproduction of full-colour images of paintings or photographs became next to impossible; normally to achieve this, four different colours are printed one on top of the other in various proportions: cyan, yellow, magenta and black. So I didn't have this option. I discovered, however, that the photogravure process could print deeper, brighter and more solid colours than any off-set litho machine. It was this potential that I opted to exploit when I designed my first stamp. I depicted, using bright and contrasting colours, a weather map of Europe, and when it was printed, I was delighted with the result.

If asked at the time to describe my sense of pride and accomplishment, I would have said that it was probably the artistic equivalent of being chosen to play international sport for Ireland. For all that, I was made well aware of the unpalatable reality that whenever an artist's work enters the public domain, there are always those who are ready and willing to denounce the effort.

The day after the stamp was issued, a disgruntled native of Cork wrote to the *Irish Times* complaining that I had created a depression over his county, and in the House of Commons the Reverend Ian Paisley demanded that the home secretary, Sir Alec Douglas-Home, object to the fact that the Republic of Ireland had issued a stamp which featured a map of Ireland without the border. Thankfully, the Department of Posts and Telegraphs paid little attention to such criticism and retained confidence in me as a stamp designer.

A stamp may be a small piece of printed paper, yet few people are aware of quite how much goes into its creation. An obvious question is: what do countries say about themselves through their stamps? In his essay 'The Semiotics of the Irish Postage Stamp' David Scott suggested that 'Stamps are – or can be – semantically anything but simple. They constitute the tip of the iceberg of a complex mass of cultural, historical and political forces of a society to which they give expression. And this is particularly true of a small country, which has been dominated by cultural and economic influences that have their origin outside its frontiers. In attempting to assert a national viewpoint or identity without openly antagonizing the forces to which the country, out of necessity, is obliged to acquiesce, the small state is forced to invent… images which offer the possibility of a certain degree of independent or national assertion, yet at the same time do so without taking up too narrow or specific an ideological stance. It is interesting that in view of this problem, Irish stamps should in particular have had such frequent recourse to artists or to the artistic image. For what better alibi could politics invent for itself than the aesthetic?'

After my first stamp in 1973, the Department of Posts and Telegraphs entrusted me with several more commissions, which were all designed for and printed on the photogravure machine in Dublin Castle. However, some time in the 1970s, a decision was made to switch to a private off-set litho printing company, which opened up considerable possibilities for designers. Even though the facility for printing truly resonant colours was lost, the sophisticated off-set litho process was able to reproduce almost any design produced by an adventurous artist. Taking advantage of those advances in colour reproduction, I produced small paintings in both oil and watercolour. This approach conformed with the results of an international survey by UNESCO, which showed that the general public like their stamps to resemble pictures in miniature.

In 2006, An Post staged an exhibition of my stamp designs in the GPO with an accompanying catalogue, which recalled the sixty-six stamps I had designed between 1973 and 2001. It was a great honour for me to have been chosen to create so many stamps that were sent out across the world, presenting a view of ourselves at a particular moment in modern history and providing clues for future historians about Ireland's self-image in the last years of the twentieth century.

✴

By the early 1990s it had become apparent that revolutionary developments in printing and colour reproduction had made currency forgery far easier. The governor of the Central Bank of Ireland, Maurice Doyle warned that 'anyone could make a copy of an old £20 note that was good enough to be passed unnoticed across a crowded bar counter.'

The Central Bank decided to replace the vulnerable currency, which had been circulating since 1970, with a new series of bank notes, incorporating greatly enhanced security features. The Central Bank held a closed competition, in which about a dozen artists and designers were invited to submit proposals for a new £20 note. I was one of them.

Shortly afterwards, a briefing document as thick as a telephone directory landed at my studio door. It contained information about the subject of the new note, Daniel O'Connell, and descriptions of the new security features: a windowed metal security thread, a latent image of the letters IR, microlettering, and a tactile mark to aid recognition by partially sighted and blind people. Finally and ominously, there was a copy of an article written by the director of the German Bundesbank in which he pointed out that 'a bank note is a security document, and not a work of art'.

I don't know whether it was the sheer immensity of the project or my own lack of imagination, but I simply couldn't get started and, as the deadline approached, feared that I would have to inform the Central Bank that I couldn't rise to the challenge. As a last resort I wandered into the National Gallery of Ireland, hoping to unearth some inspiration. As luck would have it, I came upon a mezzotint portrait of the young Daniel O'Connell by John Gubbins, which really took my fancy. I thought that the artist had given O'Connell a curiously whimsical expression that I liked because it was slightly irreverent. Inspired by Gubbins's mezzotint, I went back to my studio and rapidly put together a submission for the competition.

The Central Bank set up an independent jury to judge all the entries anonymously and, considering the rushed nature of my submission, I was surprised to learn that my design had been chosen. A meeting with senior staff was arranged at the bank's headquarters in Dame Street, where my contract of employment was discussed and agreed upon. Then at the Currency Centre in Sandyford, Co. Dublin, I met the team I would have to work with in bringing my design to print. The Currency Centre was where Irish bank notes and coinage were produced at the time, and was heavily protected. Surrounded by high perimeter fencing, it was patrolled both by Gardaí and a permanent contingent of the Irish Army. Access was through a double-lock entrance hall where visitors were held until their invitation was confirmed from within. Once past security, the visitor entered a very pleasant campus of fine buildings, surrounded by well-tended gardens, and it was in one of those buildings that I first sat down with people who came to work every day in order to print money.

I was taken on a tour of the printing facilities, where I was amazed by the complexity of the operation. I was shown sheets of cotton rag paper, incorporating the watermark and the metal security thread, stored under strict security and only released subject to controlled conditions. And I hadn't realized that in the course of the actual print-ing, the sheets of paper had to pass through three separate processes:

letterpress to print the serial number; off-set litho print for most of the detail on the front and back of the note; and finally an engraving process called 'intaglio' to print the dominant feature, the portrait.

The currency printers explained that, even though they were fully equipped to print bank notes, they didn't have the capacity to make the actual printing plates. Since the portrait of O'Connell was the main element in my design, we knew we had to find a good portrait printer. We settled on a German company, Giesecke and Devrient, that not only printed the German mark but, of more interest to us, also produced many other bank notes embellished with excellent portraits.

I met the printers at their headquarters in Munich. We agreed that I would prepare most of the artwork for the manufacture of the plates but that a different approach was necessary in the case of the portrait. The image had to be hand-engraved, at the same size that it would appear on the finished bank note, onto a copper plate by a master craftsman who would closely follow my portrait design. Wondering why he wasn't present, I asked if it would be possible to meet the engraver, so he was sent for and joined our discussion. His name was Antonio Lopez. Up until then a lot of translating was going on – English to German, German to English, but hearing his name I blurted out, '¿Habla usted español?' to which he quietly replied 'Si.' And thus began a fantastic working relationship.

For each of the portraits, I began by painting a small oil portrait that had to be approved by the board of the Central Bank. I then made an accurate drawing of the approved painting, which I sent to Lopez. He, in turn, made a drawing of my sketch which he transferred to a copper pate and began engraving. This process is both slow and cautious, simply because the engraver cannot make a mistake – one slip and the job is ruined.

After several months, Lopez would print a proof of what he had done thus far and send it to me. If I felt that small changes were required – for example, a tweak to the side of the mouth – I would introduce a suggested correction and send the proof back to Munich. This process continued for almost six months until the engraved portrait was completed to everyone's satisfaction.

The front of the £5 note featured a portrait of Catherine McAuley, foundress of the Sisters of Mercy. It was set against a view of the Mater Misericordiae University Hospital in Dublin. A classroom with three children was featured on the back of the note.

A portrait of James Joyce was on the front of the £10 note and was set against a panoramic view of Dublin City and parts of Co. Dublin and Co. Wicklow, drawn in the nineteenth century by T. R. Harvey. The back of the note carried a reproduction of Anna Livia (the River Liffey) one of the fourteen heads representing the rivers of Ireland sculpted by Edward Smyth for the Custom House in Dublin. This head and the opening lines of *Finnegans Wake* were overlaid on a nineteenth-century map of Dublin.

The front of the £20 note featured a portrait of Daniel O'Connell set against a landscape drawing of O'Connell's home, Derrynane Abbey, Co. Kerry, the original of which is held by the National Library. The back of the note bears a 'Repeal the Act of Union' pledge signed in 1845 by O'Connell, overlaid by a drawing of the Four Courts, hinting at the fact that O'Connell was a great lawyer.

The front of the £50 note had a portrait of Douglas Hyde, the founder of the Gaelic League and the first president of Ireland. In the background was a drawing of Áras an Uachtaráin, the presidential residence in the Phoenix Park, Dublin, set against a design based on the interior of the base of the Ardagh Chalice. On the back of the note was a drawing of an uilleann piper and the crest of Conradh na Gaeilge (the Gaelic League) overlaid on a sixteenth-century manuscript from the collection of the Royal Irish Academy.

The £100 note featured a portrait of Charles Stewart Parnell. In the background was a view of his family home, Avondale House in Rathdrum, Co. Wicklow. The back of the note displayed elements of the Parnell monument, located at the junction of Parnell Street and O'Connell Street in Dublin. It included the statue, the bronze torch on the top of the monument and metalwork bearing the names of the four provinces. These features were laid over an extract from one of Parnell's best-known statements, itself inscribed on the monument: 'No man has a right to fix the boundary to the march of a nation. No man has a right to say to his country – thus far shalt thou go and no further.'

These were the last Irish bank notes issued before the introduction of the euro.

As an artist who always sought to bring art to the widest audience possible I appreciated the ubiquitous nature of the bank note. At the time I remarked that, 'Even with my stamp designs I never reached such an audience.' During the years when my designs were in circulation, whenever someone had to introduce me to an audience he or she would invariably say something like, 'Even though some of you might not have heard of Robert Ballagh before, I can guarantee that you have one of his works of art in your pocket,' and, after a delay of a few seconds, dramatically produce a bank note.

In 1992, when I began work on the new £20 note, I was a complete novice; but four notes later, with the help and support of the team in the Currency Centre and close collaboration with the experts in Munich I became quite proficient at currency design. So with some justification, I felt extremely proud of the final series of Irish bank notes. Certainly the portraits engraved by Antonio Lopez were of the highest quality and crucial to the success of my designs, so when I discovered that he was due to retire before the completion of the series, I became somewhat alarmed. I needn't have worried. He elected to stay on and complete the portraits of Douglas Hyde and Charles Stewart Parnell before quitting Munich and returning home to Avila to spend his well-earned retirement in Spain. He presented me with a parting gift, a wonderful engraving of Albrecht Dürer; he was well aware of my own artistic preferences. It carried the dedication: 'A R.B., *reconocido artista y estimado colega* ['renowned artist, esteemed colleague'], A.L.'

Unfortunately, not everyone shared Antonio's positive opinion of my work. The new £20 note was only a few days in circulation when Betty and I were in a cinema queue behind two young girls who were curiously examining the new note. For a split second my wanton pride nearly caused me to remark that I was the author of the piece of money in her hand, but thankfully I remained silent. Holding it aloft one girl loudly exclaimed, 'Did ya ever see anything so shite!'

There were other criticisms that were not quite so frivolous. Because the new notes were slightly smaller than the previous ones, many people complained about their size, joking that the Central Bank was literally 'shrinking the value of our money'.

Others were unhappy with the choice of people portrayed on the new notes, particularly Catherine McAuley. One journalist in the *Star* newspaper declared that he found 'it a bit odd to see a nun from the Sisters of Mercy, with their vow of poverty, decorating filthy lucre. No doubt Paisley and his unionists will have nothing to do with this "Papist money"'. Emmanuel Kehoe in the *Sunday Press* wrote that, 'putting Sister Catherine McAuley on our currency doesn't do much for our image as a non-sectarian society from which northern Protestants have nothing to fear'.

Nonetheless, my portraits were generally well received by the public, although admittedly, the depiction of James Joyce caused some puzzlement. Since the great author was rarely seen smiling in surviving photographs, people wondered why he was sporting a wry grin on the new note, and why, in spite of his poor eyesight and thick glasses, his eyes were so clearly visible.

In my defence, the unfamiliar bright-eyed smile that gave such a quizzical look to the portrait was requested by the people in the Central Bank. Stephen Joyce, commenting on the portrait of his grandfather, said, 'I have my way of looking at my grandfather, Robert Ballagh has his, and that's fine.'

Since early times money has been used to express authority and independence and Ireland has been no exception to this symbolic urge. Even though the Irish pound was linked in value to sterling until 1979, the importance of pure symbolism was not lost on the founding fathers of the state, who moved quickly to ensure that the populace did not have to keep carrying around in their pockets the British monarch's head longer than was absolutely necessary. Ever since, we have used bank notes and coins to assert our national identity. I am humbled by the fact that I was involved in the creation of the last series of Irish bank notes that expressed our difference, and pride in our history and culture.

When a majority of the Irish electorate voted for the Maastricht Treaty in the 1992 referendum, not many were aware that they had voted for the introduction of a single European currency, a decision that would have far-reaching consequences years later. In the course of the referendum debate the controversial topic that engaged most people was abortion: whether Ireland's constitutional position on the issue could be safeguarded from European law. Only a handful of voices questioned the implications of abandoning the Irish punt.

Certainly, in the period that followed the referendum, few people paid much attention to that particular aspect of the treaty but, even so, the authorities in Europe lost no time devising plans for the implementation of the single currency.

It was only when I became involved in the design and production of the Irish bank notes that I was made aware of the sheer complexity of establishing an economic and monetary union. Unsurprisingly, most of the conversation I overheard in the Central Bank canteen centred on whether Ireland should take part in the new currency arrangement. It seemed to me that my colleagues were fairly cautious about the advisability of such a move and felt that Ireland should only join if Britain did the same; yet, in spite of such reservations, the politicians opted to sign up to what had been designated the euro. To this day I believe the decision to become a member of the eurozone in 1999 was a political decision and not an economic or financial one.

Personally, I was disheartened by the outcome, and not just because it signalled an untimely end to my bank note designs. As an artist I always took for granted the important role played by bank notes in defining a nation's identity, but by adopting the euro, which by its very nature could not express a national identity, Ireland relinquished that vital cultural signifier. However my aesthetic discomfort was dwarfed by my apprehension at what I viewed as a major threat to Irish sovereignty.

All well-founded sovereign states have their own currencies and there are sound reasons for this. By abolishing its currency, a country gives up the ability to control the rate of interest or the exchange rate. It can no longer control credit internally or influence its competitiveness externally by altering its exchange rate. On the other hand, the eurozone is incapable of sustaining a single currency, with one interest rate policy and one exchange rate policy suited to all of its members, considering that each one will have different levels of development and productivity and different economic requirements. For example, a low interest rate that might be advantageous to one country could prove disastrous to the economic wellbeing of another.

The value of having one's own currency was clearly demonstrated in Ireland during the period 1993 to 1999. This seven-year spell was the only time in the history of the Irish state when it floated its own currency, giving the Irish economy a highly competitive exchange rate. This boosted Irish exports, inhibited competing imports and launched the country on almost a decade of sound economic growth. Given my antipathy to the euro I felt somewhat challenged when the Central Bank informed me that they intended nominating me to design new euro bank notes for a competition launched by the European Monetary Institute, the forerunner of the European Central Bank.

In spite of my concerns, however, it only took a moment's reflection before I decided to accept the nomination. I simply couldn't resist the opportunity to become involved once again with my colleagues in the Central Bank. And, in all honesty, to quote *The Godfather*, I was made an offer I couldn't refuse.

In early 1996 all twenty-nine individuals -or teams nominated by fourteen European Union National Central Banks were invited to the European Monetary Institute building in Frankfurt to be briefed on the competition. Once inside the towering office block, all designers were informed by a tall and impressive figure, President Baron Alexandre Lamfalussy, that the Council of the European Monetary Institute had determined that there would be seven denominations: 5, 10, 20, 50, 100, 200 and 500, and that two themes for the bank note design had been chosen – 'ages and styles of Europe' and an abstract/modern design. We were reminded that our designs should successfully combine advanced security features with artistic creativity and, significantly, that all the designs had to ensure gender equality and avoid any national bias.

The briefing document given to each designer, while emphasizing that all designs should contain no national imagery, demanded that a

quarter of the area on the back of each note be left blank to facilitate
the incorporation of national symbols of individual countries, similar
to what was being planned for the coinage: fleeting glimpses of national
cultures. While in Frankfurt this issue cropped up during an informal
discussion with a designer from the Bank of England. I confessed to
being puzzled by the decision to omit a quarter of the design on the

back of each note. He smiled and posed the question, 'Did you ever measure the size of the Queen's portrait on an English bank note?'

On my return to Dublin, the Central Bank told me that I was expected to submit two design proposals, but that I had just six months to complete the assignment. This threw me into a panic. After all, when I created the artwork for the Irish currency, each note took six months to complete; now I was being asked to design fourteen bank notes in the same time. I knew I would need help. The Central Bank appreciated my dilemma and appointed the graphic design company Image Now to assist me.

I had only just embarked on the design of the euronotes when I heard that Britain was joining Denmark in seeking a derogation from membership of the eurozone. Shortly afterwards the European Monetary Institute informed all designers that the inclusion of a blank space on the back of each note was no longer required. But designing fourteen bank notes in only six months was still a daunting prospect and required enormous reserves of commitment, hard work and determination.

Having completed my 'ages and styles of Europe' design I quickly moved on to tackle the abstract/modern theme. I decided to feature European wildlife as the subject matter. Perhaps the elegant portrayal of animals by the sculptor Percy Metcalfe on the Irish coinage in circulation between 1928 and 1992 unconsciously influenced my choice.

I was reasonably satisfied with the results, but when the winning design was unveiled in December 1996 I have to admit that I was disappointed, not just that my own efforts had been overlooked but that a truly banal design had been chosen. No doubt the people in the European Monetary Institute who devised the original briefing document hoped to encourage the creation of designs that would offend no one, but failed to recognize that the production of inoffensive notes ran the risk of ending up with designs that nobody would cherish.

More importantly, the experience of the euro has been socially and economically dire for Ireland. When the economy needed higher interest rates in order to calm the boom, perversely the Irish found that they were obliged by the European Central Bank to halve them, because Ireland had joined the eurozone. As a result, the boom became 'boomier', as Taoiseach Bertie Ahern once put it. Irish commercial banks instantly took advantage of the situation and borrowed vast sums abroad to lend recklessly to an exploding property market, but as soon as the 'Celtic Tiger' boom turned to bust in 2008, the Anglo Irish Bank, the developers' lender of choice, went bankrupt. However, the governor of the European Central Bank insisted that on no account must Ireland allow any bank to go bust, for that would mean other European countries might follow suit, and the German, French and British banks that had lent recklessly to Irish banks might not get their money back. To oblige, the Irish government slavishly took on the bad debts of private Irish banks. It loaded €64 billion of such debt onto the backs of Irish taxpayers, most of whom had played no role whatsoever in its accumulation. Two years later, those same huge debts made it almost impossible to borrow on the international market, so the government, in desperation, submitted to the direct rule of the Troika, the European Central Bank, the Brussels Commission and the International Monetary Fund, as they took over direct supervision of the Irish economy. Irish financial sovereignty was squandered in order to save the euro in its hour of need.

✳

Back in November 1979, the American government organized a thirty-day tour of the United States specially designed for artists and art professionals from Yugoslavia, Mexico, Venezuela, Chile, Zambia, Hungary, Romania, Finland and Ireland. It was part of a wide-ranging programme to bring foreign visitors to the US to acquaint them with the contemporary art scene in the US. I was fortunate to be chosen as Ireland's representative. The purpose of the visit was to be accomplished by visiting museums, galleries, art centres, art colleges and the studios of leading American artists. Not being the kind of person who keeps an interesting and informative diary, I decided to bring a camera instead and attempt to record the experience on film. This resulted in several photographs that not only communicated something of the

Top: Wendella Boat Rides, Chicago; bottom: Poolbeg Lighthouse, Dublin.

excitement of the tour, but passed muster as aesthetic images in their own right.

When I showed them to Robin Barrington, the public affairs officer at the US Embassy, he immediately suggested that, with the assistance of the embassy, I mount an exhibition of them. David Hendriks embraced the proposal and put on one of the first photographic exhibitions ever held in a Dublin fine art setting. The publisher Philip McDermott saw these photographs and this sparked an idea that resulted in the publication of my book *Dublin*.

We had previously discussed the possibility of making a book about Dublin, perhaps using drawings or paintings. Evidently the American photos convinced Philip of the possibility of a new and unconventional photographic take on Dublin. He did not prescribe any particular approach, but left everything to me. I decided, rather than adopt any preconceived notions, to simply take my camera everywhere with me for twelve months, the duration of the project. This routine gave rise to a ruthlessly subjective view of Dublin. I found myself not only photographing the ordinary places that I encountered every day, but assiduously avoiding the celebrated views that were already well represented in existing books.

It was some time before a specific characteristic became apparent. Eventually it struck me that I was unconsciously excluding people from the photographs I was taking. This seemed odd, in that my approach to painting was exactly the opposite; after all, I was a painter of the human figure. It was a rereading of Walter Benjamin's essay *The Work of Art in the Age of Mechanical Reproduction* that enabled me to make some sense of this anomaly. In writing about the early Paris cityscapes of Eugéne Atget, Benjamin remarked, 'It has quite justly been said that he photographed them like scenes of a crime.'

This view of the street as being a stage-set for the enactment of human drama seemed to justify my approach, because if I were to focus on the citizens, attention would naturally shift away from the setting; so, to get close to what D. H. Lawrence called 'a spirit of place', it became necessary to exclude the very people who make a city a living organism. The film director Kieran Hickey wrote of my photography,

'The pictures belong not to a tourist guide-book but to something more private, secret almost – a record of a genuine world, evidence of the stubborn survival of a timeless local character. Dublin has seldom been seen like this. One has to go back to the pictures taken by Robert French before the First World War, or to the work of Nevill Johnston soon after the Second to see such a record of the face and fabric of the city. But should not a series of pictures called *Dublin* show some Dubliners? Look again. People *are* there, both the living and the dead. The dead lie in state in Mount Jerome Cemetery and are commemorated in the Memorial Park at Island Bridge. And living people? They are there too, all around us, behind the curtained and ivy screened windows or leaving the human marks of time on the worn step at the entrance to the King's Inns. Ballagh's identification with his fellow Dubliners, with their values and their urban culture is a statement of where he stands, his camera in his hand, revealing a timeless stage on which Dubliners, past and present, appear.'

Even before I became an artist I was captivated by fine art prints, which I discovered not in art galleries or museums, but reproduced in books borrowed from public libraries. First and foremost, I loved the elegance of Japanese woodblock prints created during the eighteenth and nineteenth centuries by artists, engravers and printers who worked in close collaboration. The artist was the imaginer, the designer, but his idea was turned into reality by two main processes – the cutting of the blocks and the taking of impressions from them. The main characteristics of *Ukiyo-e* prints are simplicity and clarity emphasized through clean lines and bright flat colours. Precision and lucidity are also evident in the graphic work of another favourite artist of mine, Albrecht Dürer. His finely detailed woodcuts and engravings were produced in a print workshop that was an integral part of his home and studio in Nuremburg. Often one has to travel abroad to view fine art masterpieces at close quarters, but I was delighted to find that the Chester Beatty Library in Dublin holds superb examples of both Japanese woodblock prints and compete editions of Dürer's graphic art.

In my opinion the motivation behind the creation of fine art prints is never simply aesthetic. It is often driven by a desire on the artist's part to make work available to a wider audience at a more reasonable price than would be the case for original paintings and sculptures. I was originally provoked by that democratic impulse into producing limited edition prints.

Quite early in my career I found myself asked to donate work to raise funds for various causes. However, no matter how deserving the cause, I quickly realized that I couldn't possibly respond to every request. I simply didn't paint enough pictures to service that particular demand. Also I needed to sell the work myself in order to earn a living. However, as an alternative, I suggested that rather than donate an original painting, I would produce a limited edition print to be sold as a potential fundraiser. This proved a great success, and over time I produced limited editions for Justice for the Birmingham Six, the Irish Anti-Apartheid Movement, the Conquer Cancer Campaign, the Irish Traveller Movement, the Irish Landmark Trust and many others including the North Dublin National School Project.

Betty and I faced a major difficulty when it came to the education of our children. Because of our own personal experiences we were determined that they avoid any school with a powerful religious ethos. This, of course, really narrowed our options. At the time there were few schools in the country offering non-denominational education. As luck would have it, one such school had been established in Glasnevin, not too far from our home. To our relief, the North Dublin National School Project was able to provide a place for our son Bruce.

Unfortunately the state provided very little support for such schools, so parents were constantly organizing events to raise funds to keep them going. It was in that context that the principal Sally Shiels approached me and asked me to contribute a picture for an auction or a raffle. I responded by offering to create a print as a fundraiser. Given the ethos of the school, Sally insisted that the children be involved in the project. For example the decision to make the nearby Botanic Gardens the subject of the print was taken by the children themselves, and when I decided to include a boy and a girl in the composition their names were chosen by lottery.

The finished print featured two pupils from Bruce's class looking

at a pond with giant water lily pads in one of the garden's conservatories. Thankfully the edition sold out, and the money raised paid for a new classroom.

✳

On 27 December 2008, the Israeli Defence Forces invaded Gaza. Their incursion lasted twenty-two days. When they left, 1,419 Palestinians were dead, the majority of them civilians. On the other side, the Israelis suffered 16 fatalities. In addition, 3,500 homes were destroyed, rendering 20,000 people homeless. The electricity supply system and the sewage pumping station lay in ruins; 268 businesses were wrecked with damage estimated at $139 million. Eighteen schools, including eight kindergartens, were levelled. Government buildings, police stations and health centres were shattered. A rally was organized in Dublin to protest at such wanton destruction and violence. An enormous crowd turned up and marched to the Israeli Embassy in Ballsbridge. I was one of many from Irish civil society asked to speak. After the rally a trade unionist friend, Noirin Greene, came up and insisted that 'we have to do something'. She suggested that I create a limited edition print and that she and other union colleagues would sell copies to raise money for medical aid for Gaza. I created a simple but powerful image of a Palestinian woman with a tear on her cheek. It quickly sold out. A reception was organized in Liberty Hall, the headquarters of SIPTU, Ireland's largest trade union; a cheque for €56,000.00 was presented to a Palestinian doctor with the stated intention that the money help build a new operating theatre in Gaza. Later, Jack O'Connor, the general president of SIPTU, handed over a small brass plaque embellished with Irish and Palestinian flags, and inscribed with the words *The James Connolly Operating Theatre*. He requested that it be fixed to the door of the operating theatre when it was completed.

Gaza, 2010.

CHAPTER 15

All the World's a Stage

I had designed a poster for Michael Colgan when he was working for the Dublin Theatre Festival, but I was still a little surprised when, as director of the Gate Theatre, he asked me to call into his office to discuss a stage show he intended to produce.

The unvarnished truth was that I knew absolutely nothing about theatre. As a youngster I rarely went to staged dramas, but like many of my generation I spent an inordinate amount of time in the dark watching films in the various local cinemas scattered throughout Dublin. My own fleapit in Ballsbridge was never referred to as the Ritz cinema; everyone called it the Shack. I first attended the Shack in the early 1950s, and with my pals formed part of what was called the 'fourpenny rush'. This happened every Saturday afternoon when we children, having paid the four pence admission, were herded down the aisles to fill up the rows of hard seats in front of the screen. We were controlled, rather sternly, by uniformed ushers who were all known by different brands of soap powders – Rinso, Persil and so on. This I never understood, but the programme was always great value, usually two feature films and a serial or a 'follier-up', as it was called.

Our imaginations invariably were charged by what we saw on

screen and, as we made our way home, we would slap our thighs and shout, 'Hi, ho, Silver!' or 'Take 'em to Missouri!' if the main feature had been a western, or vocalize poor imitations of gun shots, 'Dar! Dar!' and creep through the bushes beside the Dodder River, living out the experiences of soldiers in the Second World War. This rich cultural education was rudely interrupted by an announcement that admission was being increased to eight pence. Up to then, the sixpenny piece I received as pocket money not only covered the price of the ticket but also purchased an ice-lolly and a single Woodbine cigarette. Naturally we protested, but eventually we succumbed, cajoling extra funding out of our parents, and continued our regular Saturday-afternoon adventures. Some kids, however, were able to make up the difference themselves by exploiting a vulnerability in the layout of the cinema. The men's toilet was outside the building, so you had to pass through the foyer and exit the cinema to use the facility. An opportunity was spotted. For every two or three kids who went out, four or five re-turned. This continued for some time before the ruse was rumbled. The toilet was immediately ruled out of bounds. This, of course, had unpleasant consequences, with minor flooding occurring in the area of the front stalls. Management quickly reverted to the old system, but with much improved security. In 1976 the Ritz stopped showing films and became the Oscar Theatre until it closed in 1985, soon reopening as Ireland's first Sikh temple.

Occasionally my parents took me with them to another cinema, the Stella in Rathmines. Unhappily, as far as I was concerned, they were not there to see movies but to learn ballroom dancing. The cinema was equipped with a spacious ballroom, which featured a maple dancefloor supported on steel springs, where my exceptionally glamorous aunt, Evelyn Burchill, ran dancing classes. On each visit, with mounting boredom, I gazed at the sight of dancing students being put through their paces, 'Slow, slow, quick quick, slow,' wishing I were downstairs watching a film in the cinema. But the Theatre Royal, sited on Hawkins Street near O'Connell Bridge, which was opened in 1935, was much more to my taste. Its striking art deco exterior was floodlit at night to emphasize the elegance and scale of the building. Once inside the massive auditorium, decorated in an exuberant Moorish style, over 3,000 patrons, accommodated on three levels, could enjoy a combination of live stage acts and the latest films. The Theatre Royal had a resident twenty-five-piece orchestra under the direction of Jimmy Campbell and a troupe of dancers, the Royalettes. It also boasted a splendid Compton organ, which, during live performances, rose gracefully from the orchestra pit with the organist Tommy Dando playing his sprightly theme tune, 'Keep Your Sunny Side Up'.

The enormous size of the venue made it difficult to run profitably, so big international artists were booked in an attempt to boost audiences. One such star was Bill Haley who came to Dublin in 1958. I was determined to experience the kiss-curled rock 'n' roller with my own eyes and ears, so after repeated entreaties, I managed to persuade my father to take me to the Theatre Royal, which that night was packed to the rafters with hysterical fans. Although fascinated by the experience, my father was slightly distracted by the attendant pandemonium. For myself, I couldn't get enough of it.

Sadly, as financial pressure mounted, the Theatre Royal was forced to close its doors in 1962 and the profitable site was sold for redevelopment. It says something about the Irish state that this magnificent palace of entertainment was demolished to make way for a featureless, ugly office block, which in turn became the offices of a hopelessly dysfunctional Department of Health.

Samuel Beckett, oil on canvas with mixed media, 167cm x 23cm, 2018.

My only real experience of live theatre was a night at the Olympia Theatre when I was a schoolboy. I had been taken by my parents to see my aunt, Ruth Durley, playing the mother in *Stephen D.*, Hugh Leonard's adaption of James Joyce's *A Portrait of the Artist as a Young Man*, so given this minimal exposure to the world of serious drama, I approached my meeting with Michael Colgan with some trepidation.

'Why on earth do you want me to design a show for the Gate?'

His reply was short and to the point. 'I thought you'd be good at it,'

He went on to explain that the Gate Theatre had intended staging *Beginning to End*, a compilation of Samuel Beckett's work which the late Jack MacGowran, one of Beckett's favourite actors, had performed to great acclaim. Colgan planned reviving the show with the actor Barry McGovern, who had appeared in two of Beckett's plays.

Michael and Barry met Beckett in Paris and told him of their plans. He listened politely and then informed them that, since Gloria, Mac-Gowran's widow, had expressed a desire to direct a production of the compilation herself, he felt inclined to respect her wishes. However, as they were leaving he made the enigmatic suggestion that some of his other writings might be worth looking at. On their return they arranged a meeting, which I attended along with the proposed director, Colm O'Briain, who had just resigned as general secretary of the Labour Party and had previously been director of the Arts Council, and the lighting designer, Rupert Murray. On reflection, we realized that losing *Beginning to End* was perhaps not such a bad thing; it was simply a collection of popular excerpts from Beckett's work strung together, without any internal logic other than the quality of the writing. We felt we should do better. Gradually a consensus emerged that we should confine ourselves to Beckett's great post-war trilogy of novels: *Molloy*, *Malone Dies* and *The Unnamable*. We felt that there were greater theatrical possibilities in dramatizing the novels than simply dipping in and out of Beckett's writing in different genres.

Barry worked on the text with the writer and academic Gerry Dukes and came up with a selection that was not an adaptation of the trilogy, but consisted instead of extracts woven into a coherent whole that expressed the essence of the novels. Samuel Beckett was informed of our progress and replied, 'The project has my approval.'

While Barry and Gerry were working on the text, I tried to come up with some ideas for staging the show. My approach was determined by my belief in the primary role of both the text and the performance, and an acceptance that the setting should be supportive yet subordinate to the words and the action; a set should be an appropriate space for dramatic action and a visual expression of the meanings of that action. I also felt that any embellishment of the space should be minimal – 'less is more' – or, in the words of Samuel Beckett, the 'meremost minimum'.

Unfortunately Colm seemed to have other ideas. Initially he envisaged a complex chrome or aluminium structure, which I felt would be visually distracting. An impasse developed. Michael Colgan intervened, asking what I thought; I replied that even though I didn't like Colm's idea, in the interest of peace, I was prepared to deliver it.

To my surprise, Colgan replied, 'That's fine, but there is one condition. If you concede, I expect you to stand at the top of the stairs every night and greet the patrons with a sign about your neck spelling out the message – this is not my idea!'

I took the point and began talking again to Colm. We eventually resolved our differences and, with some compromises, I completed the set design to my satisfaction. Gerry Dukes described it as 'a lit space, like the corner of an exploded cube opened out for our inspection. Against the deep black of the surrounding darkness the space was outlined in white neon tubing, isolating and sealing. All the light pouring down from above, no angles, no shadows, and no concealment. An arena, a refuge, a prison cell, a room with a view to introspection and interrogation. There are no points of entry or exit. The designer did not enrich the text merely; his work made available a context of extraordinary appositeness within which Beckett's words could be dramatized. The transition from page to stage invested Beckett's words with carnal presence and moribund vivacity. And at the end, when the white light of consciousness surged to fall, the set was entirely bleached out in an intense wash of ineradicable subjectivity before the final black-out and curtain.'

In spite of my desire to avoid clutter, I accepted that Barry would need to work with several items on stage. During rehearsals an aluminium walking frame served as a seat, a bicycle, even a dead dog, but once on stage it became obvious that its metallic quality was wrong. The stage manager than produced an illustration of a carpenter's horse, saying, 'Is this the sort of thing you're looking for?'

It was, so I made a drawing and our stage carpenter built it in time for the opening night. Colm needed a raised area for the second act; he suggested a bed that was not a bed, I proposed a catafalque, drawing inspiration from the Altar of Remembrance in the War Memorial Gardens in Islandbridge, designed by Sir Edwin Lutyens. It was the only piece of furniture on stage for the second act.

Agreement about the costuming was a great deal easier. We wanted a recognizable Beckett character but not a stereotype. The heavy coat might suggest a dressing gown, but what colour? Black was wrong; dark green could suggest a mouldy black. The lining was printed with pages from the *Times Literary Supplement* and, when revealed, underscored a gag in the text. Barry tried on many different types of trousers. We opted for a pair with a big crotch and a long fly. We decided on a nightshirt for the second act and under that, a pair of long johns; a plain cream colour suggested a surgical gown or even a shroud. The show, entitled *I'll Go On*, Beckett's final sentence in *The Unnamable*, was premiered during the 1985 Dublin Theatre Festival. It was an outstanding success and was nominated for several Irish theatre awards in both the acting and design categories.

In *New York* magazine, John Simon described *I'll Go On* as 'ninety minutes of laugher, bitterness, compassion and verbal music to leave you rapt. To Beckett, mortality is a joke played on us – a terrible joke but a joke nevertheless – and McGovern delivers this epiphany in all its dizzying pain and hilarity. Robert Ballagh has made us stare into a dark corner from which two walls open up towards us; sometimes the walls are in darkness, outlined by a thin line of bright neon, and from this cornering darkness the narrator spookily emerges, and into it he will finally recede. These two walls, significantly stripped down from the usual three, are decorated with irregular wavy lines suggestive of mountains or sea on a Chinese scroll. As Rupert Murray's lighting works its manifoldness on them, the walls change colour and mood to become any setting, any season – space itself. The one prop in the first act is a trestle that impersonates a bicycle, a bench, the very concept of artefacts. In act two, the single prop is a large recumbent slab – bed, deathbed, catafalque, coffin. The costume, too, has changed, from the tramp's dark greatcoat lined with the *Times Literary Supplement* for added warmth, to a garment that is part nightshirt, part hospital smock, with a soupçon of shroud. If you want funny, take Jackie Mason. If you want funny with the increment of sublime, McGovern's Beckett is your man.'

I found my first experience of working in the theatre challenging, yet curiously exhilarating. Fortunately, because of my childhood passion for making things and my experience as a draughtsman, I was able to take on two essential aspects of set design: the production of working drawings and the creation of a model-box. This provided me with a head start in my new calling.

I'll Go On toured Ireland, the US and Europe and in April 1986, played a special engagement in the Théâtre de l'Alliance in Paris to mark Samuel Beckett's eightieth birthday. I was really looking forward to the Paris trip, especially since we were promised a meeting with Beckett himself. But two weeks before we were due to leave, disaster stuck.

After the opening of a friend's exhibition, Betty and I went to an Italian restaurant in Dublin for a party to celebrate the occasion. Shortly after we arrived, someone, white as a sheet, approached me and spluttered, 'There's been an accident – you'd better go downstairs.'

As I went down the flight of steps to the basement I recoiled at the sight of Betty's body lying prostrate in a small pool of blood at the bottom of the stairs. She had fallen down the narrow staircase on her way to the toilet. I kneeled down beside her and supported her head, but there was little else I could do but await the emergency services. A crew from the Dublin fire brigade ambulance service soon arrived, placed Betty on a stretcher and carried her to the ambulance outside the restaurant. I travelled with Betty, who was still unconscious, to the nearby Meath Hospital.

I had to wait until she was properly established in the intensive care unit before I was allowed to see her. Even though she was in a coma, I was assured she would be fine. I was not so sure. She remained in a coma for over two days, and even after regaining consciousness she was both listless and confused. The medical staff insisted that she was making good progress, but I was doubtful. And my anxiety was confirmed when I met our friend, the writer Peter Sheridan, who had just paid her a visit.

'Well, what do you think?' he asked.

'I'm not happy with the way things are going.'

'You can say that again. You'll have to do something.'

That short exchange left me in a panic. I didn't know any medical people. I was in despair, but I remembered Dr Eoin O'Brien, an eminent cardiologist and a leading expert on blood pressure. The reason I hadn't immediately thought of him was that our friendship was based, not on medical matters, but on a mutual interest in Samuel Beckett. He wrote and produced a magnificent book, *The Beckett Country*, in which he charted with maps and photographs the landscape that inspired and informed the novels, plays and poetry. Eoin had commissioned me to create seven illustrative maps for the book. I called him and he promised to visit Betty during his lunch break. At about half-past two, Eoin phoned to say that Betty was on her way to the Richmond Hospital, where she should have been in the first place, since it was the main Dublin hospital that specialized in head injuries. Betty had been the victim of an idiotic policy where, on weekends or at night, ambulances were required to deliver patients to the hospital that was on call, and not necessarily to one best suited to treat their injuries.

Eoin said that Sandy Pate, a consultant neurosurgeon, would contact me. With his distinctive Scottish burr, he assured me that Betty was stable, but added that he required my permission for 'a small intervention'. He explained what he meant: 'Well, most people would call it an operation.'

Since he deemed it absolutely necessary, I reluctantly agreed to the procedure. At about half-past seven that evening, Sandy Pate phoned to say that there had been a blood clot in Betty's brain, which he had dealt with just in the nick of time. Now Betty, being the strong person she was, decided with her usual resolve she would make a swift recovery and put the sorry incident behind her. She got over the physical aspects of the accident fairly quickly, but the brain injury was another matter entirely. I remember Sandy Pate warning me, 'A brain injury is not like a broken arm; it's far more complicated than that.' For example, because of the nature of her injury, Betty had a strong chance of developing epilepsy.

Tragically, she drew that short straw. And we were warned about possible personality changes. We quickly became aware of unaccustomed addictive behaviour, particularly in relation to alcohol; as it turned out, Betty, her family and her friends had to cope with the fallout from that disastrous accident for the rest of her life.

Some people, particularly those fortunate enough to have had no personal experience of alcohol abuse, often labour under the misconception that an alcoholic is a woebegone creature who is permanently drunk, dishevelled and disorderly. Nothing could be further from the truth. As a matter of fact, many alcoholics appear quite normal on the surface but their impaired control over how they drink inevitably results in persistent difficulties in many aspects of their lives. Obviously nobody sets out to be an alcoholic, so in order to learn how to deal with the condition it's vital to recognize it as a chronic disease in which genetic, psychosocial and environmental factors come into play. Even though every individual who abuses alcohol will do so in a different way, with differing consequences, all addicts, without exception, will have one factor in common: and that is an overwhelming propensity for denial. When Betty came home from hospital in a fairly weak state, her head swathed in bandages, she was under strict instruction to take things easy and allow nature to take its course. Yet on her first day of convalescence, when I returned from work I was shocked to find her unsteady and confused. I remember thinking, *Jesus, is this some sort of relapse?* But then it dawned on me that she was pissed – she had raided the booze cabinet. I put her to bed and immediately removed all alcohol from the house, naïvely thinking that I had solved the problem. I had yet to learn how cunning and manipulative a drinker can be.

The next day, as soon as she was alone, Betty inveigled a neighbour into buying a naggin of whiskey from the local pub. This difficult behaviour continued for a few days; but thankfully, as her physical health improved, the frenetic desire for alcohol seemed to abate and, as a family, we were able to revert to an almost normal existence. But the experience was an ominous portent of trouble ahead.

Gradually Betty resumed cooking as well as other light domestic tasks, and even returned to work on a part-time basis. At the time I was optimistic that we had put the whole sorry business behind us and that the alcoholic frenzy after her return from hospital was simply an aberration. Certainly, as we began to socialize once more that seemed to be the case, until one night at a party in a friend's home, Betty became hopelessly intoxicated and I had to literally carry her home. Once again, this bout of heavy drinking was followed by a period of calm, normal behaviour.

It was a friend of my parents, herself a recovering alcoholic, who speculated that perhaps Betty had become a 'binge' drinker – a binge being a period of time, sometimes lasting several days, in which the drinker will disregard family, friends and all responsibilities in their desire to consume as much alcohol as possible. Unfortunately, the interval between binges may become shorter. In most cases binge drinking is linked to depression, which in turn results from stress, mood swings and other psychological factors. Because a binge can be triggered by so many different symptoms, the family of an alcoholic lives in constant dread of the next unpredictable outbreak. It's worth remembering that, for most of their drinking careers, alcoholics can exercise a measure of control and for that reason will deny the existence of any problem. A close friend managed to persuade Betty to accompany him to a meeting of Alcoholics Anonymous; but after a few visits, Betty announced, 'I'm not going to any more meetings. They're all alcoholics!'

On another occasion, when Betty and I went to see a counsellor, she blamed me for her drinking, contending that I ignored her because I devoted too much time to painting. She suggested that if I were prepared to give up art she would stop drinking. Of course I didn't stop painting and Betty, in turn, didn't stop drinking; that is, until our granddaughter Ava was born. Betty adored the little mite, but Bruce, our son, made it quite clear that she would only have access to the baby if she stopped drinking. Hard to believe, but she instantly quit, and alcohol never again passed her lips.

Obviously as a result of Betty's misfortune there was no question of me travelling to Paris with the team from the Gate Theatre installing *I'll Go On* in the Théâtre de l'Alliance. As expected, given his fondness for privacy, Beckett did not attend the performance but instead agreed to meet everyone for breakfast the following morning at the Café de Paris on Boulevard Saint Jacques, a favourite haunt of his located near his apartment, with a back door through which he could enter without much fuss.

Beckett quietly joined the assembled company but didn't utter a word. No one else seemed prepared to break the ice. Silence prevailed. A Beckettian moment. Eventually he turned to Michael Colgan and, in a hushed tone, inquired, 'Are we waiting for Ballagh?'

*

Michael Colgan's wish to produce Oscar Wilde's *Salomé* at the Gate Theatre in 1988 was fundamentally an idea that originated with his predecessors, Hilton Edwards and Micheál Mac Liammóir, who presented *Salomé* in the course of their first season in 1928; and it was to celebrate their vision and courage that, sixty years later, the Gate set about mounting a new production of the play. Initially Colgan was unsure as to how to make it work, but after the English actor Steven Berkoff had a hit with his show *Decadence* in the Gate, Michael felt he had his man. He was certain that Berkoff was well suited to the richness, excess and almost velvety feel of Wilde's *Salomé*, and because my views on theatre design were not dissimilar to those of Berkoff, he felt that I would make a perfect collaborator. However, when Colgan sat down with Berkoff to discuss his direction of the play and proceeded to recommend me, Berkoff insisted that he didn't want a designer. 'Designers always promise to produce something simple and then go on and create a monument to themselves.'

All he wanted was a black box. Eventually, after some discussion, he agreed that one black box was not quite the same as another and that he would meet me; but only, he stressed, to discuss whether the black box would be matt black or gloss black. When I turned up with a plan that was minimal but obviously not a black box, Steven Berkoff, with close-cropped hair, bullish personality and, in the words of the *Guardian* dressed 'like a Lithuanian coal miner in a leather waistcoat, black shirt and baggy trousers' instantly rejected it, but afterwards complained that I had not brought more ideas.

I decided to attend a few rehearsals to get a feel for Berkoff's interpretation and was immediately struck by his 'Last Supper' scene at the beginning of the play. The talented cast that Colgan had assembled were seated upstage behind a wide table, partaking in a lavish banquet but with no goblets, no grapes – everything was mimed in slow motion. It was mesmeric.

Steven Berkoff explained, 'As a director I have chosen to bare the text and let the words crawl inside the spectator's and the hearer's mind. Rather than crowd the stage with purple cushions and burning tapers I would rather let Wilde's images do that for you. I would rather let the audience use their unrivalled imagination to see the wines and fruits, the carpets and the tables of jasper.'

Even though they had only rehearsed the opening sequence, I knew exactly what to do. I set about designing a raked or sloping performance area decorated with large marble-like slabs laid out in receding perspective, and edged with marble steps rising to a surrounding level platform accommodating the 'Last Supper' table and a piano for composer Roger Doyle to perform his original music. This minimal layout was set off by a massive backcloth featuring a romantic purple moonlit sky inspired by the paintings of the German artist Caspar David Friedrich. ·

I constructed a model-box and brought it to a meeting with Berkoff and Colgan. Berkoff seemed pleased, although he didn't say so. He

Oscar Wilde, oil on canvas, 92cm x 61cm, 1990, The Gate Theatre, Dublin.

suggested a few minor alterations. Colgan then asked if anything else should be changed. Berkoff said no; the production manager was instructed to begin building the set. Meanwhile rehearsals continued in a somewhat fraught atmosphere.

Berkoff asked to meet me, and confessed that he was stuck trying to stage the scene where Jokanaan or John the Baptist is released from incarceration. He asked if it might be possible to create a cell-like structure that would be positioned centre stage during a blackout, and from which Jokanaan would emerge. I said I thought that this was a terrible idea, reminding him that he had already set the template for the show where all movement was mimed, and that the introduction of a major piece of stage furniture would be a violation of the trust established with the audience.

Not saying anything, he returned to rehearsals and successfully choreographed a dramatically mimed ascent from Herod's dungeon. There were a few other moments of doubt, but thankfully Berkoff adhered to his original vision and created a stunning piece of theatre that was both elegant and spellbinding. A few days before the first preview, with the almost completed set in place, Berkoff saw it for the first time. I happened to be sitting in the stalls and saw him walking on stage.

Nervously I asked, 'Well, Steven, what do you think?'

He roared back, 'I fuckin' hate it!' and began to rant and rave, pacing back and forth. 'I should have listened to myself; all I wanted was a black box – this is shit!'

As he stormed off, he instructed the production manager to pick the set up and throw it out. According to the *New York Times*, Berkoff is a 'volcanic, intuitive director known to reduce grown actors to tears of fury'. Well, as I had just learned, designers are also subject to his explosive volatility.

The crew were aghast at this astonishing performance and asked, 'What will we do?'

I replied, 'We'll do what we're paid to do. We'll finish the build.'

The next evening the dress rehearsal took place on the completed set and afterwards, much to my surprise, Berkoff exclaimed, 'What a marvellous set.'

The production proved to be an enormous hit with the Irish theatre-going public; in fact it was sold out for the entire run. Critics also responded with considerable enthusiasm. Kevin Myers in the *Irish Times* declared that *Salomé* 'is that kind of astounding production where all kinds of variables have come together perfectly. Robert Ballagh's set is truly marvellous, stark and simple, to compensate for the florid lusciousness of the Wildean language; there is a pure genius at work in this production such as has seldom, if ever, been seen on a Dublin stage.'

News of the runaway success of the Gate's production of *Salomé* spread and, in no time at all, offers from abroad landed on Michael Colgan's desk. The first one he accepted was an invitation to stage the play at the 1989 Edinburgh Festival. Once *Salomé* had opened at the Royal Lyceum, all seats were sold out and people formed long queues in the forlorn hope of purchasing returned tickets. Michael Billington in the *Guardian* said that 'Berkoff gives us a controlled dream that in its reined-in eroticism and disciplined frenzy suggests that Wilde's tragedy is less a piece of Biblical exotica than a dramatized symbolist poem. Alan Stanford's Herod, a figure of Wildean bulk with carmine lips, holds every syllable up to the light in a memorable display of heavyweight camp.' Billington also singled out Olwen Fouéré's Salomé for her obsessive quality and said, 'Her famous dance of the seven veils, done without removing a _single stitch of clothing, is a wonderful piece of striptease.' Charles Spencer in the *Daily Telegraph* admitted that despite it being 'played in agonising slow motion, against all the odds, it works. Berkoff's mannered approach with its mime sequences and frozen tableaux creates a dream-like atmosphere that becomes increasingly hypnotic.'

There were many other equally flattering reviews. Naturally all of us were buoyed up by the extremely positive reaction to the production, so you can imagine how deflated we became on seeing a bizarre interview which Berkoff gave on BBC television about the Edinburgh staging. Asked if he had any problems communicating with the Irish cast, he replied, in a stage 'Oirish' accent, that he had trouble pulling them out of pubs and that the only way he could get them to visualize dramatic values was to imagine they were drinking a pint of Guinness very slowly. The cast was hurt and humiliated by this bizarre rant; in Dublin, however, the response was one of seething anger at his racist and libellous remarks.

Kevin Myers in the *Irish Times* stated that, 'It is inconceivable that the racial characterization of the Irish that Berkoff indulged in would be permitted of any other ethnic group. If Berkoff had said he had trouble getting Jewish actors out of their money-lending offices or West Indians from smoking dope, the BBC would not have transmitted it.' The end result was that an unbridgeable rift between Berkoff and the Gate cast had been created; and perhaps, in a way, this suited Berkoff, because he was already planning to restage *Salomé* in the National Theatre of Great Britain, but this time with an English cast.

*

I have to say that at the time, I paid scant attention to the various disputes. I had other things on my mind. My parents, who by then were quite

On the set of *The Importance of Being Earnest* in the Gate Theatre, Dublin.

elderly, were completely taken aback to find themselves in fairly desperate circumstances. My father had worked in the same firm for over forty years, always paying his taxes and pension requirements, yet shortly after his retirement, the company went into bankruptcy and his pension entitlements went with it. At around the same time a landlord took a case to the High Court pleading that tenant protection be put aside in favour of the right to levy rents at market values. The court found in his favour and, as a result, my parents could no longer afford the rent on their flat. Eventually, they managed to obtain rent support and were able to remain in the home that they had lived in all their married lives.

However, all the anxiety and stress was having an effect. For the first time, I noticed that my mother's mental health seemed impaired. She was forgetting things and became unable to cope; and as my father struggled to look after her, his own health deteriorated too. They were lucky, in one respect, to have access to lunches provided by the Irish Red Cross in a nearby hall. They had been self-sufficient all their lives, yet at a time of real vulnerability were forced to depend on welfare and charity. Like most proud people they were embarrassed by having to seek help. There was little I could do, as our own financial situation was very precarious, but we visited them on a regular basis to check that they were all right. However, on a particularly cold winter afternoon I was shocked to discover them huddled in front of an unlit fire wearing their overcoats. There was no central heating in the flat, but usually there was a roaring fire in the living room. When I asked why the fire wasn't lit, my father replied that he was too tired to fetch the coal. I realized we were in trouble.

One evening a few weeks later, my mother phoned to report that my father 'looked funny'. We needed no prompting. On arrival, once I saw the perplexed look on my father's face, I knew that he had suffered a stroke. We called an ambulance, which took him to St Vincent's Hospital, and while there he began to make some progress under the diligent care of the nursing staff; on the other hand, my mother's condition meant that she couldn't be left on her own. We had to introduce a rota system where Betty attended my mother while I looked after the kids and then, after a few days, we exchanged roles. After a week or so I was asleep in my parents' flat when the phone rang. It was a nurse from St Vincent's. In tears, she informed me that my father had just suffered a massive heart attack and had died. I was devastated.

I lay awake all night thinking of what I might say to my mother in the morning. I made breakfast, and when she joined me, I stammered out, 'I've terribly bad news. I'm afraid Dad died during the night.'

'Oh, really,' she replied, and continued eating her cereal.

It was then that I grasped, for the very first time, the full extent of her senility.

I remember her doctor telling us, soon after my father's funeral, that since she was in fairly good shape physically and could live for many more years, we had better find someplace where she could be looked after. We knew she couldn't come and live with us as our house was far too small; thus began one of the most stressful experiences of my life. Most of the nursing homes I visited were dreadful, and those that were half-decent were full. Then to my delight I stumbled on one that was rather attractive and had several vacancies. I immediately asked them to put my mother's name down on their list and rushed home to tell Betty the good news.

'How much does it cost?' she inquired.

In all my excitement I had neglected to ask that salient question.

After she had phoned the home Betty turned to me and exclaimed, 'You feckin' eejit.'

The annual fee was twice what I earned in a good year. I was in despair. What could we do? Thankfully the pressure was lifted, if only temporarily, when my mother was admitted to St Vincent's Hospital for tests. This break in caring for my mother allowed me to travel to the US to do some business for the Gate Theatre, but I was only there a few days when Betty called from the hospital to say that my mother had just died in her arms. In my opinion, she died of a broken heart. Wracked with guilt, I returned to bury a second parent in just over a month. I would miss them terribly, especially the leisurely walks with my father when we discussed and then solved all the problems of the world.

Michael Colgan had already accepted an offer from Charleston to present Salomé as part of their annual Spoleto Festival, so in May 1990 we all set out, this time under the direction of Alan Stanford, for South Carolina. Once again the production was a remarkable success, but there were a few dissenting voices. In the southern states of America there are many who take their Bible literally and I overheard some patrons complaining that the show from first to last was inauthentic. After all, 'There were no dinner jackets or bow ties in the time of the Old Testament!'

I'm afraid nothing short of a Cecil B. DeMille production would have satisfied those Bible-thumpers.

In the meantime, Steven Berkoff was auditioning actors for his London production of Salomé. All the roles were cast except Herod, which he intended playing himself. Even though none of the Gate cast were involved, he elected to retain the services of both Trevor Dawson as lighting designer and me as set designer for the new production. He also decided, wisely in my opinion, to use Roger Doyle's original music.

It was a real privilege to work in the Lyttelton Theatre, part of the National Theatre complex on the South Bank of the Thames. The staff couldn't have been more welcoming, and when I began to discuss my design with them they told me about facilities that simply didn't exist in Ireland. For example, up until then, each time we built the Salomé set we had to construct a raked performance area, which involved many hours of tedious carpentry. In the Lyttelton, a button was pressed, causing the entire stage deck to adjust to the required angle. As a result we were able to install the set without much difficulty.

Unfortunately, that was the easy part. As everybody gathered for the dress rehearsal, nothing happened. We waited and waited and the stage was still empty. It transpired that the young costume designer had become the latest victim of Steven's volatility.

'My cast are not going on stage in those shite bags!' he roared.

I couldn't fathom his objection, since the new costumes were not unlike those in the original Gate production. It took the intervention of Richard Eyre, a senior director in the National Theatre, to calm things down and get the dress rehearsal started. Afterwards there was no mention of the costumes.

Following a successful run in the National Theatre, the production transferred to the Phoenix Theatre in London's West End. I know I will be accused of bias, but I felt that Berkoff's productions of *Salomé* in London were not as successful as the original versions in Dublin and Edinburgh. The edge was blunted. Several years later the Gate put on a revival of the original production, but without either Olwen Fouéré or Joe Savino as Jokanaan; I felt a spark was missing. Perhaps like Oscar himself, the Gate Theatre's staging of *Salomé* was destined to shine brightly but briefly, then, like a dream, fade away.

✳

I always hated the Eurovision Song Contest. The cheesy, formulaic songs and the camp performances invariably left me cold, so in 1994, when the contest was due to be broadcast from the Point Theatre in Dublin, I resolved to keep a respectful distance. However, to my horror, on the night in question, Betty turned on the television set and sat back to enjoy the spectacle.

'Fuck me,' I muttered, 'I'm out of here.'

I made my way to my local pub, hoping for more congenial company, but unfortunately it was already stuffed with Eurovision fans, all eagerly waiting for the dire saga to unfold on several TV screens. I stole away to a quiet corner, but while sipping a slow pint or two I was advised by a few sensible souls to watch out for the interval act. They had been told that it was something special.

On hearing the presenter Gerry Ryan declaim, 'Ladies and Gentlemen – *Riverdance!*' I rose to my feet and from the back of the crowd watched, with growing amazement, an extraordinary seven-minute compilation of Irish music and dance. And when it reached a breathless climax, I joined, not only the roars of approval in the pub, but also those of the 300 million viewers across the globe. I was certain that I had witnessed an extraordinary phenomenon.

The only person I knew who had been involved with *Riverdance* was the composer of the music, Bill Whelan. He had played keyboards with the folk group Planxty and had composed 'Timedance', which the band had played as an interval piece for the 1981 Eurovision Song Contest. He also scored Pat O'Connor's 1984 film *Lamb* with Van Morrison. After phoning to congratulate him I thought it would be the last I'd hear of *Riverdance*, but some time later, I received a call from Moya Doherty, RTÉ's producer of Eurovision. She was considering staging a theatrical show based on *Riverdance*.

'Would you be interested in becoming involved as a designer?'

Naturally, I replied, 'Yes.'

When she was given the job of producing the Eurovision Song Contest in 1994, Moya Doherty was determined to come up with something radically different. The seven-minute interval slot offered

Riverdance on the Great Wall of China.

an opportunity to grab the attention of viewers with an electrifying dance number that would be Irish in a modern and exciting way. She was convinced that with champion Irish-American dancers Michael Flatley and Jean Butler and composer Bill Whelan, she could deliver the effect she sought. The choreography broke away from the stuffiness of competitive Irish dance, using leaps and expressive gestures from the principals, but also a high-kicking chorus line. Gone too were the traditional elaborate costumes with interlaced Celtic patterns and Tara brooches, to be replaced by plainer, more modern dance attire.

When Flatley and Butler burst onto the vast stage of the Point Theatre, in an exhilarating act of liberation they rebranded popular Irish culture. Fintan O'Toole acknowledged that, 'When *Riverdance* first opened in Dublin, you could hear, even above the pounding feet and the swirling music, the audience gasping for breath. And then an explosion of shouts and whoops as all that air burst out again in a wave of wonderment. It was, of course, the sheer force and energy of the dancing, the rapture of the music, the fantastic sight of so many bodies in motion. But there was something else as well, some long-submerged emotion breaking the surface and gulping in the oxygen.'

Considerable time had passed since her phone call so, with some regret, I presumed that Moya had either forgotten me, or that the project simply wasn't going ahead. But then she phoned once more.

She explained, 'We're having great difficulty getting finance in place, but we still want you to be involved. Please be patient.'

Moya and her husband John McColgan, the putative director of the theatrical version of *Riverdance*, had approached RTÉ for support, only to be rebuffed. The rejection letter read, in part:

> Thank you for telling us about your project to
> put on a theatrical show based on *Riverdance*.
> We regretfully have to decline because we
> see no commercial future in such a project.

Moya wasn't prepared to leave it at that. Her persistence eventually convinced RTÉ to come on board and, as it turned out, their investment in *Riverdance* was one of the most lucrative ever made by the TV station. After receiving the support of several other backers, Moya finally gave the green light to the project.

Because part of RTÉ's contribution to *Riverdance* was to design the set for the Point Theatre, I immediately questioned whether I had any possible role to play. Moya insisted that she still wanted me to be part of the production. Right from the start, her idea was to use projection as an integral element of the design. She felt that the really important thing was the dance, the notion of scenery or anything else getting in the way of the dancers was unacceptable. So to underscore the required scene changes she envisaged the use of massive images projected behind the dancers, and asked if I would be prepared to create the necessary artwork. Once again, without a moment's hesitation, I agreed.

Because of the late start, everybody working on the show had less time than they might have liked. Bill Whelan recalled, 'I started writing it in October and it opened the following February.' In my case, up to fifty images were required. I knew I couldn't possibly achieve that target using my normal laborious technique, so I suggested using photographs or computer graphics as an alternative; but Moya Doherty was adamant that all the images had to be hand-painted in order to realize her vision, which respected the integrity of the music and the dance. I realized I'd have to take a different approach. Using oil paint on canvas I reverted to the wet into wet method that Renaissance artists called *alla prima*. You literally paint a picture in one go, mixing the different colours together while the pigments are still fluid. When it works, it's great; when it doesn't, you throw it in the bin. I made fifty or so small oil paintings, which were photographed and then converted into large-format slides to be projected onto a giant screen erected at the back of the stage.

Some of the images were determined in consultation with the director John McColgan, others were created in response to Bill Whelan's music. On one occasion a courier arrived at the studio with a cassette tape of Bill's latest composition. While painting, I listened to it carefully, wondering if it sounded blue or perhaps even green. My hand-painted images reflect the many elemental forces that are part of *Riverdance*: fire, ice, water, gold, thunder, the sun and above all the moon, which like the river motif appears and reappears throughout the show.

History is written mainly in terms of politics and personalities, but in Ireland the importance of the land itself can never be overstated. The spirit of place remains an essential key to understanding the Irishness of the Irish. Yet this special sense of belonging must be set against the experience of those other Irish, the millions who found themselves in exile as a consequence of famine and economic stagnation or failed rebellions. I felt that representations of landscape should form an essential part of the visual inventory of *Riverdance.*

What would become *Riverdance* was being pieced together with great skill and determination in various Dublin locations, by an extraordinary team of talented people; yet, as Bill Whelan later recalled, 'It would be folly to suggest that we all knew exactly what we were doing or that there was some kind of grand design. But there is no doubt that as the pieces began to fit together, there was a sense that something unique was happening, and that whatever it was, it worked.'

Naturally the hugely successful Eurovision routine was integrated into the programme for the first outing of the theatrical version of *Riverdance,* and its pounding rhythms, exuberant dance routines and, above all, the obvious star quality of its principle dancers, Michael Flatley and Jean Butler, quickly became emblematic of the show itself. However, it would be a grave mistake to conclude that *Riverdance* was simply an Irish dance show; in fact it incorporated several quite disparate elements. The Celtic choir Amina sang some haunting melodies specially written by Bill Whelan, and drawing on past experience when he created *The Seville Suite* as part of the celebrations for Ireland's National Day at Expo '92 in the capital of Andalusia, Whelan composed two new numbers, both inspired by flamenco music, which were sensuously performed by the Spanish dancer Maria Pages. He also wrote a whirling composition prompted by the musical rhythms of Eastern Europe, which successfully accompanied the amazingly energetic members of the Moiseyev Dance Company of Moscow.

Until *Riverdance* came along, most of my experience of working in the theatre was that you got one chance at designing the set, and even if you felt you could have done better, it was only up for a few weeks or months and then it vanished. But the wonderful thing about the success of *Riverdance* has been that, right from the start, we had the opportunity to develop and improve it. For example, early on, Michael Flatley came to me and expressed some disappointment with the slide that accompanied his first entrance. He felt it was a bit dull. He said that when he came flying out from the wings, the moment had to be like the arrival of the Ice King in a musical or ballet. He had already spoken to the lighting designer, who had agreed to augment the scene with more smoke and brighter lights. My own response, inspired by Caspar David Friedrich's painting of a ship trapped in ice, was to create a bluish-toned slide of broken-up ice sheets, which augmented the drama of his entrance.

The first full-length *Riverdance* opened at the Point Theatre on 9 February 1995, and was a sell-out for its five-week run. At the time, I reflected that it was far from a finished product, but that it was as good as we could make it in the time available. For myself, I was unhappy with the quality of the projection, but it really didn't matter. People were so enthralled and excited. There were standing ovations every night. Flatley and Butler could have been dancing in a barn and nobody would have noticed.

The reviews confirmed my belief. The *Irish Times* noted that 'Riverdance is a remarkable and scintillating show, which will linger long after the last tap has faded away. It is a celebration of Irish dance and culture presented with sophistication and vibrancy,' and the critic in the *Sunday Independent* enthused, 'Riverdance was an exhilarating experience with stunning dance sequences which left the audience dazzled and mesmerised.'

After the huge success of *Riverdance* in Dublin, Moya Doherty decided to gamble on taking the show to London. She sent John McColgan and myself to check out two possible venues, Wembley Arena and the Odeon in Hammersmith. The problem with Wembley was that audiences had to go through turnstiles to get in – not exactly a theatrical experience. John was very much against it. On the other hand, the Odeon in Hammersmith was an extremely bedraggled theatre. It was originally an art deco cinema but more recently had become a venue for late-night rock concerts. Nevertheless, the Apollo group, who owned it, suggested that if *Riverdance* made a booking, they would do a complete refit. On the basis of that promise, the newly renovated theatre in Hammersmith, renamed the Apollo, was chosen as the London venue for *Riverdance.*

There were other developments that had a direct influence on the show. Because RTÉ had only been involved with the set design in Dublin, I found myself charged with devising a completely new set for the show in the Apollo. This was an enormous challenge, but one I fully embraced. The first thing I was determined to address was the unsatisfactory nature of the projection in the Point Theatre. We engaged the services of Imagination, a London-based company with a deserved reputation for projection work. Soon after I discussed the project with their designer, Chris Slingsby, an outline plan began to crystallize in my mind. Firstly I appreciated that we couldn't use back projection because the Apollo had limited stage space, having been a cinema and not a proper theatre; so the screen had to be placed against the back wall of the building. As a result, we had to use front projection, and in order to house the projectors we would have to construct a large false proscenium. Since coping with projection played such a determining role in the design process, perhaps some explanation of the technology involved might contribute to a clearer appreciation of the difficulties involved.

Obviously back projection was the most satisfactory system because dancers could perform without fear of casting distracting shadows. With front projection this was always a danger, especially if performers came close to the screen. However, back projection requires considerable space behind the performance area and, as we were to discover to our cost, very few venues had such space available. In the early days of *Riverdance* we used large analogue projectors, which had a tendency to overheat and as a result, malfunction. Occasionally one of the large-format slides would jam in its carriage and, as a result, buckle and burn. Also, in order to ensure a smooth transition from one slide to another, we had to house two projectors side by side and cross-fade one image to the other between the two projectors. We persisted with this fairly primitive technology for some time, mainly because it produced really bright images and, at the time, we felt that the first digital projectors were too weak for our purposes.

Eventually digital technology caught up, and we switched from analogue to digital. At first we continued projecting still images, but then we realized that by using digital programs, we could animate our images for greater effect. I decided to keep the animation simple. For example, if there were clouds in the original image we would gently move them, or make water ripple. The next step in technological progress saw us move away from projection to LED screens, which produce really bright and vibrant images. This technology was originally developed for outdoor use in places like Times Square in New York. In a way, the story of *Riverdance* has played out in parallel to a technological journey of discovery in new and exciting ways of representing images.

Meanwhile back in Hammersmith in 1995, all the elements of my design for the Apollo began to fall into place. There would be a series of steps leading up to a raised platform positioned in front of a large screen resting against the back wall of the theatre. At either end of the steps and platform there would be two entrances, left and right. This layout was to accommodate the existing choreography that had been so successful in Dublin, and which would remain unaltered in London. There would be four large flats or scenic pieces, two on the left-hand side and two on the right, to mask various entrances and exits, and a large false proscenium would be built to accommodate two projectors throwing images behind the dancers.

One final task remained. What to do about the bandstand? Because of the large scale of the Point Theatre, the bandstand was easily accommodated on stage; but since that bandstand was the same size as the entire Apollo stage, the band would obviously have to go somewhere else. The only solution available was to extend the stage into the auditorium on the left-hand side of the theatre. This, of course, resulted in a loss of seating, or seat 'kills' as they are known, which, understandably was not a popular solution with the promoters. To accommodate the band over 300 seats became unavailable for every

Riverdance in the Apollo Theatre, London.

performance. In order to help us with the installation of sound and lighting equipment and the building of the set, the English promoter Barry Clayman had appointed a dapper curly-haired Londoner called Colin Hannah; when I expressed concern about the appearance of the bandstand extension, he looked at me and with a twinkle in his eye said, 'Don't worry, we'll dress it up with a piece of tat, throw down a few artificial flowers and it'll be the dog's bollocks!'

Because I hadn't heard that particular expression before, I must have looked slightly perplexed. Colin exploded with laughter. Of course he had been taking the piss. When *Riverdance* began to tour both Britain and Europe, Colin became both production manager and a valued colleague.

In the course of a meeting with Chris Slingsby we made the decision to overlay all the flattage, including the false proscenium, with projected images using the old cinema projection booth at the rear of the auditorium, rather than engage teams of painters to cover acres of material with scenic art. I knew that this additional projection would require new artwork.

The first successful image I came up with was inspired by the spiral patterns carved into the large stones of the megalithic passage graves at Newgrange, Knowth and Dowth in the Boyne Valley; and remembering earlier conversations with Moya Doherty in which she articulated her wish for the look of *Riverdance* to be recognizably Irish, but not of the shamrock or shillelagh variety, I sensed that perhaps I had stumbled on to something interesting. Never mind that the passage tombs were built long before the Celts arrived in Ireland, the spiral motifs just seemed right. *Riverdance* was to turn them into a widely recognized symbol of Irishness.

I also decided, influenced by the slanting corbelled architecture of those mysterious structures, older than the great pyramids of Egypt, to frame the new setting for *Riverdance* in a similarly angled fashion.

Even though the slide with the spiral motifs became the image most frequently used in the show, I painted several other images including water ripples, depictions of a starry night scene and autumn leaves. After the new set was installed in the Apollo and the dancers and musicians began to strut their stuff, I felt quite proud of the overall effect. The whole installation was a changing mosaic of projected images. It created a wonderful sense of intimacy.

Once again *Riverdance* was a spectacular sell-out. Then, after its successful run in London, it returned once more to the Point Theatre. I was determined that, after coping with the Apollo's hopelessly confined spaces, we should fully exploit the Dublin theatre's vast stage. Since the choreography was not going to change, the general layout of the steps, the platform, the upstage entrances and the performance area remained largely unaltered. But given the width of the stage I made the decision to add two extra screens to the left and right of the main centre screen. This created a wonderfully panoramic effect, greatly enhanced by back projection, which was possible because of the depth of the stage. I clearly remember the backstage environment at the time, with

six large analogue projectors humming and clattering away in their own separate areas, each delineated by plastic tape, rather like a police crime scene. This was to prevent the unwary stagehand from walking in front of a projector and casting huge shadows on a screen for all to see.

Extra projection naturally meant extra artwork so, together with Chris Slingsby, I created new slides for the side screens to complement the main image on the centre screen. The effect was breathtaking, though I say so myself: a panorama of constantly changing images, almost 30 metres (100 ft) wide, projected behind the dancers. I was enormously gratified when Moya Doherty thanked me for realizing her original vision for *Riverdance.*

Once again, *Riverdance* at the Point was a sell-out. It seemed that the Irish couldn't get enough of it; and, less predictably, the theatre public in London were similarly enthralled. *Riverdance* was invited back to Hammersmith but almost immediately ran into its first crisis. Even before the show opened, a dispute with Michael Flatley became embarrassingly public. Apparently as a result of his enhanced stature, he was making more and more demands, both creative and financial. The promoters, fearing that the show might fail without its star performer, urged concessions; but at a certain stage, Moya just said no, that's the final offer – if he doesn't accept it, he's out.

After a rehearsal in the Hammersmith Palais, an old dance hall across the road from the Apollo, Moya gathered everyone together and announced that Michael was no longer part of the show. There were tears but, true to theatrical tradition, the show went on. Colin Dunne, another champion dancer, replaced Michael. No one asked for their money back.

Nevertheless, I was disappointed to see Michael go. I found him fine to work with and I knew I would miss his energy and charismatic performances. On the other hand, I accepted Bill Whelan's observation that he was 'not a team player'. As far as Michael was concerned it was all about him, so when he left, the show was liberated from being dependent on any individual performer. Nevertheless, even though Michael Flatley danced for just twelve weeks with *Riverdance,* for many people his name remains synonymous with the show.

Michael went off to start his own show, the messianically modest *Lord of the Dance*, which became extraordinarily successful in its own right. It seemed that *Riverdance* had pioneered a global audience for a dance genre rooted in a new understanding of Irish culture.

It was the hope of tapping into that curiosity and energy that made Moya Doherty and John McColgan gamble on taking *Riverdance* to New York in 1996. Moya's intention was to book the legendary Radio City Music Hall for the week that included St Patrick's Day.

'Just do a weekend,' Radio City management advised. 'You'll never fill it for a week. Six and a half thousand a night is a lot of people.'

But Moya was optimistic and absolutely insistent.

'OK,' they conceded. 'It's on your own head.'

Riverdance went on to sell out the whole week.

'Triumphant! A perfect gem!' cried the *New York Post*. 'This celebration will steal your heart away and make you get up and dance with them… an entertainment mammoth!'

Of course, I was already well aware of Radio City Music Hall, having seen it many times in the movies of my childhood, but I never dreamed that one day I would find myself working in the magnificence of such an art deco masterpiece; although 'work' is probably the wrong word to describe my role. Radio City Music Hall is a union house and only union members can work on the premises, and since I was not a union member I couldn't work; in fact I couldn't even talk to the crew. The solution for us was to employ a union carpenter, and if I wanted something done I would tell him, and he would then impart the information to the crew.

That's how it started out, but I quickly learned that if I respected their system, the rules were relaxed, and as a result we developed a good working relationship. By the end of the week in Radio City I began to appreciate that the American way of doing things in the theatre was conducive to sensible and efficient schedules and safe and productive working conditions. What we installed was pretty similar to our last set in the Point Theatre except, this time, we framed the design with a huge portal fashioned to complement the theatre's splendid circular proscenium. All of the construction and scenic work was carried out in a union workshop in the Bronx and delivered to Radio City in 12-metre (40-ft) trailers driven by members of the Teamsters Union, a complete service that guaranteed a job well done. The extraordinary success of *Riverdance* in both London and New York triggered the idea of touring the show throughout Europe and the US; so, in consultation with international promoters, it was decided to establish two companies: the Shannon to tour the US and the Liffey to tour in Europe. All *Riverdance* companies are named after Irish rivers.

The Liffey tour presented few logistical problems because there were a significant number of large arenas in Europe that were well capable of accommodating our extremely large set. To my great surprise, however, things were quite different in the US. Because of the scale of our show, there were only about a dozen theatres large enough to stage it; after we had played each of them about three times, a decision was made to devise a version of the show that would be just as exciting but could play smaller theatres with smaller stages. The lighting designer Rupert Murray and I were asked to produce a design for a reduced theatrical version. Right away, and with some regret, we realized that we had to jettison the projection. It simply took up too much space. But as a substitute for the mosaic of projected images, we introduced a multitude of traditional theatrical effects, like flying colourful transparent cloths, painted scenery or even a *Kabuki* drop – an effect taken from Japanese theatre in which a series of beautiful silk cloths cascade from above down to stage level, creating a transcendent moment.

Another problem was the number of seat losses caused by putting the band on a specially built bandstand in the auditorium. As this was unacceptable to the promoters we opted instead to build a two-storey bandstand, sited centre stage behind the performance area, which not only accommodated all the musicians on two levels but also incorporated theatrical lights and several mobile scenic pieces. Vancouver was the first city to see this new theatre-friendly *Riverdance* and naturally there were concerns that people might feel it was a diminished version of the original. We needn't have worried. Right from the start, the new show called the Lagan was a great success and toured the US and Canada for the best part of ten years.

Working with *Riverdance* has been for me a deeply rewarding experience, probably because it never appears quite finished. We always seem to be adjusting it to suit new and different circumstances, or to be introducing new numbers with new accompanying images. I have travelled with the show across the globe, to Australia, New Zealand, Japan, China, Mexico, the United States, Canada, the United Kingdom and many countries in Europe, each time confounded by the capacity of the show to transcend the local and become universal.

I remember Native American musicians in Connecticut telling me how the percussive rhythms of Bill Whelan's music felt so familiar to them; and Yuka Timori, a student of traditional Japanese music, noted the similarity between Japanese *taiko* drumming and the tap-dance rhythms of *Riverdance*: 'The combination of the sounds, the deepness of the. drums and the hardness of the dancing – add to the connections that the Japanese feel.'

While in Japan, I was interviewed by a journalist who innocently inquired, 'Which of the images were specifically painted for Japan?'

'Well, none,' I replied.

'But what about the rising sun and the gold-panelled images?'

I had to admit that they had always been in the show.

'But they're so Japanese.'

All I could do was shrug.

Fintan O'Toole in the *Irish Times* wrote how '*Riverdance* has taken that unlikely link between ceilis and chorus-lines and reworked it into the most joyous reconciliation of Irish piety and American pizazz imaginable.'

This seems about right.

I remember once going to a scenic workshop in upstate New York to check out how they were progressing with my designs. One of the scene painters, working on a Newgrange pattern, asked, 'Is this for some Native American dance show?' To him, the spirals and chevrons looked like Native American iconography.

Riverdance, whether because of the music, the dance or the imagery, always manages to touch a universal chord. Back in Ireland it came to be seen by some as embodying a newfound national confidence, but, to others, it represented a 'Disneyfication' of Irish culture. In their sociological study *Cosmopolitan Ireland* Carmen Kuhling and Kieran Keohane acknowledge that *Riverdance* brings millions of spectators to their feet with waves of rapturous applause, cheering and weeping hysteria, but wonder, 'When audiences leap to their feet, what is it that they are straining to see or hear?' Some might argue, they suggest, that it's 'a mass-produced global product cynically created for a homogenised global audience' while cultural nationalists accuse it of being 'inauthentic', but somehow these perspectives do not capture the way in which it has become a source of a positive identity for Irish people.

CHAPTER 16

A Very Reverend Gentleman

I was totally gobsmacked when, one winter morning back in 1982, I received a letter from Sweden inviting me to stage a mid-term retrospective exhibition in the Municipal Art Gallery (or Konsthall) of Lund. As far as I knew, I had no previous connection with Sweden and certainly none with the southern university town of Lund. Nevertheless, at that particular time, this unexpected offer was extremely welcome.

My career in Ireland had become more than slightly becalmed, largely due to my positive response, along with several other artists, to the urgings of the Arts Council of Ireland to establish an artists' representative organization. Accordingly, we founded the Association of Artists in Ireland in 1980, which took on the lofty mission of improving the welfare and status of the visual artist in our country. It was the first such body to be established in the history of the Irish state. At our first meeting I was elected chairperson, and this launched an incredibly active decade in which I found myself engaged in a constant struggle to advance artists' rights, both nationally and internationally. One obvious outcome was that I had less and less time for my own work, so the Swedish invitation provided a unique solution to a personal dilemma; I now had the opportunity to put on a major exhibition without having to make any new work.

I immediately embarked on a working relationship with the director, Marianne Nanne-Brahammer, who turned out to be a true professional. An attitude, I might add, that was fully in accord with our notions in Ireland about Scandinavians in general, though when I finally met Marianne I was to discover that she was anything but the stereotypical Scandinavian. She was not tall, she was not blonde, and certainly she was not the athletic type. She was a small elfin woman, with a dark pageboy hairstyle and an almost permanent impish smile. And to my amazement she was already quite familiar with my work;

With Marianne Nanne-Brahammer at my exhibition in Lund, Sweden.

as a result we were able to settle on the choice of pictures for the exhibition without much difficulty.

The first tangible evidence that things were on the move, literally, was the arrival in Dublin in early 1983 of something I had never seen before: a professional art transporter. This was a specially fitted-out climate-controlled vehicle, with two specialists who were charged with collecting the work and ensuring its safe delivery to the Konsthall in Lund.

As the date for the opening of the exhibition approached, Betty and I set off for Sweden. We flew to Copenhagen and then caught the ferry that would take us across the sea to Lund; in those days, the idea of building a bridge from Denmark to Sweden was simply a utopian dream. Once on board, we were bewildered by the inebriated state of many of our fellow passengers. These were, we discovered, Swedish dipsos who, unable to obtain sufficient alcohol in the land of their birth, temporarily took to the sea in order to acquire their drug of choice. The fact that they could purchase it at duty-free prices was an added bonus. Ah, human ingenuity! There was a time in Dublin when the pubs were closed on the national holiday, St Patrick's Day. This was more than inconvenient for the city's drinkers, but salvation was at hand. The annual dog show at the Royal Dublin Society's grounds in Ballsbridge on St Patrick's Day obtained a special licence each year to dispense alcohol to those attending the event. It was amazing to observe how so many thirsty Dubliners became ardent dog lovers for just one short day in March.

When we arrived at the Konsthall, a modern, well-appointed building on the corner of the main square in Lund, the very capable gallery staff had already hung the exhibition, so, apart from a few minor adjustments, there was little else for me to do.

On our second night in Lund, Marianne invited us to a dinner party in her home with several of her friends. After some idle chit-chat we all took our places at the well-laid table, where Betty and I spotted at once the peculiar presence, at each place setting, of a very small glass filled to the brim with little more than a mouthful of wine.

Across the table we glanced at one another and silently concluded that this practice probably represented some eccentric Swedish custom, or perhaps, and more likely, was an internalized acceptance of official antagonistic attitudes to the consumption of the demon drink. Undeterred, we ate our dinner, making polite small talk and avoiding any mention of the dearth of alcohol, when, after what appeared like a self-imposed silence, Marianne suddenly blurted out, 'This is terrible – I'm so embarrassed. I'll have to tell you.'

Betty and I were aghast at this outburst, and nervously awaited what promised to be an awkward revelation. Marianne began telling us how in 1970 she travelled to Dublin determined to seek out new Irish talent to exhibit in the Konsthall, and, after spending some time exploring the local art scene, she finally decided on one artist – me. I have to tell you I was fecking astonished on hearing this, because I had no previous knowledge of Marianne's interest in my work, an interest all the more remarkable considering the brevity of my artistic career up to 1970.

Marianne continued her story with a description of her visit to the Arts Council of Ireland, the purpose of which was to inform them of her plans. Once inside their impressive Georgian townhouse on Merrion Square, she found herself in the office of the serving director, Father Donal O'Sullivan. This tall, imperious Jesuit, dressed all in black apart from a snow-white dog collar, must have cut a strange figure indeed to this visiting woman from secular Sweden.

Anyway, on being told of her intentions, his response was immediate and to the point: 'No, no, no. He's far too young, too inexperienced.'

He then proceeded to name all those artists favoured by the establishment, who in his opinion should have been on her list in the first place. Refusing to be deflected, Marianne persisted with her original choice, to which the reverend gentlemen replied with a certain finality: 'Well, I'm afraid we can't help you there.'

'That's all right,' responded Marianne. 'I'll contact Robert Ballagh myself. Can you give me his phone number?'

'Oh, as far as I know he doesn't have a telephone.'

'Well then, can you give me his address?'

'Sorry,' insisted the director of the Arts Council, 'I'm afraid we would be acting irresponsibly if we did that. You see, he is a chronic alcoholic and unfortunately he can become quite violent.'

With those chilling words my retrospective exhibition in Sweden was delayed for over a decade. Thankfully Marianne remained interested in my work and courageously reissued her invitation to me in 1982, but sadly she had not forgotten the slanderous remarks about my alleged alcoholism; hence the embarrassing farce at the dinner party that night in Lund. However, after I confessed to being a moderate drinker and explained that the calumny sprang from the politics of the Irish art scene, wine and glasses were produced and we raised a toast to the success of the exhibition.

✶

On returning home I found I couldn't get what had happened in Lund out of my mind. In my naïveté I had always thought that in order to succeed in the arts, all one had to do was to work hard, develop one's skills and count on the support of those charged with the arts' stewardship. Unfortunately I now learned that things could be far more complex, often with malign forces hidden from view. As I dwelt on these matters a distant memory floated to the surface of my mind, a story picked up when I used to frequent various bohemian watering holes in Dublin. This was years before I finally decided to try 'pushing the brush', as the painter Micheal Farrell was fond of describing it.

As I remembered, the gossip among artists at the time was that people from the Guggenheim Foundation had come to Dublin with the intention of awarding an important prize to an Irish artist and, having surveyed the scene as best they could, they chose the painter and printmaker John Kelly. On informing the Arts Council of their decision, however, they were subjected to a barrage of criticism and then supplied with a shortlist of artists who were deemed more worthy of the honour. Shamefully they succumbed to this pressure, changed their original decision, and awarded the prize to one of the officially preferred artists.

Now, all of this is simply hearsay, based on that most unreliable of sources – pub talk – but many years later, when I myself joined the ranks of the standing army of artists, I learned the true story. One night I found myself at a dinner party beside Michael Scott, the architect. To my great surprise, and out of the blue, he resurrected the Guggenheim story. He was a member of the Arts Council in the 1960s and he confessed to being astonished by the unilateral rejection of the choice made by the Guggenheim people; so he resolved to confront his friend, the reverend gentleman, on the matter.

Michael Scott's question was simple: 'Fr Donal, why did you oppose granting the prize to John Kelly? After all, is he not a perfectly good artist in his own right?'

Fr Donal replied, 'Of course he's a good artist, but that's not the point.'

Puzzled, the architect inquired, 'But what is the point?'

The Jesuit, clearly irritated, disdainfully remarked, 'We couldn't possibly allow him to have the prize. He's working class!'

Donal O'Sullivan joined the Jesuits when he was nineteen. He studied at University College Dublin and at Egenhoven in Belgium, and went on to teach at Clongowes Wood College, an elite private secondary school. In the 1940s he was in charge of preparing novices at St Stanislaus, a Jesuit seminary in Co. Offaly. In appearance he was tall, with dark grey hair firmly combed back, rather like Bela Lugosi in the film *Dracula*, and his head, normally held erect, was centred on a nose of distinctly aquiline profile. He was extraordinarily elegant for the time, sometimes wearing garments quite unusual for a cleric, such as shot silk waistcoats with jet buttons.

His public image was often haughty and overbearing and frequently disdainful of those he disagreed with; yet on a personal level, he could be pleasant and engaging. As Adrian Frazer, in his biography of the sculptor John Behan, ruefully observed, 'Only in the Ireland of the time, or perhaps also in the Italy of the Medicis, is it possible to imagine such a priest.'

Prior to Fianna Fáil's departure from office in 1946, minister Patrick Little mooted the idea of a cultural institute or a council of national culture. He was clearly influenced by the establishment of the Arts Council of Great Britain in 1945; nevertheless, his suggestions fell on deaf ears. John A. Costello, the taoiseach in the new interparty government, sensing that something had to be done, commissioned Thomas Bodkin, former director of the National Gallery, to write a report on the arts.

The final document was scathing about the condition of Irish cultural institutions and the neglect 'almost amounting to contempt' for art in the educational system. His definitive conclusion was a damming one. 'No civilized nation of modern times has neglected the arts to the extent that we have done over the past fifty years.'

The government's response was the 1951 Arts Act which set up a weak and underfunded Arts Council. Bruce Arnold, the writer and journalist, maintained that 'From its inception it was set adrift on a course that left it at the mercies of its members and more importantly

My exhibition in Lund, Sweden.

its Director,' and this, in turn, provided 'a kind of absolution for the politicians'. The first director was Patrick Little, who was replaced in 1956 by the writer Seán Ó'Faoláin, whose early enthusiasm quickly evaporated. He resigned in 1959, describing the work as 'futile since there was so little money'. Ó'Faoláin was followed by Monsignor Patrick Browne, the former president of University College Galway, who died after only a year in office and who was swiftly replaced by another priest, Fr Donal O'Sullivan, who immediately became controversial due to his championing of the visual arts to the exclusion of all other areas.

This bias was probably a result of his lifelong friendship with the artist Evie Hone. Under his directorship, the Arts Council neglected music, drama and dance and instead promoted an understanding and acceptance of modern art in Ireland. Unfortunately, however, many examples of Irish visual art simply did not seem to qualify for support. The exclusion of artists practising more conservative styles or the emerging expressionist painters led to accusations of not only confusing artistic merit with private taste, but failing to represent and foster the full range of painting styles in Ireland.

In the active promotion and support of a specific type of modern art, Fr O'Sullivan was unfortunately aided and abetted by Michael Scott, later my informant on O'Sullivan's prejudices, to the considerable annoyance of several other members. Terence de Vere White believed that 'the Arts Council was run by Fr O'Sullivan and Michael Scott. I objected to the Director's one-man-band style. He only consulted Scott and meetings were a farce – I resigned.'

Another council member, the composer Brian Boydell, wrote, 'I have the impression that everything was fixed beforehand by Fr. O'Sullivan. Things on the nod without any hitches. Michael Scott was in collusion with Fr. O'Sullivan and they decided things together.'

In his defence, Michael Scott later contended, 'The international mood of the time favoured abstract works. We bought the painters we thought were good and they were good!'

The director insisted that, 'The council has consistently endeavoured to buy good Irish painting irrespective of its origins. Unfortunately in the world of art, as in any of the professions in any country, the unpalatable truth is that there are those whose ambition runs far ahead of their talent; they are just bad at their job.'

However, in the opinion of Brian Kennedy, the former assistant director of the National Gallery, 'Too often it appeared that "bad" painters were simply those whose paintings Fr O'Sullivan disliked.'

Eventually the autocratic nature of Fr O'Sullivan's Arts Council became politically unsustainable, and in 1973 a new Arts Act introduced a new and more accountable authority. With this mordant verse the artist Michael Kane bid farewell to the old regime.

> A group thus passes from the scene
> Whose likes again shall not be seen
> For casual heroic waste
> Of public money on private taste
> Complacence, arrogance, self-contentment,
> Begrudgery and pure resentment
> We raise a cheer as it departs
> The Inquisition of the Arts.

⋆

When the writer Graham Greene died in 1991 and biographers began to investigate his remarkable life, they unintentionally unearthed a tantalizing episode in Fr O'Sullivan's story.

Greene came to Achill Island in 1947 to pursue his affair with Catherine Walston, the very beautiful American wife of Harry Walston, a wealthy Labour MP and later Lord Walston. She had met Greene when she asked him to act as her godfather, saying that his books had influenced her decision to become a Catholic. Within months of meeting they had embarked on an affair that lasted more than a decade. While on Achill, Catherine met Ernie O'Malley, the republican and author of the great revolutionary memoir *On Another Man's Wound*, and developed a close friendship with him. O'Malley introduced her to the artist Evie Hone, who took Catherine to see the stained-glass windows she had made for St Stanislaus Chapel, and which had been commissioned by Fr Donal O'Sullivan. The following week, O'Sullivan took Walston to the Dawson Gallery in Dublin to see a painting by Jack B. Yeats. According to Greene's biographer Michael Shelden, Fr Donal, who was fond of a drop himself, encouraged Walston's long drinking binges, and one consequence of this was that he had a sporadic affair with her in her Fitzwilliam Street flat. It is commonly believed that she is the inspiration for 'the saintly and promiscuous Sarah' in Greene's novel *The End of the Affair,* though the difference between events in the novel and the lives that inspired them is considerable. Certainly, Fr Crompton, the priest in the novel, is not at all like Fr Donal, but Greene does refer to 'his Torquemada nose'.

*

In 1916, after the surrender of the provisional government, some prisoners were marched to a little patch of green in front of the Rotunda Hospital. The officer in charge, Captain Percival Lea-Wilson, decided to humiliate some of the leaders. Tom Clarke and his brother-in-law Ned Daly were stripped naked and verbally abused. Unfortunately for Lea-Wilson, one of the prisoners who witnessed this unnecessary abasement was Michael Collins. Later, in 1920, when Lea-Wilson was serving as a district inspector with the Royal Irish Constabulary in Gorey, Collins had him shot.

Lea-Wilson's widow Marie suffered a severe collapse, but was helped to recover by a Jesuit, Fr Thomas Finley, who offered her solace and spiritual guidance. In gratitude, she gave him a painting with a biblical theme, which he in turn passed on to the Jesuit residence in Leeson Street in Dublin. In 1990 Fr Noel Barber, the rector of the residence, asked his friend Brian Kennedy from the National Gallery about having some of the paintings in the residence cleaned. On viewing the paintings, Kennedy and the gallery's assistant restorer, Sergio Benedetti, felt that one of them deserved closer inspection. They took it to the gallery. After considerable cleaning, restoration and an exhaustive amount of research it turned out that the picture in question was the long-lost masterpiece *The Taking of Christ* by Caravaggio.

I tell this tale because for years, this masterpiece hung in the front parlour of the Jesuit residence; and one of its prominent occupants – Fr Donal O'Sullivan, someone who claimed to know a good picture when he saw one – failed, time and again, to recognize the quality of the painting hanging on the parlour wall.

CHAPTER 17

Union Dues

On a cold, miserable winter morning in 1976, feeling cold and miserable myself, I made my way to a large grey stone building at the bottom of Gardiner Street. It was the labour exchange. Being broke, I was hoping to sign on the dole.

The woman behind the counter snapped, 'Name?'

'Robert Ballagh,' I replied.

'When did you stop working?'

After I told her I hadn't actually stopped working, she pushed aside the form she had started to fill in and, with mounting exasperation, told me irritably that I couldn't make a claim if I hadn't stopped working. I tried to explain that an artist doesn't stop working; he might stop selling, but he never stops working.

She gave me a withering look. 'We have no form for that sort of thing. You'll have to see a supervisor.'

After waiting some time, I was finally received by a senior official who politely explained, 'You're not really entitled to claim, but we can appreciate your situation. Would you be agreeable to a means test?'

I nodded positively.

He added, 'One more thing. I can't sign you on as an artist because no such category exists. Would you mind being an unemployed self-employed labourer?'

The following week, at hatch 11, I joined a queue of travellers – my fellow unemployed self-employed labourers. In contrast, I experienced no real difficulty in making a claim seven years earlier, not as an artist but as an unemployed draughtsman. My categorization as a non-person by the Department of Social Welfare spoke volumes about the state's perception of the status of the artist in Irish society. I was determined to question such negative attitudes, but it wasn't until the end of 1981, when we formed the Association of Artists in Ireland (as I mentioned in the previous chapter), that a practical challenge became possible. This was the first time in the history of the Irish state that artists combined together to improve their lot. This first committee of artists, Jim Allen, Cathy Carmen, Ken Dolan, Patrick Hall, Leo Higgins, Eithne Jordan, Michael O'Sullivan and Vivienne Roche elected me as chair, and affiliated to the cultural division of the Irish Transport and General Workers' Union, which already included Actors Equity, the Society of Irish Playwrights and the Association of Irish Composers. Offices were provided in Liberty Hall, headquarters of the union, Betty Ballagh was employed as administrator and two members were appointed to the committee of the cultural division.

At the time I wrote: 'By avoiding all the usual aesthetic arguments and by concerning ourselves instead with strictly professional matters, we've managed to appeal to the whole spectrum of artists whether academic or avant-garde.'

Meetings were held with various government departments on issues like income tax, VAT, social welfare and customs and excise regulations; and drawing on EEC and UNESCO documents, the association presented detailed, urgently needed legislative changes to bring the status of Irish artists into line with that of artists in other European countries. Some of those recommendations included the artist's resale right – his or her right to a small percentage or royalty if a work is sold on by a buyer – and the percentage scheme for art in public buildings. With the help of solicitor John Gore-Grimes, legal advice was provided to help artists in their dealings with galleries and the public. I remarked,

'Some people don't seem to appreciate that buying art is no different to buying anything else. When you buy a suit, you don't expect to get it for months on approval and then be allowed to give it back.'

The association also took successful action on behalf of artists in a number of cases of non-payment for paintings.

The International Association of Art, a UNESCO affiliate with eighty-one member countries, had an Irish national committee; but unfortunately it had been inactive for several years. The few surviving members of that committee decided to hand over responsibility for its operation to our new organization.

The first opportunity we had to participate in the affairs of the IAA was to send a delegation to the General Assembly held in Helsinki in 1983. As chair, I headed the Irish delegation, which included the artist Samuel Walsh and Betty, our administrator. Without any real expectation of success, we decided to put my name forward in the election for the twelve-member international executive committee. I was, to my surprise, elected to serve on the committee for a three-year term of office. It was wholly against the odds. After all, we were only newcomers among the more than eighty countries in contention. On reflection, I think we were welcomed by the various blocks as an independent voice.

Overnight I had become a spokesperson for the arts not only in Ireland, but throughout the world. An early example of this new responsibility occurred when, quite soon after the General Assembly, I found myself addressing a UNESCO meeting in Paris on the role of culture in third-world development. I think I just about managed to bamboozle my audience by conjuring up Ireland's colonial past and by quoting freely from James Joyce.

Intergrafik was an international exhibition of graphic art held once every three years in East Berlin, the capital of the German Democratic Republic. The artist Käthe Kollwitz's declaration, 'I will be active in these times,' had been chosen as the inspiration for the undertaking. Since 1976 my work had been shown in Intergrafik, but I never had the chance to go there; so I was delighted to accept an official invitation to show in the 1984 exhibition and to attend the symposium that was always held in conjunction with it.

On a Monday morning in June, I flew to Tegel airport in West Berlin and then took a taxi to Checkpoint Charlie. Having no idea what to do, I approached a black US soldier who seemed to be on duty.

'Which way to East Berlin?'

'If you wanna give those commie bastards your money, it's that way!' he snarled, pointing to the actual crossing point.

My hotel was situated on one of the main streets in Berlin, Unter den Linden, a fifteen-minute walk from the border. The following morning we were taken by bus to lay wreaths at the memorial to Käthe Kollwitz, a fine artist who was highly regarded in the GDR. This was a duty I was honoured to perform, since one year earlier, I had included one of her powerful drawings of a mother and child on a poster for the campaign against the Eighth Amendment, which was a bitter and divisive struggle fought over the insertion of a ban on abortion into the Irish constitution.

The opening of Intergrafik 84 took place at three o'clock in the afternoon. The works were displayed in a quite dramatic exhibition space at the base of the enormous TV tower, East Berlin's answer to the Eiffel Tower, which had a revolving café at the top with stunning views of the city.

The exhibition featured over 3,000 works by 900 artists from more than 60 nations. Ireland was represented by Cecil King, Alice Hanratty, Theo McNab and myself. The symposium proper began at nine o'clock on Wednesday morning in the Artists' Union building. To my considerable dismay, I discovered that I was listed as the first contributor. I began by speaking quite slowly, not just because my speech was being simultaneously translated into four different languages, but also because I was convulsed with nerves. Nevertheless, after a jittery start, I managed to get through the thirty-minute illustrated talk. The theme of my presentation was the political wall murals that had been created in the North of Ireland in response to the 1981 hunger strikes. I argued that they represented an almost unique approach to visual expression, in that they were an example of ordinary people, feeling totally ignored by mainstream media, turning to art to tell their story.

My contribution was well received and resulted in three radio interviews and the publication of my text in *Bildende Kunst*, the leading art journal of the GDR under the heading 'Politische Wandmalerei in Nordirland' ('political murals in Northern Ireland').

On Friday morning 300,000 members of the FDJ, the Free German Youth organization, descended on Berlin to attend a massive youth festival, which took place every four years. The main streets were closed to traffic and every hundred yards or so there were bands playing all sorts of music from rock to Dixieland, jazz and folk. Tents and stalls displayed books, posters and craftwork. During the day, in a large square called Bebelplatz, the Red Army choir sang; and later that evening, in the same square, Mikis Theodorakis conducted his oratorio *Canto General*, a requiem for the coup d'état in Chile, for an audience of 60,000. This was a beautiful and moving work, set to a text by Pablo Neruda and performed by a symphony orchestra with added traditional Greek instrumentation. On Sunday morning, my last day in Berlin, I decided to visit the Palast der Republik, a modern building opposite Berlin Cathedral. It contained not only the parliament chamber but also bars and restaurants, which were open to the public. The walls were hung with enormous paintings specially commissioned from leading artists like Willi Sitte and Werner Tübke. At three o'clock I had to leave to catch my plane home. I crossed the border at Bahnhof Friedrichstrasse and took the train to West Berlin, which passed through several abandoned underground stations, bathed in ghostly light. This gave them an eerie, surreal appearance underscoring the unnatural reality of the divided city.

★

The first meeting of the new executive of the IAA was hosted by the artists' union of the Soviet Union in Baku, now the capital of Azerbaijan, in October 1984. The committee members came from disparate places and cultures, so considerable time was invested in getting to know one another. The Soviet Union, Bulgaria, Romania, Sri Lanka, Ireland, Nigeria, Burkina Faso, France, Tunisia, Iraq, Norway, Cuba and Japan were represented at the meeting.

However when we finally got down to business, we were faced with the challenge of adopting measures to deal with the impending departure of the US from UNESCO, and the inevitable loss of funding. President Ronald Reagan was not a fan of UNESCO, and when the organization declared the old town of Havana part of the 'patrimony of the world' and gave grant aid for the restoration of some of its buildings, he was furious. 'We're not giving money to an organization that gives money to communists,' he fumed.

A few months later, in December, I was invited by UNEAC, the writers and artists' union of Cuba, to explain the role of the IAA at a conference in Havana. On a personal level there was nowhere I wanted to visit more. Ever since the revolution that overthrew the Batista regime in 1959, Cuba had caught the popular imagination, and it had certainly captured mine. On my first visit to Cuba I found few of the consumer goods that we in Western developed societies take for granted, but on the other hand, I didn't find the chronic poverty, class exploitation, racial prejudice, illiteracy, corruption and endemic diseases prevalent elsewhere in Latin America. What the Castro government seemed to have established – despite attempted invasion and a prolonged economic blockade by the US, but, admittedly, with considerable support from the Soviet Union – was something approaching a society in which everyone was assured a tolerable existence, adequate healthcare, full education and the dignity of work. This remarkable achievement was brought home to me when, travelling in the countryside, I encountered an old peasant aged about eighty. He was obviously living much the same way he had always lived, so I asked him, 'Has the revolution meant much to you?'

'Well, I have electricity now,' he said, gesturing to a small television set in the corner of his shack.

'But your life hasn't changed?'

'No, I live the way I've always lived.'

'So the revolution hasn't really meant that much to you.'

The old man smiled. 'My two grandchildren are engineers.'

When I visited Havana's art college, which was sited in what used to be an exclusive country club, I asked about the fees paid by the students.

'There are no fees,' I was told. Materials were supplied free, and students from outside Havana were entitled to free accommodation. An image that symbolized the educational opportunities freely available was that of a black girl I glimpsed through a window, practising her cello in a space that had been the dining room of the old country club. I remember thinking, *The only way she'd have got in before would have been by cleaning the floors.*

The actual conference took place in the auditorium of the Museo Nacional de Bellas Artes, and in the course of the first morning session I addressed a modest crowd, explaining the work of IAA and UNESCO. As the morning wore on, however, I began to notice the slow arrival of more and more people until, finally, by lunchtime, the place was full to capacity. I was at a loss to understand what was happening until someone explained that the organizers, foolishly, had put it about that anyone attending the conference could avail themselves of a free meal in the nearby Hotel Sevilla. As a result, practically every artist in Havana turned up just in time for lunch. Overwhelmed by this crowd, the hotel closed its restaurant, but, not to be outdone, the organizers called in a fleet of coaches to ferry everyone to the nearest place that could cope with such numbers. This turned out to be a hotel in Santa María del Mar, a seaside resort about 12 miles (20 km) from Havana. There, while waiting for lunch to be prepared, many people decided to pass the time by having a drink at the bar and in no time at all, and not surprisingly, a party atmosphere had begun to develop. It was about eight in the evening when the coaches finally returned their inebriated passengers to Havana. I remember asking one of the organizers about the lost afternoon session. 'Oh, don't worry, we'll work harder tomorrow!'

The Cubans were very generous hosts in that they not only flew me to Cuba but they also invited Betty, who was able to share the unique experience with me. UNEAC, the artists' union, maintained a retreat house high up in the Escambray Mountains near the south coast of Cuba. We were invited to spend a weekend there. The house was originally built for an opera singer who was the mistress of a sugar baron. We travelled by coach to Trinidad, a beautifully preserved old city, nearly 300 miles (480 km) south east of Havana. There we were to change to a smaller bus, which could tackle the steep mountain roads. Unfortunately the small bus was not there to meet us, so we stood about in the street waiting for it to arrive.

After some minutes a woman came out of her house and invited us inside, saying *'Mi casa es su casa'* ('My home is your home'). She plied us with coffee and homemade biscuits as the grandfather of the family sat watching a new version of *King Kong* on the television and the teenagers noisily prepared themselves to go out for the evening. At the time, I was unable to recollect where I had previously experienced such spontaneous hospitality. Later it struck me. It was in the Ireland of my youth. In those far-off days a weary stranded traveller could always depend on a welcome at any door, and perhaps even a cup of tea.

Time-keeping in Cuba was a fairly relaxed affair; an East German artist we met found this extremely frustrating and continually complained about schedules not being kept. Eventually he was told very firmly by someone from the artists' union, 'This is the tropics, not Germany. Things are different here. However, if you insist on exact timekeeping, there is a flight to Berlin tomorrow morning and it will definitely depart on schedule!'

Ireland may not be in the tropics, but Betty and I had no great difficulty adjusting from Irish to Cuban time-keeping. Yet one evening, even we were surprised. The occasion was the museum opening of the salon of the artists' union, a huge show with 800 exhibits, which was also a big social occasion. We were told that we would be collected from the hotel at eight o'clock. However, when we came down from our room to the lobby we noticed that the entire staff were watching Fidel Castro on television. By 9.30p.m. I had become a little concerned, and spoke to our driver. I gently hinted that we might miss the opening. He immediately responded, 'Oh, don't worry, nothing will start until Fidel has finished!'

One morning we visited the Escaleras de Jaruco, a beautiful nature park not too far from Havana. We had been advised to drop into a certain open-air restaurant which boasted spectacular views of the countryside, but when we arrived, it was closed: a teachers' trade union was holding an end-of-term party. However, when they saw us outside they insisted that we join them and shared food and drink with us. At four o'clock, we finally extracted ourselves from the drinking and dancing and reeled back to our hotel.

On a personal level, my first visit to Cuba was a memorable experience. I loved the people, the country and above all the culture, and I was delighted to be able to take advantage of this short visit to organize an exhibition exchange which involved a tour of fifty Cuban graphic works to Ireland, and a reciprocal tour of fifty Irish works to Cuba.

*

It was in 1986 that I attended an executive meeting of the IAA, hosted by the Bulgarian artists' union in the small town of Smolyan, which, for whatever reason, had been singled out for special treatment by the authorities. Even though it was a fairly isolated hamlet in the Rhodope Mountains, close to the Greek border, it boasted a museum, an art gallery, a library, a community centre and a modern hotel, which was the venue for the meeting.

The first morning session was completely taken up in setting out procedures for the next General Assembly, which was to take place later in the year. I suggested that, over the lunch break, copies of what had been agreed should be made and then distributed to all committee members. This was met by a crestfallen expression on the face of my Bulgarian colleague, who quietly informed me that there was only one photocopying machine in the town, which belonged to the Communist Party, and their offices were closed. However, with telling effect, his frown converted to a smile as he informed me that the local head of the Communist Party was a personal friend and that he would give him a call. As a result, when we returned after lunch, a neat copy of our agreed procedures had been placed on the table before each committee member.

After a few days the food in the hotel restaurant, which had been pretty good, radically changed; all fresh food disappeared, to be replaced by canned milk, canned vegetables and preserved meat. Of course, we made inquiries. Rationing? We got no answers, just quiet murmurings about the threat of possible contamination. It wasn't until I arrived back in Ireland that I discovered the real reason behind the altered menu. While we were in Smolyan the nuclear catastrophe at Chernobyl had taken place and, as a result, precautionary measures had been imposed all over Bulgaria.

✳

In October 1986 more than 300 artists and art critics went from all over the world to Iraq to attend the largest art festival ever held in the Middle East. They were invited by the minister of information and culture, Latif na Sayif Jassim.

The festival staged an international exhibition of over a thousand works installed in a brand-new gallery, the inevitably named Saddam Centre. Several of my prints were on display. Apart from hosting the festival, the minister of culture also invited the International Association of Art to hold its eleventh General Assembly in Baghdad and, in spite of the refusal of some national committees to send delegations, it turned out to be the best-attended General Assembly in the history of the association.

After our work was done, we were able to enjoy the activities laid on by the Iraqi artists' association. We visited museums containing magnificent treasures from ancient Mesopotamia, and the homes and studios of contemporary Iraqi artists. We were also taken to see the ruins of Babylon, some 55 miles (90 km) south of Baghdad, which were under restoration at the time. Nearby lies the holy city of Karbala and it was there that I was made aware for the first time of the radical divisions in Islam between the Shia and Sunni branches of the faith.

As guests of the Ministry of Culture, we were supposed to visit the main mosque in the city, but the *mullah* absolutely refused to allow 'infidels' into his holy place. It was explained to me that, even though the government of Iraq was ostensibly secular, it was perceived as Sunni by most Shias; whereas in Karbala Shia clerics were wholly in charge, at least of their holy places.

We traipsed around the many mosques in the city until our harassed guide eventually came across a cleric willing to allow us to enter a small one, but only on condition that all the women in our company were fully covered. I was astonished at how busy the mosque was, but then it was explained to me that every day was taken up with the funerals of soldiers killed in the bloody yet inconclusive war then being fought between Iraq and Iran.

The government of Saddam Hussein was, at the time, an ally of the West, which backed his war against Iran and the Ayatollah Khomeini; and, to my surprise, I discovered that the Irish were everywhere in Baghdad. The Industrial Development Authority was out in Iraq promoting Irish goods and services; PARC, an Aer Lingus subsidiary, ran their hospitals; and Larry Goodman, the Irish beef baron, sold them meat. Yet in spite of this cosy set-up, I felt ill at ease. I had never been in a country where the cult of personality was so inescapable. We arrived at the Saddam Hussein International Airport, drove into the city along the Saddam Hussein Boulevard, couldn't help observing the giant murals and statues of the great leader, and attended meetings in the Saddam Hussein Conference Centre. When I got back to Ireland I wrote a piece for the *Irish Press* about my visit, detailing our many wonderful experiences, but finishing with some criticism of the regime. For this I was denounced by figures from the political and business establishment, who insisted that Iraq was the most progressive and pro-Western state in the Middle East. However, in 1991, when Saddam Hussein invaded Kuwait and the US launched Operation Desert Storm, and I supported the anti-war movement, the same people attacked me for being a stooge of Saddam.

During my time in Iraq in 1986 I visited a leading Iraqi artist, Laila Al-Attar. In the course of the first Gulf War a cruise missile struck her studio and her home. She was vaporized. Sadly, nobody seemed to care about such collateral damage.

✳

In the course of my involvement with the International Association of Art I had the good fortune to make the acquaintance of several distinctive individuals. One such person was Tair Salahov, the first secretary of the artists' union of the USSR. He came from Azerbaijan and was slightly swarthy in appearance, with neat black hair and a well-groomed black moustache. He cut an imposing figure and, even though he was a working painter, he always wore a dark suit and tie. I remember on one occasion, when we were strolling along a street in Moscow, becoming conscious of the odd person paying him deference. Later it was explained to me that they had probably spotted a small insignia on his jacket lapel, which indicated that he was a member of the Supreme Soviet.

I'm sure it was on account of Salahov's good offices that I found myself invited to an international forum in Moscow in 1987 which had as its theme, 'A non-nuclear world and the survival of mankind'. The organizers invited over a thousand people from over eighty countries, representing the disciplines of science, medicine, religion, commerce and culture with a view to holding frank discussions about the state of the world.

In Shannon Airport I boarded an Aeroflot plane and curiously found myself directed to a first-class seat. I hadn't expected the people's carrier to exult in luxury travel and this initial disquiet was reinforced when Noël Browne, the legendary socialist doctor and politician, who had been invited to the forum as well, came up from economy to interrupt my Russian champagne and caviar lunch with the sardonic comment, 'Wait till the comrades back home hear about this!'

I was picked up at Moscow Airport and taken to the Cosmos Hotel, where most of the cultural attendees were staying. This is a huge modern semi-circular building constructed for the 1980 Olympic Games and located beside Vera Mukhina's celebrated sculpture, *The Worker and the Collective Farm Girl*, above which soars the colossal titanium monument honouring the first man in space.

I will never forget my first breakfast at the Cosmos. Having been directed to a particular table, I settled myself in and then looked across at my fellow guest, who was none other than Gregory Peck. I was almost dumbstruck, but I needn't have been, because he was, as I expected, a charming, genial individual who made conversation flow. One of the topics discussed was the making of the movie *Moby Dick* in Youghal, Co. Cork, in which he played Captain Ahab.

I can't say the same about my lunchtime companion, Yoko Ono. I attempted to strike up a conversation about John Lennon, but she didn't appear in the least interested in talking about the working-class hero or anything else.

The cultural forum was held in three separate sections and each participant could choose which one to attend. As it happened, the one I chose was the one attended by the majority of writers and artists. Our theme was 'The role of culture in protecting civilization and universal values'. An early speaker was the celebrated poet Andrei Voznesensky who, in the course of his address, explained the attitude of Soviet writers and artists to the massive changes that were taking place in the Soviet Union under Mikhail Gorbachev. He said that it was not a cultural revolution, but a revolution by culture. Voznesensky had been involved in getting many banned writers published, and one of his achievements had been the first publication in Russia of Boris Pasternak's *Dr Zhivago*. He finished his contribution with a poem he had written the previous night. In it he cleverly employed the numbers contained in the year 1987 to echo the countdown to a missile launch – destruction, or the launch of a boat – construction: 10–9–8–7.

Another speaker was Hermann Kant, a writer from the German Democratic Republic. He said that he was delighted to see Gregory Peck at the forum, and noted that if fate had decreed otherwise, Peck would be in the White House and Ronald Regan would be at the forum.

During the first lunch break I bumped into Tair Salahov, who introduced me to the first secretary of the writers' union of the USSR. In the course of our conversation, he inquired if I would do him a favour. He told me that the chair for the afternoon session had become ill and, since I spoke English, he asked if I would be willing to replace him. Of course I responded positively, but when we assembled back in the conference hall I was more than unnerved to discover that the three main speakers were Graham Greene, Norman Mailer and Gore Vidal.

In a short intervention, Graham Greene compared Mikhail Gorbachev to William Shakespeare. Norman Mailer made a strong, intelligent speech, but finished with what I considered a rather patronizing request. He asked that the Soviet Union continue with *glasnost* ('openness') for just two more years, because it would take that long for Americans to recognize the thaw as genuine; he seemed to suggest that the only reason for changes by the Soviets was the desire to impress the American people. Gore Vidal made a skilled and humorous presentation tracing the billion-dollar quest for some imaginary protective shield against nuclear weapons back to 1942, when Ronald Reagan, in a movie role as an FBI agent, saved the US and mankind by capturing a gravity-defying machine. Vidal suggested that this moment in B-movie history sowed the seeds in the future president's brain for the necessity of acquiring the ultimate weapon. I'm afraid I only moderated the session. I was too in awe to make a contribution myself.

Smolian '87, painted during the artists symposium in Bulgaria.

The atmosphere at the forum was of genuine openness with everyone displaying a generosity of spirit, exemplified by the decision by some of the performers present to stage an impromptu concert. No promoter in the world would have been able to assemble such a cast list. Michel Legrand played a number of his compositions, including 'The Windmills of Your Mind', and Karel Gott, Czechoslovakia's most popular singer, sang several songs, as did the singer-songwriter Kris Kristofferson. Maximilian Schell gave a short poetry reading, and was followed by Yevgeny Yevtushenko.

The high point of the evening, however, was Gregory Peck's reading of William Faulkner's Nobel Prize acceptance speech from December 1950. This was particularly apt, since in it, Faulkner spoke movingly about the nuclear threat to the survival of mankind.

Apart from the formal activities of the forums, there were many less structured gatherings. The artists' union held a reception for the visual artists, and the following night I was invited to a party given by the Georgian artist Zurab Tsereteli in his apartment. On both occasions I relived the Russian passion for making elaborate toasts, which I have to confess I enjoy greatly. On such occasions hyperbole is not only permitted but actively encouraged.

The final day of the forum was a meeting in the Hall of Columns in the Kremlin, where eight speakers summed up the work of the separate sessions, followed by a wide-ranging speech by Mikhail Gorbachev, secretary general of what was still then the Communist Party of the Soviet Union. At the start, he outlined his fears for the survival of civilization in the face of the nuclear threat, but then went on to describe the changes taking place in the Soviet Union. He emphatically stated that its international policy was more than ever determined by domestic policy, which was aimed at bringing out the potential of socialism through activating the people's strengths. After the speech, all one thousand of us were invited to a banquet hall for a buffet lunch. At this point, Gorbachev and members of the government came into the hall and started an informal walkabout. As he neared me I thought I might have an opportunity to meet him, but, unfortunately, like a rugby second row forward, Peter Ustinov plunged in ahead of me, forming a scrum with other interested parties. At that stage, I decided to move away, but a backward glance disclosed a sight I will savour for a long time: Marcello Mastroianni emerging from the scrum, holding aloft a treasured autograph of the secretary general.

I heard and met more interesting people during those few days in Moscow than one could possibly encounter in a normal lifetime. At the banquet in the Kremlin, I was briefly chatting to Kris Kristofferson, and he summed up the atmosphere quite succinctly, turning to me and saying, 'It's a great time to be in the USSR.'

✳

Dimitri Ostoich, a sculptor and vice-president of the artists' union of Bulgaria, was a stocky individual and certainly looked like someone who could handle large heavy sculptures. His grey hair was cut short and he sported a casual grey beard, but his most outstanding feature was an enduring propensity for merriment.

In the course of our work on the executive committee of the International Association of Art we became good mates and, probably as a result of that friendship, he arranged for Betty and me to attend a painters' symposium organized by the Bulgarian artists' union which took place in Smolyan during the summer of 1987.

The deal was simple enough: the artists' union took care of flights, accommodation and materials, and in return, participating artists were obliged to donate one painting to the local art gallery. The artists' union maintained a large traditional house on the outskirts of the town, which had been converted into an artists' retreat; there, we joined our fellow painters who came from Cyprus, Bulgaria, East Germany, Greece and Denmark.

About halfway through the symposium I received a communication from Ostoich suggesting that since we probably needed a break from painting, he planned to take us hunting in the forests of the Rhodope Mountains the following weekend. It sounded so exciting that I deliberately neglected to mention that we had never been hunting before, or that we disapproved of the bloodthirsty practice. We picked up our hunting companions, the director of the Smolyan art gallery, the chief of police and the head of the local Communist Party, and set out for a remote hunting lodge located in the middle of a dense forest. As it was evening when we arrived, a fire was lit and supper was laid out, consisting mainly of what would be our next day's quarry: wild boar. Abundant supplies of beer and wine were also on hand. Once we finished the spread of ham and pâté, we attempted to dispose of the remaining stock of alcohol. Someone produced a guitar, and the air soon resounded with Bulgarian melodies. Thankfully, apart from Betty, no one from Ireland was present to witness me butchering several Irish ballads.

Eventually we were forced to call it a night, as we were supposed to be 'fit and well for the next day's hunting. After a late breakfast, we set about our preparations. Perhaps recognizing my unmistakable unease, my fellow hunters, with mischief in mind, decked me out in a hunts-man's vest, a bandolier stuffed with cartridges and a weapon pressed into each hand, so that I closely resembled a Balkan bandit. Once they had finished hooting with laughter and I had divested myself of most of the military hardware, we set off into the forest. It was explained that since Betty and I were inexperienced hunters, we were not going to hunt boar on foot, which would be far too dangerous. Instead we were going to trek to a clearing in the forest and climb into an elevated hide and wait for prey to come to us. We waited and waited for hours, talking only in whispers, but no animals of any kind ventured into the clearing. Then, just as light was fading and we were about to depart, we heard a faint rustle coming from the undergrowth. A tiny fawn emerged. I remember thinking, *They'll never shoot such a small creature.* Then I heard the quiet click of several safety catches being released.

'Jesus,' I groaned. 'They're going to kill Bambi!'

At that moment the fawn turned and scampered back into the forest. The hunters moaned with disappointment, whereas both Betty and I expelled sighs of relief. We made our way back to the hunting lodge for another night's merriment. The following morning, Ostoich drove us back to Smolyan to re-engage with the symposium. On our return, however, it was explained that even though Betty was an arts administrator, she was a participant in the symposium and as such she was expected to paint a picture and donate it to the art gallery. Betty rose to the challenge and produced the second picture she had ever painted: a simple landscape, *Moon over the Rhodope Mountains*. In the course of the symposium I managed to paint two pictures, both of which I donated to the gallery.

*

A new committee would be elected at the twelfth General Assembly in 1989, so I approached the gathering in Madrid, hosted by the Spanish artists' association, with feelings of both regret and relief.

Betty painting her picture for the Smolian art gallery.

I have to admit that my work as treasurer proved to be an uphill task, largely due to the withdrawal in 1985 of the US from UNESCO and the subsequent non-payment of its subvention. UNESCO, in coping with the financial shortfall, decided to cut its subventions to all non-governmental organizations; for the IAA, this entailed a 22 per cent drop in funding. But the situation was even worse than that. UNESCO made it quite clear that since the organization itself was having financial difficulties, all non-governmental organizations would have to adopt programmes closely in line with UNESCO's own. This meant that rather than working on measures to improve the status of the artist, the IAA found itself engaged in organizing exhibitions and festivals designed to reflect well on UNESCO. I was not happy with this development, and was glad to get out. Yet, in spite of many frustrations, the AAI and the IAA worked to improve artists' lives in Ireland and around the world, and we did make a difference. I'm proud to have been involved in that effort. Nevertheless, I was relieved to take a rest from such preoccupations and spend more time in my studio.

The artists' resale right or 'droit de suite' was first introduced in France after the First World War to render assistance to the widows of the many artists who perished. The operation of this right allows the artist or the estate of the artist to benefit from the sale of a work on the secondary market, by assigning a small percentage of the purchase price to the artist.

Both the AAI and the IAA campaigned long and hard for the comprehensive implementation of the scheme. I remember meeting officials from the cultural section of the EEC, as it was known then, who at the time assured me that the community fully supported the measure. However, it wasn't until 2005 that the European Union finally adopted the resale right in an official directive. Following on from that decision, each member state was given five years to prepare the necessary legislation to facilitate the effective operation of the directive. It was that long-awaited development that encouraged some people, who were already concerned with artists' rights, to establish the Irish Visual Artists Rights Organization, IVARO, in 2005. This new body was charged with informing artists of their rights, acting as a licensing agency and collecting royalties on behalf of artists; I was elected as its founding chairperson.

The Irish government did absolutely nothing to prepare for the operation of the new rule. The deadline of 1 January came and went. IVARO decided that as soon as a major auction took place, and an Irish artist was unable to collect his or her royalty, we would urge that particular artist to take a case against the Irish government.

A large painting of mine was sold at auction on 5 February 2006 so, rather reluctantly, I elected to take a case. I claimed that I was incurring financial losses because of the non-implementation of EU law by the government, and sought damages from the state for its failure to vindicate my property rights under the Irish Constitution and the European Convention on Human Rights. The High Court agreed that I had been wronged and awarded me €5,000 damages, plus my legal costs.

However, even before I got to court, the government, so that it wouldn't be politically embarrassed, rushed through legislation to make it compliant with European law. The only way it could do this was by using what is called a statutory instrument, where the relevant minister can introduce minimal legislation by diktat. This measure is supposed to be used only in an emergency. One unfortunate consequence is that the Irish resale rights legislation, because it was so rushed, is probably the least effective in Europe. Nevertheless, in the first two years of the scheme, IVARO collected and distributed to artists a bounty of over €200,000.

CHAPTER 18

Behind the Curtain

I n the 1980s most people in the Western world had no real contact with those who lived behind what Winston Churchill originally termed 'the iron curtain'. It was a bipolar world. Over many decades, misunderstanding, ignorance and fear had flourished on both sides of a divided world.

When I was a kid in the late 1950s I had direct experience of this altogether unreasonable behaviour. One day while walking home from town I chanced upon a small bookshop in Pearse Street with a discreet sign calling itself *New Books*. At the time I had no idea that it belonged to the Communist Party of Ireland and even if I had been aware of that fact, it wouldn't have meant much to me; what did matter however, was that I spied, in the window, a book on space exploration, a subject that intrigued me. I went in and exchanged one shilling for an illustrated volume on rockets and sputniks.

Layer that evening, as I sprawled on the living room carpet gazing at the photographs and drawings in my newly acquired book, my mother entered the room and asked, 'What are you doing?'

'Oh, reading about rockets and sputniks.'

'Let's see.'

My mother casually flicked through the pages until her eyes fixed upon an imprint on the title page: *Published by The People's Press, Moscow, U.S.S.R.*

To my horror, my mother abruptly crumpled up the book and threw it into the blazing fire. 'There will be no communist propaganda in this house!' I was stunned; after all it was only a book about sputniks. But that was the way it was, particularly in the Ireland of the 1950s when the Catholic Church held sway and maintained a virulent opposition to anything associated with communism.

On another occasion the Catholic Archbishop of Dublin, John Charles McQuaid, urged the faithful to stay away from an international football match between the Republic of Ireland and Yugoslavia on the grounds that attendance would be tantamount to supporting atheistic communism. Thankfully, in matters of sport, the Irish public was disinclined to accept guidance from the Catholic Church, and, as a result, 22,000 people turned up for the match in Dalymount Park. Regrettably the Irish lost by four goals to one.

✶

Even by the 1980s, things hadn't changed that much. Certainly, in the world of art, most of us in the West still hadn't a clue about what was being created by artists in the socialist countries.

For me this changed when I became involved with the International Association of Art and UNESCO in 1983 and began to meet many fellow artists from Eastern bloc countries. This contact exposed me to work that was different but also skilfully executed and often challenging in content. I became determined to bring some of this work to Ireland. Over the next few years, in spite of scarce resources, the Association of Artists in Ireland managed to organize several exchange exhibitions including one with UNEAC, the writers' and artists' union of Cuba, and another with the artists' union of Hungary.

Perhaps it was the success of those cultural exchanges that prompted the Polish artists' union to invite me to stage an exhibition of my own work in Warsaw.

Роберт Баллах

/Ирландия/

Живопись Графика

Catalogue cover for my Moscow exhibition.

When Betty and I arrived in Warsaw in time for the opening in December 1987, we were more than pleased to discover that my paintings were already hanging on the walls of Galeria DAP in the centre of Warsaw.

The opening itself was a well-attended affair with several speeches followed by much informal conversation. I particularly remember meeting a well-known actor, who was extremely complimentary about the work, especially my portrait of Noël Browne.

The next day we were invited to lunch at the home of a family of artists whose various members made paintings, sculptures, ceramics and mosaics. They were generous hosts. Travelling back to our hotel we called into a Catholic church to view some of the family's commissioned work which included a ceramic *Stations of the Cross* and a large golden mosaic of Pope John Paul II. The church was packed and as we moved about trying to glimpse the art work some of the faithful began to express obvious disapproval by indicating that we should be down on our knees, praying for our eternal salvation and not gawking about the place. As far as I was concerned the experience was a bit too much like 1950s Ireland – I couldn't get out fast enough.

Before we began our return journey, we visited the old town of Warsaw, in the company of a local artist. Almost everything we were looking at had been levelled in the course of the Second World War but, as a matter of national pride, each building had been lovingly reconstructed with reference to paintings, drawings and photographs of the old city. As I stood there I couldn't help but draw an invidious parallel with Dublin, which, even though it escaped the ravages of the war, still managed to demolish vast tracts of its previous architectural heritage to make way for dreary and unimaginative modern office blocks.

On my return from Warsaw I had barely resumed my normal working routine when a letter arrived from the Artists' Union of the Soviet Union. It contained an invitation to stage a mid-term retrospective of my work in Moscow during May 1988. The proposal was clear enough – the union in Moscow would organize the exhibition and cover all costs – once the work landed on Soviet soil. However, one question immediately dominated my thoughts. Who would provide the funding for the transport and insurance involved in getting the work from Ireland to the Soviet Union? With that financial worry in mind I contacted the Department of Foreign Affairs. Contrary to my modest expectations the department officials responded quite positively, saying that, with the recent establishment of an Irish embassy in Moscow, an exhibition by an Irish artist would be an ideal project, worthy of support. They suggested that I put together a detailed proposal and submit it to the cultural relations committee. This was a committee appointed by the Minister for Foreign Affairs and charged with promoting Irish culture abroad.

Comforted by such assurances I told the Artists' Union in Moscow that I accepted their invitation and then set about preparing the relevant material for my grant application.

Having obtained quotes from all and sundry, including one from an Irish shipping company that offered to deliver a container holding all the paintings protected in packing cases to the Baltic port of Riga, I felt I was ready to submit my application, costed at about 4,000 pounds, to the Cultural Relations Committee.

I was informed that my application could not be processed at that stage as the Cultural Relations Committee no longer existed. Its term of office had expired and a new one had yet to be appointed by the minister. Seeking clarification, I was firmly told that only the Cultural Relations Committee could award grants; all I could do was wait for a new committee to be appointed and then reapply.

It seemed to me that I was left with two stark choices. I could either cancel the exhibition or pay the expenses myself and hopefully recoup the money at some later date. As I had just found out that I was only the third Western artist to be granted a major official show in Moscow – Francis Bacon's exhibition in 1987 was the initial breakthrough followed by a display of work from the American artist Robert Rauschenberg – I decided the opportunity was too important to let pass, so I dug deep and paid the bills myself.

*

In May 1988 Betty and I flew to Moscow and checked into a massive hotel close to Red Square that had been reserved for us by the Artists' Union. The *ROSSIYA* was an enormous yet bland, square modern structure twelve storeys high containing at least 3,500 bedrooms. It had similar entrances on all four façades, but, as I was to discover, if you went in the wrong one you could become hopelessly lost, as the four quadrants of the hotel did not interconnect. When we took the lift to the fourth floor we immediately become aware of another salient feature.

On each landing there was a sour-faced woman keeping a beady eye on the comings and goings of all the guests.

Early the next morning we were driven to the headquarters of the Union to meet those officials who were involved with my exhibition and then travelled with them to the Central House of the Artist overlooking Gorky Park, where the exhibition was due to take place. On arriving at the gallery, however, we were met with a situation that was in stark contrast to our experience in Warsaw. Nothing had been prepared and nobody seemed to know anything about the whereabouts of the paintings. I was told not to panic, everything would be OK. Nevertheless, the impasse persisted for two more days.

Finally, Elena Militanian, an administrator with the Union and a personal friend, confessed that they were having tremendous difficulty in getting a state transport company to bring the work from Riga to Moscow, but she assured me that they had an alternative strategy in place. They were planning to use a 'co-operative' carrier to do the job. I later realized that the designation was probably a euphemism for a private business, one that was possibly engaged in the black market.

Anyhow this 'co-operative' company successfully completed the task by delivering the paintings to the gallery just two days before the opening. I breathed a massive sign of relief. And when I watched the gallery staff, armed with the latest electric screwguns, begin dismantling the packing cases I was mightily impressed. But then I heard the whirring sound slowly abate as the batteries ran flat and watched as one by one they resorted to the trusty screwdriver; I was perplexed. It turned out that the new tools had only just arrived and the person responsible for their purchase had neglected to get chargers for the batteries. Nevertheless, after much manual labour, the pictures were eventually unpacked and ready to be hung on the walls of the gallery. This job was done by lunchtime the following day and, as it turned out, well in time for the official opening that evening.

The opening itself was a rather formal affair with speeches from Tair Salahov, the First Secretary of the Artists' Union, a representative from the Ministry of Culture and, at the request of the Irish embassy, the ambassador Charles Whelan. Despite the stiff atmosphere at the opening we were all able to let our hair down at a reception held afterwards in the Artists' Union building where there was a profusion of vodka, a multiplicity of toasts and, of course, repeated shouts of 'nastravia' and 'sláinte!'

It was there that I became reacquainted with an old friend and colleague, the art historian and critic, Alexander Roshin. Sasha, as he was called, had a prodigious capacity for vodka, which was surprising considering his rather slender frame and customary neat appearance, but this was something I was already familiar with, having revelled in his company on several previous visits to Moscow. He had written an extensive illustrated article on my work for a Soviet art journal.

During our stay in Moscow Sasha invited us for dinner to the small apartment he shared with his mother. There we enjoyed a delicious chicken dish prepared by his mother, washed down with copious glasses of full-bodied red Georgian wine. As always happens on pleasant occasions, the time flew and regrettably we had to depart to catch the tram back to our hotel. On the short walk to the tram stop and out of earshot of his mother Sasha confided that she had risen at five o'clock that morning to queue for the necessary ingredients for the supper. We were astonished that someone would have to go to such lengths to produce a decent meal for her guests and embarrassed by the fact that she had done so for us.

*

Another private social event took place in an altogether more extravagant Moscow apartment. It was a party thrown by a very successful

Georgian artist, Zurab Tsereteli and he did not skimp in serving his guests wine, brandy and wonderfully fresh produce delivered straight from Georgia.

During the course of the evening he presented me with a huge signed and dedicated copy of an illustrated volume celebrating his artistic career. When I finally got it home I quickly discovered that it was far too big for any normal bookshelf and that the only suitable place for it was on an actual coffee table.

As a sculptor he had completed many public commissions throughout the Soviet Union which were often monumental abstract works, colourfully enriched by the use of mosaics. Many years later he radically altered his style, producing large figurative works in bronze, including a colossal, controversial statue of Peter the Great in Moscow and a huge portrait in bronze of Vladimir Putin. Some people are born survivors.

With Zurab Tzereteli and my translator Marsha Federova.

*

Sadly all good things must come to an end but before we departed for home Tair Salahov contacted me to say that he had been talking to Dimitri Ostoich, the vice-president of the Bulgarian Artists' Union and together they had hatched a plan to bring a selection of my work to Sofia and display it in the gallery of the Artists' Union. I was assured that this proposal would only cause a slight delay in finally returning the works to Ireland and that the two unions would cover all costs involved. As far as I was concerned all of this made perfect sense, so I accepted the proposition and promised that I would do my best to attend the opening in Sofia.

All things considered the visit to Moscow was a truly exhilarating experience and, most importantly, the exhibition itself seemed to have been a popular success. I gleaned this positive information from the contents of a container that had been positioned close to the exit from the gallery where visitors were invited to post comments, rather like ballots in a ballot box.

*

Shortly after I returned from Moscow I heard that the Minister for Foreign Affairs, Gerry Collins TD had, at last, appointed a new Cultural Relations Committee so I immediately submitted a fresh application, but, this time one that, instead of quotations, furnished receipts to the tune of almost 4,000 pounds, for bills that had already been paid. I was not best pleased when eventually I received an offer of only 800 pounds from the new committee. My immediate reaction was to tell them where to stuff their miserable money but thankfully Betty's common sense prevailed: 'take it and get on with your life'. Sometimes, however, such magnanimity is difficult to sustain, especially in my case, when I later learned about a Louis le Broquy exhibition that had been arranged for the Picasso Museum in the south of France at about the same time as my exhibition in Moscow, and which ran into similar difficulties with the non-existent Cultural Relations Committee, except that, in this case, the Department of the Taoiseach intervened and instructed foreign affairs to ignore the regulations and hand over 15,000 pounds, the amount requested, so that the exhibition in Antibes could go ahead.

I was still feeling raw when I happened to bump into Joseph Lynch, a civil servant with Foreign Affairs and Secretary to the Cultural Relations Committee. There and then I decided to make him aware of my bitter resentment at what had happened. I finished my invective with the comment, 'It's simply not fair'. At the time I was surprised by the candour of his reply. 'Of course it's not fair, but we had no choice. If we hadn't given over the money for the exhibition in France we'd have never heard the end of it.' Undoubtedly the whole wretched business had sapped my morale, so, to avoid any future repetition of such humiliation I resolved henceforth to never again apply for Irish official funding.

✶

Towards the end of June in 1988 I flew out to Bulgaria for the opening of my exhibition in Sofia and when I set foot in the Bulgarian Artists' Union building I was more than relieved to discover that the pictures had arrived safely from Moscow and were hanging in some style, on the walls of the gallery. There was a big crowd at the opening and the usual ration of speeches, including a contribution of a different kind from a young art student who had been commissioned by the Union to deliver a short paper on my work. After the speechifying was done several people approached me to have a conversation about the show and other matters, yet, in spite of the conviviality, it slowly began to dawn on me that I hardly knew anyone at the opening and I realized that Dimitri Ostoich was nowhere to be seen; after all it was his prompting that had led to the exhibition in the first place. Towards the end of the evening I came across a familiar face. It belonged to a woman called Julia who worked as a translator. She whispered that Ostoich would like to meet me for lunch the following day and slipped me an address scribbled on a piece of paper which turned out to be the directions to a slightly shabby hotel. When I got there Ostoich was already installed.

He quickly jumped to his feet, embraced me and welcomed me to Sofia. He told me that he had visited the exhibition that morning and that it looked marvellous; a compliment that prompted me to ask, 'Why weren't you at the opening?' He quickly responded, 'I wasn't invited.' Rather perplexed I asked, 'And why was that?' With some reluctance he explained that there had been recent developments in the Union and, as a result, he had been sidelined.

I was flabbergasted, because in my judgement he was an unflinching champion of Bulgarian art and culture. Obviously I was keen to find out what had led to his undoing. Initially he was hesitant but eventually he intimated that perhaps some of the new people at the top in the Union weren't pleased with his connections to the old Communist Party and were happy to see him go. All I could do was offer my sincere commiserations. We finished lunch with a few toasts to the artists of Bulgaria and Ireland then embraced once more and, with considerable emotion, made what would most likely be our final farewell. Walking back to my hotel I was not too surprised to find myself humming quietly the chorus of the Bob Dylan song 'The Times They Are a-Changin''.

The following morning, at their request, I met a group of young artists and students and change was most certainly on their minds.

After some warm remarks about my exhibition they proceeded to talk about how eagerly they were anticipating the arrival of what they referred to as 'the market', insisting that it would usher in all kinds of freedoms. I wished them well but added a note of caution. 'Who will pay for education, healthcare, housing and all the other social services currently provided by the state?'

They appeared bemused by my question and struggled to come up with an appropriate response before finally mumbling something like, 'But of course those services will still continue to be provided.'

I smiled and, as I turned to depart, declared 'Well, good luck with that!'

Back in my Dublin studio, anxious to make up for lost time I became totally immersed in painting, to the extent that I thought of little else, until the plight of the over fifty paintings that I had borrowed for the exhibitions in Moscow and Sofia flashed across my mind. It only took one phone call to the Irish shipping company to discover that the paintings had failed to arrive back in Ireland as promised. I was alarmed. I decided to make a phone call to the Artists' Union in Moscow which, in those days, was easier said than done. First I had to book a call with the international operator, wait patiently for a connection and then if I was in luck, hope that the person at the other end in Moscow could speak English. After several attempts I was told that the paintings had returned from Sofia to Moscow but after that nobody seemed privy to their whereabouts. It was like a depressing repetition of the nightmare before the opening in Moscow except this time it was dragging on, not for days, but for weeks and even months. I was panic-stricken, imagining how I might explain to the lenders from Ireland's leading cultural institutions that I had lost their precious pictures. But just as I was about to give up hope of ever seeing them again, Elena Militanian called to report that they had tracked down the paintings.

They had been sitting in a container on the docks at Riga for months simply because some lazy bureaucrat charged with completing the necessary paperwork hadn't bothered to get up off his arse and do the job.

To my great relief the container arrived back in Dublin a week later so finally I was able to return all the pictures to their rightful owners.

My exhibition in Sofia was the last of my adventures behind the iron curtain, adventures that proved invigorating yet also revealing. I had the unique opportunity to observe at first hand the significant role played by culture in those societies while, on the other hand I witnessed the contradictions and frustrations experienced by so many ordinary citizens in their daily lives. But I never dreamt that the entire communist project would be swept away in a few short years.

Postscript

Some considerable time after my exhibition in Moscow I received an unexpected phone call from Mairéad Breslin Kelly, the wife of a good friend, the artist John Kelly, asking if she could bring a Russian visitor to my studio. This unusual request stirred a memory of Mairéad's fascinating family history. Her father Patrick Breslin was an Irish socialist who, out of a sense of solidarity, travelled to the Soviet Union in 1928. While there he foolishly gave up his Irish passport and became a Soviet citizen. This unfortunate decision made it well nigh impossible for him to return home and tragically, as so often happened under Stalin's oppressive regime, he managed to fall foul of the authorities, was sent to a gulag and died in 1942. Thankfully however the story did not end there. Many years later Mairéad learned that she had a Russian half-brother, Genrich Kreizer so, as soon as she could, she travelled to Moscow, met him and, as fate would have it, a true friendship blossomed.

My Russian visitor Piotr Guverov or in English, Peter Goold-Verschoyle, had a similarly complicated back-story in that he was distantly related to the Sealy family, descendants of the first President of the Irish republic, Douglas Hyde. It was probably because of this Irish connection that he developed a keen interest in Irish history and culture. As a result when he visited my exhibition in the Central House of the Artist in 1988 he was dismayed to find that many viewers were unfamiliar with some of the characters in the paintings, so, on the spur of the moment, he decided to explain the historical background to anyone who would listen. He quickly drew a crowd. The gallery was delighted and invited him back each week to repeat the performance. This experience was the reason why he was so keen to meet me on his visit to Dublin. He wanted to tell me about his unofficial role in explaining my work to the Russian public. Naturally I thanked him profusely and apologized, saying that I would have done so earlier had I known about his efforts on my behalf. He insisted that apologies were not necessary, as he had thoroughly enjoyed the opportunity to talk about Irish history and culture.

It was at this stage in the conversation that I noticed one of the lenses in his glasses was cracked and that his jacket cuffs were frayed. Wondering about this threadbare appearance I asked what seemed an obvious question, 'How are ordinary citizens faring in Russia, today?' His frank reply was 'For many people life is very difficult – especially the old and the infirm.'

He then explained that when he retired from university employment his pension was sufficient for his needs, but after the collapse of the

Soviet Union and the massive devaluation of the rouble that pension was reduced in value to about 50 cents a month. Hence his straitened circumstances. Mairéad had previously told me that the Sealy family had helped pay for his Irish trip.

It all seemed so terribly unfair especially since, at that time, incredible fortunes were being accumulated by the new Russian oligarchs. Later I pondered on the untold stories of the many millions of former Soviet citizens struggling to survive in the brave new world of the Russian Federation.

CHAPTER 19

Every Picture Tells a Story

M y experience in Belgium in 1976, when I discovered that the gallery wanted me to go on repeating myself, convinced me that whatever I was going to do next, it was not going to be determined by others. I was not going to be swayed by either the vagaries of the art market or the latest concepts promulgated by the legion of disputatious theorists and critics.

To tell the truth, I was fed up with endless debates about what was good and what was bad art. In response, I chose to do something quite simple. I would paint an autobiographical portrait of myself and my family outside our terraced home in Dublin's inner city. A simple image, almost like a snapshot, telling a very simple story. I confess that to follow through on the idea took a fair amount of soul-searching. I knew I'd be branded by some as a conservative, even a reactionary. At the time, modernist dogma still ruled the roost, insisting that the only valid subject matter for painting was art itself – arguing that the introduction of anything else, particularly narrative, was intellectually dishonest. I didn't give a damn. In fact, I felt my newfound attitude to be strangely liberating, and the most natural to adopt. In addition, I drew considerable comfort in my new role – painting my

Inside No. 3, acrylic and oil on canvas, 182cm x 182cm, 1979, Ulster Museum.

own story – from the fact that the Irish are acknowledged across the world as gifted storytellers.

The title of the actual painting was chosen with some sense of irony. In the past, many abstract paintings were given pretentious numerical titles, whereas my painting was called *No. 3* simply because the subject was the third house on the street and the number three was on the door.

Rambling about Dublin, I noticed small blue plaques on certain buildings, each bearing information about a famous former resident. What really surprised me, however, was where many of Ireland's most renowned artists had lived: Jack B. Yeats on Fitzwilliam Street, Mainie Jellett on Pembroke Street and Andrew O'Connor on Merrion Square, among others. These had all been exclusive and expensive properties for many generations. Consequently, I thought it might pose a challenge to paint my modest home near Broadstone, and, by way of contrast, draw attention to the reality that most young artists were forced to experience.

Even though the painting incorporated portraits of my wife, my daughter and my son, I chose to hide my own face behind an open book, which was, in fact, a real publication with the curious yet optimistic title *How to Make Your Art Commercial*. My intention was to comment on the precarious nature of many artists' lives. In spite of having achieved something of a reputation, I still found myself signing on and off the dole.

By far the most radical aspect of the painting for me, however, was the switch to the almost exclusive use of oil paint. I found that with oils, with their slower drying time and with the help of paint rollers and sponges, I was able to simulate the appearance of many textures – for example, brickwork and concrete – and for the first time, I began painting with transparent colours or glazes to create tones and shadows. This is a technique where any pattern in the under-painting will necessarily show through the darker coat of glaze, which is applied last.

There is no doubt in my mind that the technical advances facilitated by oil paint gave my pictures a richer and more radiant appearance. (There was a downside; it now took almost the same amount of time to paint one picture as it previously took to paint enough work for an entire exhibition.)

To start the next chapter in my story all it required, literally, was just a few steps past the hall door and into the front room of No. 3. As everyone knows, the home is the place where intimacies can take place, so bearing that in mind, I embarked on the formidable challenge of painting the female nude: a great and controversial tradition in Western painting. I felt a certain humility following in the footsteps of artists like Rubens and Rembrandt. My model was also my wife.

In compositional terms *Inside No. 3* defies conventional visual logic, using several vanishing points to evoke the claustrophobic sense of being enveloped in a small room. The curved lines of the ceiling pull the eye around in a circular motion, echoing, in a way, the spiral staircase, which conveys a naked Betty downwards into the room. This turning movement was important because it underscored my reading of John Berger's contention that the female nude in Western art has often been depicted frontally, looking straight out from the canvas, the subject of the male gaze. By turning Betty away, my intention was to subvert that tradition. She is literally ignoring the male gaze. Once again, as in *No. 3*, my painted likeness is missing. All that can be seen of me are my white shoes resting on a couch, but on the other hand, though my face is unseen, my photographic image appears on the TV screen in the far corner.

Near my feet a bag with the brand name Fender emblazoned on its side lies at the base of the spiral staircase. It's simply a nostalgic reference to my earlier career in music when I played a Fender bass. However, much later, its inclusion led to a comic response. My daughter Rachel had taken a part-time job with the Douglas Hyde Gallery in Trinity College and on one occasion, when she was sitting at the desk, she observed a guided tour of an exhibition that included *Inside No. 3*. The presence of that picture prompted someone to ask, 'Can you explain what Fender means?'

Not to be caught out, she swiftly improvised, 'Oh, Robert Ballagh loves basketball. He keeps his boots in that bag.'

Upstairs No. 3, oil on canvas, 183cm x 183cm, 1982–3.

At that stage I found that on trips abroad I tended to visit the great museums and carefully inspect the work of the old masters, rather than spend my time in modern art galleries as I'd done in the past. I particularly appreciated the early Dutch and Flemish painters, who, of course, were the first to work with oil paint. I loved their meticulous precision and their greedy eye for detail. There was a sense of interior worlds closely observed; the kind of claustrophobic experience that had stimulated the obsessive detail in Celtic manuscripts. Johannes Vermeer was a special favourite, and I felt it was time to meet him. I painted *The Conversation* as a record of that imaginary occasion.

On the extreme left of the 8 x 6 foot (2.5 x 2 m) oil painting, through a narrow doorway, an interior room is glimpsed, with black and white floor tiles as in most of Vermeer's paintings. I am portrayed listening to Vermeer who is seated across a table with his elbow resting firmly on a closed book entitled *Modern Art*. He is obviously in an argumentative mood. On the patterned wall outside there is a lighter rectangle indicating a missing picture, which can be seen face to the wall in the bottom right-hand corner. A small signature is just legible: the capital letters R.B.

The Conversation not only raised issues that were of considerable importance to me, but also helped signal the future direction of my work.

*

As far as I was concerned, postmodernism was always a bit of a puzzle. Perhaps in architecture it made most sense. After all, modernist architecture, as in the work of Le Corbusier and Mies van der Rohe had very strict rules – adherence to functionality and no ornamentation – so when those rules were broken by, for example, the introduction of ornamentation or a departure from minimalism, the results were obvious and plain to see. But in painting, postmodernism made no sense. All it seemed to do was facilitate more bad painting. What else could happen if there were no rules?

The much-needed renovation of our home provided a unique opportunity to question the relevance of the philosophy that was beginning to dominate discussion in the world of art. I decided to paint a picture with a clear pun in the title, *Inside No. 3 After Modernization*. Since postmodernism promised freedom from any one dominant convention, the painting seized the opportunity to allow a plethora of styles to co-exist in a way that made some visual sense. Looking slightly mesmerized, and with my figure painted in a strictly realist manner, I sit at the centre of a visual whirlwind containing elements of pop art, cubism, art deco and abstract expressionism, which, breaking all the rules, should have ended up a mess; yet, for some unexplained reason, the painting seemed to work. At the time I remained confused as to whether I had confirmed the appositeness of the philosophy in terms of the visual arts, or its irrelevance.

At last, the time arrived to climb the spiral stairs and enter the privacy of the bedroom. It slowly dawned on me that having painted a descending female nude, the next challenge would have to be an ascending male nude. Worst of all, since Betty had only grudgingly agreed to model for the first piece, I knew that I really had no choice but to model for the second. My initial apprehension was due to the fact that the last time I dared depict the male genitalia there was a very public hue and cry. It happened in 1977 when the artist Barrie Cooke proposed, as part of the Kilkenny Arts Week, an exhibition he called *Artists Make Kites*. He invited me to take part and suggested I make a figurative kite. Having considered several options, I finally settled on the choice of a flasher. With arms outstretched, the male figure made an almost kite-like form, with the real possibility of actually being flown. At the time, however, I conceded, 'I'm not so naïve that I didn't think the subject might be controversial. So I deliberately adopted a very stylized and non-realistic treatment that I thought wouldn't cause offence.'

Nonetheless, hours before the official opening the Protestant dean of Kilkenny and chairman of the arts committee, the Rev. Brian Harvey, climbed up a ladder and personally removed my kite on the grounds that 'its display under the circumstances would be inappropriate'.

Barrie Cooke denounced the action as censorship. Theo McNab, a close friend, withdrew his kite in protest, as did Camille Souter. Micheal Farrell telegrammed from Paris demanding that his kite be removed.

Overnight the kite became a *cause célèbre*. 'Flash of Inspiration Doesn't Get a Chance,' joked the *Daily Mail*. Bob Fannin, the cartoonist in the *Evening Herald*, depicted two girls ignoring a flasher; 'Definitely not an original Ballagh!' one of them says, and in the *Sunday Independent* Hugh Leonard quipped that Robert Ballagh has 'the most public private parts in Ireland'.

The final act in the drama, or farce, took place when a policeman, following a complaint from some religious group, entered Eason's bookshop in O'Connell Street and removed from the shelves all copies of the *Grapevine* magazine, which had reproduced the kite on its cover.

✴

In terms of composition I decided to emulate the spiral movement of *Inside No. 3* by creating a circular canvas, a *tondo* which, in turn, would become an imaginary stage for a performance by only two players. In the finished canvas *Upstairs No. 3*, Betty is lying naked holding a book of Japanese erotic illustrations and, like my own in *Inside No. 3*, her head is cropped out of the picture. This creates the impression that, like the spectator, she is also watching the story unfold. Meanwhile, having arrived at the top of the staircase wearing only socks and T-shirt, I timidly engage the gaze of either the spectator or my wife. The contrast between the shameless depiction of sex in Japanese *shunga* art and the nervousness evident in Western attitudes to sexuality is obvious. On the wall facing Betty is a print of Gustave Caillebotte's painting *Rue de Paris, temps de pluie*, a spectacular picture that dazzled me when I first saw it in the Chicago Art Institute. Next to Caillebotte's masterpiece, the bedroom window offers a glimpse of James Gandon's magnificent building, the King's Inns. As a comment on increasing

Upstairs No. 4, oil on canvas, 198cm x 152cm, 1989, National Gallery of Ireland.

global militarization, I painted a US combat helicopter, like the ones that appear in Francis Ford Coppola's *Apocalypse Now*, scudding past the window. At the time, critics described its inclusion as 'rather fanciful'. They must have been unaware that as the Special Criminal Court was a near neighbour of the King's Inns, Irish army helicopters regularly swept the area during political trials. At my shoulder hangs a small portrait of James Connolly, the socialist activist and writer and one of the leaders of the 1916 rebellion. He's there to remind me not to lose the run of myself, 'The game may get more complex, but my views remain the same.'

Thankfully, most of the responses to the picture were positive and relatively calm, but there were a couple of amusing reactions. When the painting was shown in the Hendriks gallery, I spotted my good friend Gerald Davis at the opening, chatting away on the far side of the room. Gerry was a fascinating character: he painted, he owned a gallery, he wrote as an art critic, he even started a record label to promote jazz, his favourite music; but most of all, being Jewish, he loved to dress up as Leopold Bloom and parade about on Bloomsday, the day when James Joyce's extraordinary novel is celebrated in Dublin.

On seeing me, he immediately dashed over and exclaimed, 'Bobbie, I never knew you were Jewish!'

Some time later, a gallery in Galway hung a print of *Upstairs No. 3* in their window. A policeman arrived, acting on a complaint from a member of the public, and removed the offending picture. Once it was accepted that the complaint was unsustainable, the print was returned; the gallery owner instantly placed it back in the window, but this time placed a feather over the offending part, like the fig leaves of old.

✶

Our next-door neighbours, the Hyland family, told us that they were planning to leave the area and offered us first option to buy No. 4 Temple Cottages. Even though it took considerable time and effort to secure the necessary financing, we jumped at the opportunity. After all, the existing two-up, two-down houses were incredibly small, so to be able to join two together represented a real opportunity to better our own cramped living conditions. Luckily, as far as I was concerned, it also facilitated the conversion of two upstairs bedrooms into a studio; a pressing necessity, since I had just lost the lease on my space in Parliament Street. I couldn't wait to get started on a painting that would reflect this exciting development. Strangely, it was Brian Friel's play *Philadelphia, Here I Come!* that provided the initial inspiration.

On stage, the principal part of Gar is played by two different actors, one performing as the private Gar and the other as his public manifestation. For the new painting, I decided to feature two Robert Ballaghs, one an artist and the other a citizen. To reflect this dichotomy the picture was literally composed in two halves: the studio in No. 4 on the left and the bedroom of No. 3 on the right. The scale drawings, once begun, took on a life of their own and quickly evolved into quite a dynamic composition, which ultimately required the manufacture of a canvas with a complicated shape. On the left of the completed painting, Robert Ballagh the artist stands, brushes clenched in his teeth, wearing a kimono. I don't even own a kimono, but its presence recalls an exciting visit I made to Japan as a guest of the Japanese artists' union. My signature, in a cartouche on the top left, is also in Japanese. The inclusion of such exotic elements was deliberate, to reflect the stereotypical view of the artist as an eccentric bohemian. Meanwhile, to the right of the composition, citizen Ballagh, dressed quite normally, stands poised to descend the staircase. He has obviously read the disheartening news about unemployment, headlined in the discarded newspaper, and must also be aware of the unfulfilled aspirations of the 1916 Proclamation, which hangs on the adjacent wall. Nevertheless, he begins his descent to exit the house and engage with the world outside.

So far, you might be forgiven for thinking that the only location for the unfolding of this narrative was a small dwelling in Dublin's inner city, but, of course, that's not the full story. There were other addresses to investigate.

Some time in 1974 we were told about a cottage in East Cork, just outside the village of Ballycotton, which was up for sale at a very

reasonable price; so, feeling slightly flush after the successful exhibition in the Galerie Isy Brachot, we decided to become the owners of a rural retreat. Highfield, as it was called, became a welcome escape from the city, especially during summer when the children were on school holidays.

In spite of such rural exposure, I remained perplexed by the preoccupation with landscape that possessed so many Irish artists irrespective of their own particular origins. In the early twentieth century, it became almost compulsory for artists who considered themselves relevant to travel west and paint both the natives and the landscape. It was as if the soul of Ireland resided in the countryside, well beyond the pale.

The obvious question: why did so few visual artists seek to emulate the example of James Joyce, whose own writings drew almost exclusively on his urban experiences in Dublin? This was the dilemma, the glaring absence that impelled me to paint *Highfield*.

On the surface, the painting appears quite simple, showing me standing in the doorway of my new rural studio, gazing across the countryside to the sea. But once again, the full story turns out to be more complicated. In the first place, the setting provided me with an opportunity to paint in the style called *contre-jour*, which I had wanted to do for many years. This is where daylight streams into a darkened interior casting interesting and complex shadows, while at the same time highlighting the edges of all obstacles in its path. On the floor lies a torn-up Picasso poster, *Portrait of Jacqueline*, illuminated by the stream of light; but the real story revolves around the relationship between the artist, contemplating the landscape, and the unprimed canvas resting on the easel in the studio, which remains resolutely blank. It seems to me that while *Highfield* asks many questions, it provides few answers.

The cottage in Ballycotton, or rather its back garden, provided the setting for another painting in which the various elements depicted could not possibly co-exist at the same time and in the same place. The final canvas, a horizontally disposed elongated diamond, has a

High Field, oil on canvas, 185cm x 137cm, 1983.

hammock positioned on its central axis in which I am both relaxing and reading. The book, featuring a portrait of Che Guevara, is included to draw attention to the optimism of the 1960s, when young people, including myself, were convinced they could change the world.

To my left on the grass lies a childhood memory, a model airplane, while to my right my father stands – not as I knew him, but as an international sportsman of the 1930s equipped with the tennis racquet and clothes of the time. I called the painting *The Orchard of Nostalgia*.

Our cottage in Cork is a surviving example of nineteenth-century vernacular architecture, so, in making it habitable, we were determined to maintain the original structure. I felt this achievement was worthy of celebration, along with my sixtieth birthday, which was the original inspiration for the painting: *Still Crazy After All These Years*. When drawing up the composition of the proposed painting, I placed the point of view at the top of the small ladder-like staircase on the end wall, so that the whole roof structure opens out, fan-like, in a most dramatic fashion. I then figured that to contain this dynamic composition I would once again use a circular format. All that was left to do after that was to literally drop me into the picture, relaxing on the sofa and wearing a T-shirt printed with the slogan 'Fuck the begrudgers'.

★

In the course of the 1980s a curious intellectual atmosphere began to permeate southern Irish society, largely in response to the conflict in the North. It was spearheaded by the government of the day, which insisted on a strict implementation of Section 31 of the Broadcasting Act, which proscribed interviews with spokespersons from illegal organizations. The clear objective was to deny aid and comfort to republican politicians and paramilitaries, but insidiously the operation spread to include many others who, though not directly involved themselves, were deemed sympathetic to the nationalist or republican cause. This long list included, among others, trade unionists, historians, Irish language activists, artists and musicians. As always with such bans, some of the results were absurd: Paul Robeson's stirring rendition of 'Kevin

Barry' was considered too subversive to be included on the national radio station's playlist.

I decided that it was time for another conversation, so I hatched a plot to convene a meeting with two individuals who undoubtedly would have been on a similar list in their day: Patrick Pearse and James Connolly, leaders of the 1916 Rebellion. To emphasize the clandestine nature of the hypothetical meeting, the two protagonists are portrayed at either end of a small narrow table constrained tightly by the corners of a triangular composition. I sit in the middle on the other side of the table, listening intently to their conversation. From the apex of the triangle, illuminating the claustrophobic setting, hangs a single light bulb. The whole scene is rendered in a dark sepia monochrome replicating the mood of an old photograph, perhaps suggesting that a true reading of history is the only way to avoid repeating the mistakes of the past.

I submitted the final painting, *The History Lesson*, to the Oireachtas art exhibition, part of the annual Irish language festival, and was flattered to be awarded the Douglas Hyde gold medal for history painting. That outcome, perhaps, encouraged Pat Cooke, director of both the museum at St Enda's, the school originally established by Pearse, and Kilmainham Gaol, to call me and propose the purchase of the painting. He pointed out that although the necessary funding was available, approval had to be obtained from the art advisory committee established by the Office of Public Works, the body responsible for both institutions.

The committee rejected the proposition, with one member vehemently snorting, 'Over my dead body will that artist or that painting be purchased!'

Surprisingly, I wasn't too upset, because at that juncture I was preoccupied with commissioned work and had little time for such vexations. However, this lack of time also had the unfortunate consequence of a temporary lull in my own storytelling project. There's always a price to pay.

CHAPTER 20

A Bespoke Artist

F or as long as I can remember, the business model followed by most artists has been to devote a considerable amount of time, with no immediate financial return, to building up a body of work to take to a dealer or gallery in the hope of an eventual exhibition. In this process, the artist pays all the costs including framing expenses, and if a successful show happens to be the end result, the dealer walks away with at least 50 per cent of the total take. This practice has never served artists well, but in the absence of any real alternative it has endured.

Certainly the early course of my own artistic career was marked by a treadmill of exhibitions – a few successful, many less so, but all both physically and mentally draining. The first glimmer of a possible alternative emerged when Gordon Lambert not only commissioned me to paint his portrait, but some time later, on finding a battered old screen in his attic, came up with the off-beat notion of asking me to consider remodelling it as an artwork. When I first saw the tattered remnants of the four-part folding screen, I sensed that a successful outcome was improbable; but after cleaning it and stretching it with canvas I gradually began to see some potential in the idea.

Screen for Gordon, 1976, Irish Museum of Modern Art.

In searching for a theme, my mind unconsciously drifted back to the old cowboy films, and that moment when the heroine, often the singer in a saloon, modestly undressed herself behind a screen, while at the same time talking to the gallant hero on the other side. This whimsical memory gave rise to the concept of a double-sided painting. Viewed from one side, recently divested lingerie is draped casually over the top of the screen, while the other side frankly portrays a young woman in the very act of undressing.

Late one night I received a telephone call from an excited Gordon Lambert. He had just experienced Bernadette Greevy singing the title role of Hérodiade at the Wexford Opera Festival and was convinced that her many achievements as a singer were worthy of a portrait. He asked me if I would take on the commission, and even though I knew little about classical singing, I immediately accepted. My initial efforts, based on visiting her in her home, were fairly conventional, and pushed me in an entirely different direction. I began to catalogue in my mind her successful international career, and as a result came up with the idea of creating an imaginary cabinet with its shelves displaying the high points of her musical life, all exposed by drawing back a red velvet curtain.

Knowing Gordon Lambert's fascination with kinetic arts, I included within its frame a looped tape of Bernadette singing Brahms, which was set off by anyone approaching the picture.

The experience of those commissions slowly brought me to an appreciation of the practical benefits for artists willing to work in a similar way. Working to commission normally guarantees payment, thus releasing the artist from the psychological torment of placing work on public display in the forlorn hope that someone, someday, might buy one of his or her pieces; and without question, a creative relationship with a client can often turn an artist's work in a radical new direction not previously considered.

Perhaps a useful analogy might be with the tailoring business, where most garments are manufactured for retail outlets to be sold on to customers who have absolutely no association with those who made the garments in the first place. Success is determined entirely by the whim of the market. On the other hand, there are specialists, bespoke tailors, who make garments designed specifically for individual clients. In this more privileged context, unique relationships can develop that are mutually beneficial to both client and designer.

★

It was late January 1975, and Betty had started to go into labour when the phone rang.

'My name is Ciaran Costello and I'd like to discuss a commission.'

'Sorry, can't talk now,' I snapped, more in panic than anything else.

Betty then intervened. 'Perhaps we should go to the hospital?'

I replied, 'Remember the last time – let's wait a bit.'

Shortly afterwards Betty insisted, 'I think we should go now.'

We got into the car and began the short drive to the hospital when Betty, quite calmly, informed me, 'The baby is coming now.'

'Jesus Christ!' was my response, as I broke several red lights and finally mounted the pavement outside the Rotunda Hospital.

We jumped out and went straight to reception where the porter gave Betty forms to complete. At that moment, her waters broke, so forms were forgotten and she was immediately taken upstairs to the delivery ward. I rushed out to park the car and quickly returned, only to find Betty, having already given birth, smoking a cigarette with a healthy son asleep in a cot beside her.

For his name we had decided on Robert, but then the realization dawned that with a grandfather and father named Robert the boy needed a more imaginative alternative. As it happened, Gordon Lambert's nephew Bruce was working in the hospital at the time, so we plumped for Robert Bruce Ballagh, with which we were happy, though we had to put up with some people now and then exclaiming, 'We didn't realize you were Scottish.'

★

To his credit, Ciaran Costello rang back the following day and we agreed to meet. The proposed commission was for a development in Clonmel.

A 25 metre (80 ft) mural was required for a supermarket, and several large paintings for a bar and restaurant. As a theme for the mural I decided to employ the *People Looking at Paintings* series, and as a suitable material I chose Formica laminated plastic because I felt it would stand up to the wear and tear of installation in such a public space. Everyone thinks of Formica as plastic, but it's really layers of impregnated paper laminated together by heat and pressure in a huge press. I selected a paper with a parchment-like finish, which was silk-screen printed with my design and then laminated. The finished Formica was bonded to large plywood panels before final installation in the supermarket.

For the bar and restaurant my clients suggested a theme of local interest. I knew little about Clonmel, and was struggling until a friend suggested I think about Laurence Sterne. At the time I just about knew he was an author, probably English, but couldn't make a connection until I learned that he'd been born in Clonmel. I began reading his great novel *The Life and Opinions of Tristram Shandy, Gentleman* and even though it was over 200 years old, I was instantly stuck by its contemporary relevance.

My friend, the film-maker Kieran Hickey, remarked, 'It seems to me [Ballagh] was waiting to meet Sterne and Sterne was waiting to meet him.' I loved his sense of humour, his outrageous graphic interventions,

Laurence Sterne, study, acrylic and oil on canvas 182cm x 91cm, 1975.

like the inclusion of a full black page in memory of the deceased Yorick, and his constant allusions to the fact that as a reader, you are reading a book that is in the process of being written.

'If ever a writer expressed the nature of writing and the consciousness of being a writer writing for an audience reading what one is writing, it was Sterne,' explained Kieran Hickey, 'and if ever there was a painter who paints pictures about the consciousness of a painter as he paints pictures for an audience who are looking at a painting he has painted, it is Ballagh.'

It was Kieran Hickey who advised that before even lifting a brush, I should travel to London and see Sir Joshua Reynolds's famous portrait of Laurence Sterne in the National Portrait Gallery. When I got there I walked around the gallery for an hour and couldn't find the bloody thing.

Eventually, after informing an attendant that I had come over from Dublin especially to see the picture, he explained, 'I'm afraid it's been taken down for cleaning and restoration, sir.'

He must have spotted a look of abject disappointment on my face because he surreptitiously led me through a doorway, down several corridors and into the restoration department of the National Gallery. To my astonishment, he reached up to a rack, took down Reynolds's unframed masterpiece and placed it in my outstretched hands.

But as I anxiously scanned the painting, I heard a roar: 'What the hell do you think you are doing?'

Two gentlemen in white coats came rushing up, snatched the picture from my hands and replaced it in the rack. Then, with considerable disdain, they gruffly ordered me off the premises. At the time I hoped the attendant didn't get into too much trouble, but, as I acknowledged, 'It was in the middle of an IRA bombing campaign, and there I was, an unidentified Irishman, holding, in my hands, one of Britain's great national treasures.'

For the commission I elected to create two large paintings: the first, a portrait of Laurence Sterne; the other, an interpretation of his extraordinary novel.

Being aware of the apparent spontaneity of Sterne's writing – as he himself hinted, 'Ask my pen, it governs me, I govern not it' – I chose to depict his likeness, as originally painted by Reynolds, materializing in the midst of a massive swash of paint delivered by a hugely magnified brush. The picture, on three 2 x 1.2 metre (6 x 4 ft) panels, was painted in a green monochrome. Originally I planned to use red but, learning that Sterne died from TB, decided that this was inappropriate.

Straight away I knew that taking on *The Life and Opinions of Tristram Shandy, Gentleman* would be an unreasonable task; it was too big, too complex and too unique, so, to make a feasible start, I decided to eschew any attempt to describe the narrative or to illustrate, in a conventional manner, any of the main characters. Instead the painting took the form of laid-out pages from the novel, particularly the black page, the blank page and the marbled page, plus several other pages that appear to be blowing away like leaves in the wind of time. They are interspersed with what can only be described as surrealist portraits of the main characters, which are bordered with window frames, in keeping with Sterne's speculation on the consequences of there being 'a window in every human breast through which could be seen the soul'.

When Tristram is about to be conceived, his mother interrupts his father with the untimely remark, 'Pray my dear, have you not forgot to wind up the clock'; hence, in my portrait, Tristram's head is portrayed as a drooping clock face, about to be guillotined by a window, which in turn is a reference to an unfortunate incident in the nursery when, as a child wanting to pee, he lifts a window to discover only too late that his uncle Toby has previously removed the sash weight. Like the book, the painting opens with the original title page, courses across nine 2 x 1.2 metre (6 x 4 ft) panels before finishing up with a rear-view image of myself signing the work.

*

In 1976 I wrote an article that was fundamentally critical of the art college system, which I suppose was audacious of me considering I had no personal experience whatsoever of third-level art education. Nevertheless, I offered an opinion that young artists might be better served by an apprenticeship system. Campbell Bruce, professor of Fine

Art in the National College of Art and Design, contacted me saying he had read the article. Expecting a bollocking, I was pleased when instead he declared the article interesting, and asked, 'Would you take on a couple of students as apprentices?'

As it happened, I had just been commissioned by the Arts Council to paint a portrait of Joseph Sheridan Le Fanu, so the two students sent by Campbell worked with me on every stage of the painting. I hope they found the experience beneficial; in my case, however, I discovered that I wasn't great at delegating. As I said at the time, 'I get too nervous, particularly if I've spent a long time working on something. It worries me that the other person may not understand or appreciate what I'm trying to do.'

Le Fanu was one of the great Anglo-Irish horror novelists, like Bram Stoker and Charles Maturin, with stories that stir unconscious fears in the mind of the reader. It was that atmosphere I wanted to evoke in the portrait. I placed Le Fanu standing at a window surrounded by decorative stone elements, which required the manufacture of five separate shaped canvases. He is holding a candle, a reference to his habit of writing all night invigorated by copious draughts of green tea. The casement windows are slightly ajar. Le Fanu's body becomes invisible in the gap between the two window frames and we see in the distance a ruined house isolated beneath an enormous pale blue sky. During his final illness, he dreamed of being in a decaying old house, and when he finally expired the doctor announced to the family, 'The house has finally fallen.'

*

When I met the playwright Hugh Leonard for the first time I instantly picked up on his passion for the movies, so when he asked me to paint his portrait, I knew what the theme of the picture would have to be. It would be a tribute to the old movies that we both grew up on as children, during many happy hours spent in various local cinemas across Dublin.

In the first place, the shape of the canvas conformed to the proportion of the standard projected image, called Academy ratio, where the width of the screen was a third bigger than the height. This, of course, was before the advent of wide-screen cinema when movies began to appear in CinemaScope and VistaVision.

Secondly, the portrait was painted in the monochrome tones of the silver screen; not so much black-and-white as black, dark blue, grey and white.

In the painting itself, Leonard sits alone in his study, smoking a cigar, contemplating his typewriter while behind him looms a view of Dalkey Island by moonlight. My obvious intention was to recall those countless memories from detective movies when the hero, having returned to his office at night, is disturbed by an unexpected knock on his door. A vital element in the painting is the typewriter, which dominates the foreground. In it a film script is being typed, a script which in turn accurately describes the action unfolding in the painting: 'Author sits, cigar in hand, facing artist sitting in author's chair'. To get the jargon right I borrowed a Douglas Sirk screenplay for *Captain Lightfoot* which was shot in Ireland, and to ensure total legibility I silk-screen-printed the text on to the canvas. The finished picture is not only a portrait of a distinguished Irish writer and a tribute to the cinema, but also raises questions about the relationship between the word and the image.

*

The Chester Beatty Library in Dublin boasts one of the finest collections of Oriental art in the world, but it also houses masterpieces from many other cultures. One such example is a superb collection of graphic work by Albrecht Dürer. In the 1980s the library mounted an exhibition, *Dürer in Dublin*, and when the director of the Albrecht Dürer-Haus in Nüremberg, Dr Karl Heinz Schreyl, visited Dublin to attend the opening, he chanced upon my painting *The Conversation*. Responding to the allegorical presence of Vermeer in my picture, he proposed I paint a similar tribute to Dürer for a room in the museum devoted to artists influenced by the German master.

Naturally I jumped at the offer; I had always been a great admirer of Dürer, especially his self-portraits. But for my painting I took a different tack and focused on his series of prints and diagrams illustrating the various methods used by artists to engage with perspective in their work. I settled on one where Dürer depicted an artist using a grid to draw a reclining nude in foreshortened perspective, except, in my design, I substituted myself for Dürer's artist. In the finished painting everything is black-and-white except the view through the open windows and the self-portrait, which are both rendered in full colour.

I wouldn't blame you for asking the simple question, 'Do all commissions involve portraiture?'

Well, a simple answer from my own experience is, 'Not always!'

One particular commission proved to be truly memorable. It followed an invitation from the Commissioners of Irish Lights to paint the Fastnet lighthouse, a dramatic outpost in the Atlantic Ocean off the south-west coast of Ireland.

On accepting the job, my immediate concern was, 'How do I get reference photographs of the lighthouse?'

'Oh, don't worry, we'll fly you out in a helicopter.'

So, on the appointed day, I drove to Cork Airport and got kitted out in a bright orange survival suit equipped with earphones and a microphone. I climbed into the small helicopter and sat in front with the pilot. Two lighthouse men crouched in the back, on their way to begin their shift on the rock. Even the take-off was exhilarating, as I'd never ascended vertically before, and very quickly I appreciated the earphones and microphone; without them communication was impossible due to the furious engine noise. We skidded across the countryside, then above the sea, before arriving over the lighthouse.

We then began to hover, and as I looked down on the tiny landing pad, with H inscribed within a circle, the words of Roy Scheider in *Jaws*, on realizing the true size of his adversary – 'You're going to need a bigger boat!' – seemed strangely appropriate. I needn't have worried; the pilot landed perfectly and I got out to allow the lighthouse men to disembark. Once back on board we immediately took off and the pilot told me that I had just ten minutes to photograph the lighthouse. I quickly began my task, but felt there was too much shine on the curved cockpit cover.

'Don't worry,' said the pilot. 'Just slide it back.'

I did just that and began leaning out, snapping away with no obvious obstructions. At that moment, with considerable panic, I noticed I had forgotten to refasten my seat belt, so there was absolutely nothing to stop me falling out of the helicopter and tumbling into the ocean. With a mixture of fear and embarrassment I fastened the belt and attempted to complete my mission. After the allotted ten minutes the pilot announced that we had to move on. Pretty quickly, however, I figured out that we were flying in the wrong direction, at least as far as I was concerned.

I asked in alarm, 'Are we not going back to Cork Airport?'

'Oh no! Next stop is the Bull Rock lighthouse off Kerry, and after that Galway.'

'But my car is in Cork!'

'I'm sorry, but to land anywhere else would require permission from the police.'

I must have pleaded a good case because he looked sympathetically at me and said, 'Look, there are playing fields in Schull and if we slip in quietly, perhaps nobody will notice.'

He dropped the helicopter down to what appeared like a few feet above the waves and slid in to land on an open space. Of course, every kid in the local school burst out of class and rushed down to see what was happening. As I disembarked they all gathered around me, hoping, I guess, for some celebrity; but when I extracted myself from the orange suit, I heard distinct murmurs of, 'Who the hell is he?' and the excitement quickly evaporated.

Luckily I had friends in nearby Ballydehob who drove me back to Cork Airport to retrieve my car and bring my adventure to a successful conclusion. All I had to do then was paint the picture.

I had enough serviceable photographs to be able to paint a view from the air of the lighthouse surrounded by the vast Atlantic Ocean. And because of my own personal experience, I added a small red helicopter similar to the one I flew in on that madcap day.

The Fastnet Lighthouse, oil on canvas, 92cm x 61cm, 1986,
Commissioners of Irish Lights.

I have an English friend, a dealer and collector who knows a thing or two about art. He visits Ireland on a fairly regular basis, usually to attend an auction or to view an exhibition. On one such occasion after an auction I met up with him, and noting a satisfied smile on his face, inquired, 'Well, did you buy anything?'

'Yes, would you like to see it?' He produced a tiny watercolour. 'What do you think?'

To my untutored eye it seemed fairly nondescript, but not wanting to appear disparaging, I asked, 'How much did you pay?'

'A hundred euros,' was his reply.

Relieved that he hadn't wasted too much money, I was about to respond when he interjected, 'Don't look at the picture. Look at the frame.'

He then conceded that the watercolour was indeed nineteenth-century rubbish, but the frame was an eighteenth-century gem and that, on his return to London, he would easily unload it for several thousand pounds. 'The ignorance of auctioneers, I love it. They allow me make a handsome living!'

One evening I was surprised when he phoned asking if I would accept a commission, and was even more surprised to learn the subject – none other than Fidel Castro. He had recently visited Cuba and was most impressed, to the extent that on his return, he decided to commission a portrait of Castro. He had only one request: he wanted Castro portrayed as an old man, not as the young revolutionary in military fatigues, adorned with weapons and Cuban flags. That suited me fine, as I was keen to deviate from my normal approach of revealing someone through an inventory of their life and instead to concentrate on the man rather than the myth.

I had hoped to visit Cuba and perhaps photograph the man himself, but I was firmly told by the Cuban Embassy in Dublin that he was too ill to receive any visitors. This was a disappointment because, some

Fidel Castro, oil on canvas, 183cm x 192cm, 2009.

time before, when Gerry Adams paid an official visit to Cuba, he presented Fidel Castro with a copy of *Legacy*, a print I made to mark the twentieth anniversary of the 1981 hunger strikes. I had specially signed it for him in Spanish. Adams later told me that Castro praised both the print and the artist and said he would hang it in his office. When I later met the new Cuban ambassador, Noel Carrillo, he confirmed that my picture was hanging beside the president's desk in Havana.

For the actual portrait a major influence was Velázquez's series of portraits of classical or mythological figures, in which he used ordinary people as models. He did a really fine one of Aesop – an old man clutching his fables.

Ciaran Carty described my portrait thus: 'Castro is standing alone – because in the end, you are alone – as if caught by spotlight on an empty stage. He is bare-footed and clasps a toga-like red flag around his otherwise naked body. He is facing into the wings, perhaps about to make an exit.'

✶

Of course, the middle-aged James Joyce never stood on Sandymount Strand as he does in my portrait, commissioned by his alma mater, University College Dublin. Nonetheless I felt justified in using artistic licence to place him in that imagined location; after all, so many scenes from his own imagined world took place within the compass of Dublin Bay.

In my T-junction of a painting, the horizontal section at the top features Howth Head, the setting for Leopold and Molly Bloom's first love-making, whereas the beach of Sandymount Strand, depicted at the base of the T, is where Gerty MacDowell sat, displaying her legs much to the excitement of Bloom.

On the same beach lie discarded pages from *A Portrait of the Artist as a Young Man*, *Ulysses*, and *Finnegans Wake*, with the author's right

Legacy, 2001.

foot standing assertively on a page from the 'Proteus' episode of *Ulysses*. The page from *Finnegans Wake* containing the celebrated opening lines: 'riverrun, past Eve and Adam's...' intrudes beyond the picture plane into the space occupied by the viewer.

The writer and critic Declan Kiberd, in a thoughtful comment on the portrait, wrote, 'There is a thoroughly vaudevillian element to the gent on display here: with his cane and cross-legged pose, he might well have been a figure in a soft shoe song and dance routine. The giveaway in all this is the spotted red and white bow tie of the circus clown, whose eyes project an inner sadness but whose mouth traces the beginnings of a sardonic smile. Every Ballagh portrait tells us something of the painter as well as the subject, and the mix of melancholy and jauntiness, of fragility and defiance in Joyce's pose may hint at an invincible sadness in the painter's own life, as he worked to complete the picture following the sudden death of his own wife, Betty.'

*

When I was approached to paint a portrait of the musician, singer and composer Eleanor McEvoy I instantly embraced the opportunity. In the first place I knew that it would allow me to address an issue that had always concerned me – the obvious gender imbalance in my commissioned portraiture. The reason for this was not entirely my fault, since males usually commissioned pictures of themselves or of other males, which is in itself a telling social commentary. Also I hoped the portrait would, in some way, reconnect me to my distant musical past. Eleanor McEvoy is unusual for a singer, songwriter, guitarist and live performer in that her beginnings were in the world of classical music. As a very young violinist she played with the National Symphony Orchestra. It was to address the fact that she could read and write music that I decided to make the painting a diptych, featuring in the background two pages from the sheet music for her song 'Harbour', written in her own hand.

Opposite: *James Joyce*, oil on canvas, 2011, University College Dublin.
Overleaf: *Eleanor McEvoy*, oil on canvas, 90cm x 120cm, 2011, National Concert Hall, Dublin.

Eleanor stands in front of the left-hand panel holding her guitar in a pose that, in the words of music critic Jackie Hayden, 'captures her unique and personal blend of defiant rock chick with a cool feminine mystique'.

On a personal level I took enormous satisfaction in lavishing meticulous care in the painting of her Fender Telecaster guitar, the same brand of instrument that I played many years before.

*

I always admired Harold Pinter. I found his standpoint on the role of the artist in society refreshingly honest. Pinter believed that an artist's primary responsibility is to make art, a complex process with its own internal energy that should never be compromised; on the other hand, he also believed that artists, being citizens in society, should, as citizens, concern themselves with social matters. In an interview with Ciaran Carty he argued, 'The citizen has responsibilities to scrutinize the society in which we live quite rigorously. I haven't stopped doing that and I don't intend to stop either.'

No one would suggest that Harold Pinter's plays are diminished by his political writings and involvement in protests against oppression and illegal wars.

You can imagine how intrigued I was to be asked by Michael Colgan to create a portrait of Harold Pinter to hang in the Gate Theatre. Because it was a posthumous portrait, I gathered a wide range of photographs of Pinter and used them to create a drawing that had the sole purpose of locking down an acceptable likeness. Having achieved that, I transferred the drawing to the canvas. My first task as a painter was to preserve the likeness on canvas, but then I began trying to push the portrait beyond a mere likeness to somewhere else. The journey was long and arduous and involved no road map, just daily applications of scumbles and glazes in the sanguine hope that something special might eventually

Harold Pinter, 2016, Gate Theatre, Dublin.

emerge. Finally, one day when I was applying one more glaze and one more highlight, the alchemy occurred. The eyes ceased to be mere adumbrations of pigment and instead changed, disclosing real emotion and becoming expressions of sadness and steely determination.

The eyes also induced a colour palette of unusual greens used in the rest of the portrait; in his casual shirt and the modulated background. At the bottom of the portrait Pinter holds two items. The first is a canvas with the back facing out, which, of course, means that only the subject of the portrait knows what lies on the surface of the painting he is holding. The second item is the first page of his acceptance speech, delivered in Stockholm, when he won the Nobel Prize for Literature. This is an exceptional document in which he not only reiterates his views on the artist's role in society, but also stridently condemns the warmongers who contrived the invasion of Iraq in 2003. In order to draw attention to this radical speech I made his hands three-dimensional, a gesture which also might suggest an escape from the world of art into our world, the citizen's world.

*

Even though it was more by accident than design that I ended up spending a considerable amount of my time working on commissions, I have to say that the practice brought not only a fair degree of financial security, but also introduced me to a wide range of fascinating subject matter that I wouldn't have dreamed of myself. Nevertheless, there is a danger in getting so involved in commissioned work. There can be precious little time or energy left for anything else; and after all, sometimes significant issues arise that can only be explored by way of an artist's personal vision.

One of those issues confronted me directly in June 2000, when I learned of Micheal Farrell's tragic death from cancer. As soon as I was made aware of the arrangements for his wake in the village of Cardet in the south of France, where he lived with his second wife, artist Meg Early, I set off, determined to attend. I almost immediately realized that it was no ordinary day: it was 16 June 2000, the first Bloomsday of the millennium, and in Micheal's case wholly appropriate, as he burned with a passion for James Joyce and his writing all his life. The obsequies in Cardet were informal. Micheal's family scattered some of his ashes over his beloved allotment just outside the village; then, according to his wishes, the rest were returned to Ireland to join his ancestors in Cortown cemetery in Co. Meath. Later that evening there was a party in the village square attended by locals and friends. The artist Brian Bourke and his son Malachy played some fine Irish music and the villagers unveiled a plaque dedicated to Micheal. The next day, as I prepared to depart, Meg told me that Micheal had promised to show his last picture in a local exhibition, but sadly had been unable to get it ready in time.

Brian Bourke and I immediately went upstairs to Micheal's studio and took great solace in stretching the last Micheal Farrell painting. It is a variation on a famous canvas by George Bellows representing the last moments from the world boxing title fight between Jack Dempsey and Louis Firpo. Micheal's title, *The Great Fight*, clearly refers to his own titanic struggle with cancer, which began when he was first diagnosed in November 1988.

I will never forget the time when Micheal told me of his diagnosis. It was a grey day, befitting the occasion. I was at home when a taxi pulled up, and a man got out. I didn't recognize him at first; he seemed so dreadfully gaunt. There was a knock on the door. I opened it and then recognized Micheal, looking terrible.

'Bobert,' he said; he always called me Bobert. 'Have you any money to pay the taxi?'

He had no Irish money and had just come from the nearby Mater Hospital. I let him in and he immediately slumped on the couch.

'Bobert, I'm fucked – it's cancer.'

I couldn't believe it. I didn't know what to say. Finally I summed up the courage to pose the obvious question, 'What kind of cancer?'

'Throat cancer; they say they are going to have to take off my whole fuckin' jaw.'

And all I could say was, 'Aw, Jesus Christ!'

Not knowing what more to say or what to do, we sat there, main-

Micheal Farrell, oil and mixed media, 244cm x 152cm, 2001.

taining an awkward silence, only broken when, with a slight glint in his eye, Micheal snarled, 'Ah, fuck it, let's go for a pint.'

I never met anyone who fought a disease as he did. Other people would have been gone in a couple of years. He just fought it and fought it. Alex Blayney, his Irish doctor, wrote, 'His vendetta against cancer was nothing short of superhuman; a lesser being would have wilted long before.'

But eventually his time had to come.

I have a clear recollection of him remarking, almost casually, 'I can't do this any more.'

I knew he was referring to his treatment, which was always desperately debilitating. In a way that was the beginning of the end, which came on 8 June 2000, just one month short of his sixtieth birthday.

I was determined to do something in his memory, but being aware that it was highly unlikely that I would receive a commission, I decided to commission myself. From the outset I knew for certain that the setting for my portrait of Micheal Farrell would have to be a Dublin pub; I could think of no other location where he would be more at home, so I decided to seat him against a partition in Ryan's of Parkgate Street, a fine old Victorian pub. And because there was never silence around Micheal – he was always loquacious, argumentative and fun to be with – I decided to surround him with a lively visual manifestation of his personality. It struck me that his *Pressé* pictures, inspired by the orange squeezers in Paris bistros, with squirts flying in all directions, would be appropriate, especially the first political one he made about the Dublin and Monaghan bombings of 1974.

I ultimately coalesced these disparate elements into a complex painting, described by the artist and writer Brian O'Doherty as falling 'with a thump into the ecumenical category of mixed media', and he explained how, 'in a massive collage, objects escape the painting and situate themselves – mutely and aggressively – in the spectators' space,' resulting in 'the painted Farrell being surrounded by a virtual hurricane of objectifications.'

His painted elbow rests on a three-dimensional counter bearing a three-dimensional pint, both produced by a wood turner to my specifications. My original intention had been to paint them, but when I saw the finished items, turned from ash, I knew it would be shameful to paint over such beautiful wood. Instead I used ebony stain on the pint shape, which allowed the beautiful wood grain to show through, giving the impression of a pint settling; and again, for much the same reason, I used green stain on the counter top.

Canvas shapes from the *Pressé* series, with their staccato shouts of terror and outrage, spin out from behind Farrell and the partition. The colours on his palette, tightly gripped by his three-dimensional thumb, are the blue, white and red of France, but the colours on the tops of the three-dimensional brushes are green, white and orange. Even though he lived for years in France, Ireland was never far from his mind.

Finally, Micheal's legs are drawn deliberately in a sketchy manner, as a riposte to his constant jibes about my meticulous all-over finish and his urgings for me to loosen up; so, for my portrait, I loosened up, for once, by sketching his legs in his own gestural style.

As for the accuracy of my depiction, Brian O'Doherty had the following to say: 'The carefully painted head of this posthumous portrait resurrects its subject with an eerie stereoscopy. The face is mapped with lines incised in gullies and rivers, mountain ranges of wrinkles, dark acres of unshaven chin. This is a face as it might be remembered by Borges's character, Funes the Memorious, who could not forget anything. Ballagh's intense concentration infuses a life-giving energy into the dead face. Madonna Irlanda herself (Farrell's version of François Boucher's salacious portrait of Mademoiselle O'Murphy) might well say, "It's the living image of him." The painted brown eyes look back at the maker and through him at us, appeasing, seeing if we're up for anything, up for a pint. The severity of the face at first glance is mitigated by the vulnerable, slightly open mouth. Portrait painting of this order is a painstaking incremental process of additions until the final hallucination appears. Ballagh has gone through something mediums go through in a séance: hazardously connecting with the spirit of the departed to shake the blue-grey ectoplasm (which is pure energy) into a living virtuality. This involved an emptying out, an elimination of self that enables the depicted subject to emerge. It is an intimate – and exhausting – exchange. Any wavering betrays itself. Knowing both of them, no such flaw is visible. Ballagh has kept faith with his friend.'

✶

In an interview with the writer and critic Ciaran Carty, Patrick T. Murphy confessed that, when he returned from the US to take up his post as director of the Royal Hibernian Academy, he was astonished 'to discover that there had been no big Ballagh show in Ireland'. He decided to put this right by offering me a retrospective exhibition in the academy's gallery in Ely Place. He had only one stipulation: because of my background in architecture and my experience in the theatre, he suggested that I contrive an imaginative design for the presentation of the exhibition.

Model for the 2006 retrospective exhibition.

My concept was to create the illusion of walking through a narrative of my artistic life. It took the form of an installation, in the main exhibition hall, of interconnecting rooms, the entrance to which was through a doorway in a pseudo-Palladian-style façade, emblazoned with the Latin phrase in chiselled lettering, *'Pittura veritas revalat'* ('painting reveals the truth').

It was plain that such an ambitious undertaking would involve serious expense, so naturally, I was dismayed when I learned that the main sponsor had pulled out. I was left with an unpalatable choice: either cancel the show or incur considerable personal debt.

It was at this point that the businessman Dermot Desmond stepped into the picture. Having already purchased some of my work, including the Farrell portrait, he wanted the show to go ahead, and provided sufficient funding for the academy, in the words of its director, to 'undertake one of its most ambitious installations to date'.

As a gesture of thanks I offered to paint his portrait.

Desmond responded, 'There's no need for that,' but I insisted.

So the picture wasn't commissioned; it was a voluntary project. The view depicted behind Desmond is, in reality, impossible. No one can look in two different directions at the same time, but an artist can always cheat. To the left, the Liffey flows out to sea through Dublin's docklands, whereas, to the right, the same river runs its course past O'Connell Bridge, Liberty Hall and the Custom House. All references for the painting were derived from photographs of both Dermot Desmond and views of Dublin taken from his office at the top of the Irish Financial Services Centre.

In order to display the panoramic nature of the composition adequately, I decided to attempt something I'd never done before – or even seen done – and that was to stretch the canvas on a ground that was curved outwards. This was a difficult task because normally canvas is stretched over a flat surface, but with considerable care and attention it eventually took up the curved shape and as a result played a significant role in the creation of the portrait.

★

In 2008 I found that the image of Théodore Géricault's epic painting *The Raft of the Medusa* kept returning to me with haunting urgency. Certain associations between the acutely shifting nature of Irish society at the time and the content of the original picture began to strike with unexpected force. When Géricault painted his picture of terrible tragedy, it was seen by French people as a metaphor for the recklessness and incompetence of the governing authorities. By painting a version of his masterpiece I hoped to allude to the failure of leadership in Celtic Tiger Ireland in economic and regulatory terms. At the time I said, 'We sit on the raft and wait, as Géricault's wretched crew and passengers did when their aristocratic captain and army officers commandeered the lifeboats and left them to drown. The Celtic Tiger bubble has burst. Our banks lent recklessly, allowing bankers to take out huge bonuses, and builders and developers borrowed recklessly. Most have now been

Raft of the Medusa after Géricault, acrylic and oil on canvas, 105cm x 203cm, 2008.

caught out. Yet those who benefited little or not at all are being forced to pay the bill run up by others during those years of excess.'

I gave my painting the same title as Gericault's masterpiece which probably prevented most people from understanding my true intention, namely a critique of those responsible for the economic crash. In fact when the picture was shown on *The Late Late Show*, Ireland's most popular TV programme, the presenter, Pat Kenny, seemed taken aback by my explanation. 'That's surprisingly prescient, isn't it?' To tell the truth, I have always found that unlike the response to journalism which is always immediate, the public usually takes considerable time to appreciate the true content of a work of art. Certainly that was the case when I painted my versions of Goya, Delacroix and David in response to the northern conflict and found them instantly dismissed as mere pastiches of old masters.

CHAPTER 21

Dining at McDonald's

Once upon a time I was quite happy to be called an artist. And, I hear you say, 'Why wouldn't you?' Yet in recent times, I frequently find myself, in response to a stranger's inquiry, replying with an alternative job description: 'I'm a painter.' Having spent almost half a century striving to develop and improve my skills as a painter, I'm now quite reluctant to be defined by such a catch-all term as 'artist'.

For example, I simply have nothing in common with someone who pickles a shark in formaldehyde or who exhibits a can containing their own excrement, or even someone who displays an unmade bed; yet, as you know, all of those practices are carried out by people who are currently described as 'artists'.

Another categorization, that irritates me is the tendency to refer to me as a 'political' artist. In my opinion, that particular definition is both narrow and limiting, yet over the years, I myself have failed to come up with an adequate alternative description. It was only when the artist and writer Brian O'Doherty wrote that 'Robert Ballagh's art is not so much a political art as an art made by an intensely political person' that I realized what I was.

Of course, you might say, it's not as simple as that. For example, what's your definition of politics? And it's true, one could be a monarchist or a republican, a democrat or a neo-Nazi, a capitalist or an anti-capitalist and so on. The political choice made by any individual is critical, for that choice will influence all his or her ideas and actions.

In my case, my own political beliefs have remained fairly constant; indeed, I can't remember a time when I didn't subscribe to the fundamental guiding principles, first laid down by the French Revolution, of *liberté, égalité, fraternité,* and those ideals have also conditioned my approach to art. I have deliberatelychosen an artistic language with universal accessibility, have frequently employed techniques and means of expression that facilitate wide dissemination, and often have tried to locate my work in situations that maximize public participation. Yet when I started out, nearly fifty years ago, the realization of such lofty ambitions seemed almost impossible. For a start, I had no fine art training. So there I was, in the late 1960s, a pretty heady time both politically and artistically, all fired up and ready to go; but sadly, in the words of Robert Hughes the art critic, describing a later generation of painters, I was stranded like an 'aircraft without an airstrip'.

But liberation was at hand. In 1967, as I wrote in an earlier chapter, the ROSC exhibition was staged in Dublin; and sifting through the amazing range of work on display, I came across the first examples I had ever seen of the new international pop art style. The fields of bright acrylic primary colours, the razor-sharp outlines, the hopelessly ironic comic book content all totally overwhelmed me. To my youthful eyes, everything else in the exhibition seemed dreadfully dull. But what was even more exciting at the time was the realization that I, with some ingenuity, would be able to have a go at this. I already knew that I was incapable of painting like Vermeer, but I was fairly confident that I could knock out a few images in the pop art style; and so it turned out to be.

By 1969, I was able to put on a solo exhibition in which my political concerns at the time, the Vietnam War and the civil rights campaign in the North of Ireland, were rendered in a pop art style. The same year, I was selected to represent Ireland in the Paris Biennale. So, in a remarkably short time I had managed not only to take off as an artist but also to establish a modest reputation, especially when you consider that I had little going for me other than reasonable manual dexterity and attitude – bags of attitude. As I mentioned earlier, gaining access to the Irish modern art scene was not as difficult as I had anticipated; and within a relatively short period of time, I had become Ireland's best-known pop artist. To be brutally frank, I was probably Ireland's only pop artist. Nevertheless, even at that early stage in my career, I was beginning to regard the vocabulary of modern art as somewhat limiting. For example, when I looked at the work of, say, Roy Lichtenstein, the comic book artist, I couldn't help speculating that his chosen approach would inevitably restrict his full development; and, sadly, such has been the case. Lichtenstein remained trapped in a prison of Ben-Day dots for the rest of his life, and he is not unique. Many other modern artists have suffered the same stylistic incarceration.

In the early 1970s, painters like Roy Lichtenstein and Andy Warhol provided the artistic template for my work, but as my ambitions grew and as I strove to extend my capabilities as an artist, I found myself searching for different models. These turned out to be painters who were working almost a half-millennium earlier – artists like Van Eyck and Vermeer. With slow determination, I managed to reach a stage where in all honesty I could say, 'I'm painting now like I'd always liked to have painted, if I'd been able to.'

Yet, inasmuch as I'd achieved a certain technical competency in an accessible pictorial language, an irritable conundrum had taken root. How was it that, in spite of all my efforts, the art establishment – which had provided significant support in my early career – now seemed largely unimpressed? Paradoxically, the work itself proved to be extremely popular with the general public. In addition, I felt little kinship with most of the art being promoted by the art establishment; a view, I have to say, endorsed by public opinion.

'How has it come to this?' I asked myself. 'Why have so many people become confused and disenchanted with the art of our times?'

How attitudes have changed from those of the past. During the Middle Ages, the objects we now consider art were produced in communal workshops and, as a consequence, had no individual authorship;

there was little discrimination between the work of an artist and the work of a craftsman. Thomas Aquinas wrote of the arts of shoemaking, cooking, juggling and grammar as well as the arts of sculpture and painting. However, things were changing, and by the end of the fifteenth century the artistic profession had begun to differentiate itself from craftsmanship. According to Arnold Hauser, the historian of aesthetics, Michelangelo became one of the first artists to claim 'independence to shape the whole work from the first stroke to the last', yet even he was severely constrained by outside pressures to paint, or sculpt in rather narrowly defined ways. Nonetheless, it's worth noting that at the time, 'such interference did not appear in the least unacceptable'. The close ties between artist and patron continued in seventeenth-century Europe, when the artist literally and also psychologically became the house guest to the nobility and the royal court.

However, in the eighteenth century, the scene shifted to the *salons* in the homes of aristocrats, where culturally minded members of the upper classes held regular meetings with selected artists and writers. In the words of the author Tom Wolfe, 'The artist was still the gentleman, not yet the genius.' However, with the social upheavals that followed the French Revolution the artist slowly evolved into what Tom Wolfe called a a 'free floating, unattached individual not bound by patron or commission'. While this situation was intellectually attractive – the artist was no longer being told what to paint – the actual separation from any clear social group or class and from any secure form of patronage left the artist in a precarious position. Many artists, feeling a sense of alienation, sought out the company of other like-minded souls. They huddled together in bars and bistros, and in their discussions and disputations the modern perception of the artist began to form.

Avant-garde artists committed themselves to making art that would baffle and subvert the cosy bourgeois vision of reality, and to realize this ambition they chose to work quite independently. Significantly, they painted for themselves alone, with no specific audience in mind. Paradoxically, the actual audience for avant-garde art was quite specific. It was a small group, who, though part of the middle classes, felt themselves to be different. Tom Wolfe argues that 'There is a peculiarly modern reward that the avant-garde artist can give to his benefactor: namely, the feeling that he, like his mate the artist, is separate from and aloof from the middle classes – the feeling that he is a fellow soldier, or at least an aide-de-camp in the vanguard march through the land of the philistines.'

Certainly such was the case during the early years of modernism, where an avant-garde art form, supported by a few enlightened souls, saw itself threatened on all sides by a massive army of the ignorant.

This standpoint of isolation and vulnerability remained unchanged until Alfred Barr, having convinced a few friends, namely, the Rockefellers, the Goodyears and others, of the significance of the new art, founded the Museum of Modern Art in New York. In fact, the founding meeting actually took place in John D. Rockefeller Jr's living room. So the unloved foundling child that was modern art found itself in the rather bizarre situation of being adopted by some of the most powerful people on the planet. What irony! Art that was supposed to be anti-establishment became established even institutionalized in the most fundmamental manner.

All that was left now for modern art to become totally dominant was the necessary development of an enabling infrastructure. Dave Hickey describes this phenomenon well in his essay *Enter the Dragon*. 'After 30 years of frenetic empowerment… the venues for contemporary art in the United States had evolved from a tiny network of private galleries in New York into this vast transcontinental sprawl of publicly funded, post modern ice boxes (and)… the ranks of the *art professionals* had swollen from a handful of dilettantes on the east side of Manhattan into this massive civil service of PhD's and MFA's who administered a monolithic system of interlocking patronage.'

For many years the towering figure of Picasso held sway over the world of modern art. He was a giant, but a giant with feet of clay according to some. They suggested that he was far too dependent on his all too obvious skills as an artist and worse, his work suffered from insufficient intellectual imput. Slowly Piccasso's influence began to be eclipsed by the conceptual principles of Marcel Duchamp, to the extent that, today, Duchamp's ideas form the dominant ideology of modernism. Duchamp's key contribution to the development of modern art has been the notion that the artist's choice imbues a given object with special properties which are tantamount to a metaphysical transformation of the object; that it ceases to be a pedestrian artefact (urinal, bottle rack, unmade bed or whatever) and becomes, by virtue of the artist's choice, art. The consequences of blanket acceptance of this doctrine are worrisome in the extreme. If, for example, everything *can* be art then how can we define that which is *not* art!

Imagine a situation where someone breaks into a parliament building and attempts to assassinate a politician but, on arrest insists that his action was an art performance and not attempted murder.

Believe it or not, this bizarre predicament came to pass when the loyalist killer Michael Stone employed artistic licence as part of his defence against a charge of attempted murder. He tried to break into Stormont (where the Northern Irish Assembly meets) while armed with a knife and homemade bombs. When a convicted sectarian killer – he had already shot three people and injured dozens more in an attack on an IRA funeral some years earlier – feels justified in claiming to be a performance artist, we must accept that the current definition of modern art has become far too porous to be of any practical benefit. Without question, an enormous chasm has opened up between what the general public recognize as art and the art promoted by contemporary galleries and museums. Can this chasm be bridged? Not if the status quo persists, where powerful unrepresentative minorities alone determine whose art is destined for greatness.

Tom Wolfe ruefully observed that 'the notion that the public accepts or rejects anything in modern art, the notion that the public scorns, ignores, fails to comprehend, allows to wither, crushes the spirit of, or commits any other crime against the art of any individual artist is merely a romantic fiction. The game is completed and the trophies distributed long before the public knows what has happened. The public that buys records by the billions, and fills stadiums for concerts, the public that spends $100 million on a single movie; this public affects taste, theory and artistic outlook in literature, music and drama. The same has never been true in art.'

An even more insidious fallout from the Duchamp 'art is what I choose' doctrine has been felt in the realm of art education, especially in the training of the artist. After all, if art can be made via the simple act of choosing an object, then why bother spending years learning and developing basic artistic skills and techniques? Robert Hughes remarked that, 'For nearly a quarter of a century, late-modernist art teaching has succumbed to the fiction that the values of the so-called academy, meaning, in essence, the transmission of disciplined skills based on drawing from the live model and the natural motif, were hostile to *creativity.* Art schools in the 1960s and the 1970s tended to become like crèches whose aim was less to transmit the difficult skills of painting and sculpture than to produce *fulfilled* personalities. At this no one could fail. Besides, it was easier on the teachers if they left their students to do their own thing. It meant they could do *their* own thing and not teach, especially since so many of them could not draw either.'

I am convinced that the problem is not really an art problem; after all, there are many varieties of art being created in the world today. The critical problem is one of administrative control. A relatively small group of art professionals worldwide maintains a stranglehold on the selection and exhibition of the art that the general public are allowed to see; and, as I have explained already, their choices are informed by a complex ideology, which promotes an art form that, by definition, is designed to challenge the public. Certainly the adoption of the 'art is what I choose' doctrine, coupled with the abandonment of any skilful engagement with materials, has resulted in the proliferation of artworks that are largely incomprehensible to the general public or utterly banal. How many people who enjoy art have traipsed optimistically through the white halls of modernism only to be disappointed and dumbfounded by arrays of builders' bricks, a crucifix steeped in the artist's urine, or a glass of water on a glass bathroom shelf? All over the world, from Auckland to Anchorage, from Sydney to Stuttgart, on entering the local contemporary museum, you will stumble across a pile of rocks courtesy of Richard Long, then perhaps a large silk-screened image of some celebrity by Andy Warhol, before your eyes shift towards a huge striped canvas courtesy of Sean Scully. And so on and so on: in each museum, the same visual menu. In terms of choice it's the equivalent of being forced to dine at McDonald's.

Those who do care about this impasse feel frustrated by their inability to express an opinion on the matter, for it seems that any public criticism of the situation is immediately rebuffed by the standing army of critics as hopelessly conservative and ill informed. The realization that such empty art is, by and large, promoted by the subsidized sector further fuels the public's frustration. The public as taxpayers find themselves paying for art that they find at best confusing, without having any possible input into the process that promoted it in the first place.

If contemporary art is to survive and prosper then the democratic deficit that lies at the heart of the modern art world must be challenged. I should stress that I am not arguing against the right of any artist to choose any art form as a means of self-expression; what I am looking for is more art, rather than less. To achieve this, change is required, and that change must take place within the controlling bureaucracy. For a start, there must be a recognition of the democratic concept that with power comes responsibility – for example, the responsibility to listen to others. The present patronizing attitude of bureaucracies – 'We know best' – is simply not acceptable. Unfortunately, if the public's right to express an opinion is ignored, then the art of our age will remain in the dark, the self-indulgent plaything of a few.

It must be accepted that there is more to art in the world today than that which conforms to modernist ideology. The museums and galleries must be opened up to a wider and more representative range of work than they currently sponsor. If such changes were made, there's a chance that our museums and galleries might become places of pleasure and enlightenment, rather than whited sepulchres.

CHAPTER 22

Great Encounters

P ainting portraits can be a fascinating pursuit; after all, how else might an artist meet so many interesting people? Certainly, in my own case, I encountered several charismatic characters who were truly memorable.

One such encounter was with Charles J. Haughey, the late disgraced taoiseach; but before describing that experience, some context is required. In 1969, when the North exploded, the Irish government was caught napping – not surprisingly, since successive governments, almost from the foundation of the state, had paid scant attention to what was happening north of the border. As the crisis unfolded the government quickly discovered that it didn't know what was going on, and, worse still, whom it could trust. A nebulous operation was established to respond to a disastrous situation that was getting worse every day. Families were burned out of their homes; whole streets in the Catholic areas of Belfast were evacuated. In response, field hospitals and reception centres were established to cater for the thousands of refugees flooding across the border, but it was appeals from besieged nationalists for assistance in defending their communities that caused most concern.

It's difficult to comprehend today the levels of fear and apprehension that were the daily experience of nationalists at that time. I remember attending a public meeting outside the General Post Office in O'Connell Street, where speaker after speaker from the North, including Paddy Devlin, later one of the founders of the SDLP, and Paddy Kennedy from the Republican Labour Party, described the vicious sectarian attacks by loyalist mobs and sections of the local security forces on their communities; then they begged anyone in the crowd with access to weapons to fetch them and said they would ensure that the weapons ended up in the right hands. That was the way it was: an atmosphere of violence, panic and fear, and this is where the story becomes somewhat murky. Even now, the full truth has yet to be told. At some stage, a decision was taken to import arms for Northern nationalists to use to defend themselves.

Charles J. Haughey, oil on canvas, 122cm x 152cm, 1980.

This covert operation was quickly rumbled, however, presumably by British and Irish intelligence, and Taoiseach Jack Lynch was threatened with exposure unless he dealt with the situation. Lynch and those closest to him decided to scapegoat those most identified with the plot; they immediately sacked ministers Charles J. Haughey and Neil Blaney, and put out their own version of events contending that they, namely the government, had no previous knowledge of the plot to import arms. Some who had originally supported the importation changed sides and signed up to the government's version of events. One minister, Kevin Boland, resigned in protest at the situation.

Eventually a trial was convened. Haughey and Blaney, together with Captain James Kelly, an Irish army officer, and Albert Luykx, a businessman, were charged with the illegal importation of arms. The 'Arms Trial' was highly controversial, with a definite whiff of perjury in the air; but ultimately the defendants were cleared of all charges. Neil Blaney decided to leave Fianna Fáil and establish his own party, based in Donegal, while Kevin Boland also resigned from Fianna Fáil and founded another new party, Aontacht Éireann.

Charles Haughey remained in Fianna Fáil and began a lengthy and arduous campaign to regain the support of the party faithful. His hard work was rewarded in 1979 with his dramatic victory in the Fianna Fáil leadership battle after the resignation of Jack Lynch. His definitive moment of triumph came in 1980 at the Fianna Fáil Árd Fheis (party conference), when he received the acclamation of the party as both president of Fianna Fáil and taoiseach of the state.

Soon afterwards the poet Anthony Cronin, who had been appointed as a cultural adviser by Haughey, called to say that the taoiseach would like to talk to me about painting his portrait. An appointment was made to meet in government buildings, but once I was in his prime ministerial office, Haughey suggested that we would be much more comfortable discussing our business at his home, Abbeville, in north Co. Dublin. We walked down to street level, climbed into the back of his state car – a black Mercedes – and were driven through the streets of north Dublin, where he took the occasional opportunity to acknowledge his constituents with a discreet wave. At some stage he asked Max, his driver, to turn on the radio so he could hear the news. As was common at the time, the main item concerned yet another controversial policy devised by British prime minister, Margaret Thatcher.

Haughey smiled, 'She's a right bitch, isn't she? I'd never get away with that!'

Eventually we arrived at Abbeville, a fine eighteenth-century country house designed by James Gandon, surrounded by extensive parkland. Haughey ushered me into the living room where we sat down, amid antiques and artworks, to discuss the commission. He was quite clear about what he wanted: a painting that would record, for posterity, his moment of triumph at the 1980 Árd Fheis; nothing more, nothing less. He stated that everything I needed would be provided – photos, videos – and that, if necessary, he would make himself available for additional photography. Then, having agreed an appropriate fee for the commission, he suggested, 'It's time for a drink!' and disappeared out the door and down a corridor. I went swiftly after him into what I can only describe as a traditional Dublin pub, re-created within the house by the architect Sam Stephenson.

'You'll have a pint?' he assumed, and proceeded, like an experienced barman, to pull two pints of Guinness.

We sat down in an alcove by a window, sipping our pints and gazing out at several horses gambolling about the paddock. Eventually it was time to depart, and Max drove me back to the city.

After carefully examining the large pile of photos that were supplied by the taoiseach's office, I came to the inconvenient conclusion that in order to properly execute the actual portrait element of the picture, I would still need to take some photos of Haughey myself. I arranged a suitable time to visit his office, and after setting things up and asking him to strike a pose, I realized to my horror that there was no film in the camera. With considerable embarrassment, I asked myself, *Do I lie and carry on, or do I tell the truth?*

I decided on the truth.

Charlie replied, 'Well, can you get some film?'

I said I had several rolls in my car, which was parked nearby.

'Fine,' he said. 'You go and get the film; I'll attend to affairs of state.'

On my return I shot off several rolls and afterwards Charlie led me to the door, remarking with his tongue firmly in his cheek, 'Well, Ballagh, isn't it lucky you don't earn your living from photography?'

I now had all the material I needed to plan a composition for the final picture, which included the full paraphernalia of a party conference: the huge magnified photo of the leader, the podium, the microphones, the colour scheme and the people cheering, waving flags and placards.

I now realized that there was a choice between two possible designs.

I phoned Haughey. 'I can paint the picture reflecting the reality of the event, with you at the podium, sharing the platform with various other politicians and ministers, or I can compose it differently and lose them.'

His reply was instant and to the point: 'Lose them!'

When the picture was completed it was agreed that Anthony Cronin would come to my studio and inspect it before Charlie took delivery. I remember asking if, by including three images of Charlie in the picture, I had perhaps over-gilded the lily.

Tony smiled. 'You could have chanced a few more!'

After the picture had been delivered, the following day a shiny black Mercedes slid down our narrow terraced cul-de-sac and parked outside the house. Max got out and handed me a cheque for the full amount. I remember wishing at the time that all my clients were as straightforward in their dealings.

Sadly, in a short few years, I was to be disabused of such a positive appraisal. In 1983 I met Anthony Cronin in a pub near government buildings. He informed me that the taoiseach was considering appointing me to the Arts Council. As far as I was concerned, that was positive news; after all, the Association of Artists in Ireland had just been formed, and one of its key demands was that professional artists should be appointed to decision-making bodies.

However, Tony then went on to describe how unhappy Charlie was with the director of the Council, Colm O'Briain. This surprised and disturbed me. I felt that, after the autocratic regime of Father Donal O'Sullivan, Colm O'Briain represented a breath of fresh air.

Then came the bombshell. Tony said that if I was appointed, the taoiseach would expect me to maintain a watching brief on the director. I was dumbstruck. Nevertheless, since Haughey's (and Cronin's) expectation seemed so vague, I decided to accept the nomination and to wait and see how things might develop. Certainly, on a personal level, I had no intention of acting as a spy.

I needn't have worried. After the subsequent general election Haughey was replaced as taoiseach by Garret Fitzgerald, who, having no interest in the arts, certainly had no need for artistic spies.

As I had been appointed to fill a vacancy, my time on the Arts Council was necessarily short – just two years – and, for whatever reason, Garret Fitzgerald chose not to reappoint me. I'm unsure as to whether I achieved anything worthwhile as a serving member of the council but I must admit that I still harbour a sense of guilt over my failure, in one particular instance, to ensure due diligence in the disbursement of public funds. In the 1980s there was no suitable public space in Dublin for major art shows, so when Patrick J. Murphy became the new chairman of the ROSC executive committee he resolved to address the exigency.

According to Peter Short, author of *The Poetry of Vision*, an account of the ROSC exhibitions from 1967 to 1988, 'the patriarchal and undemocratic nature of the post of chairman of the ROSC executive committee became apparent when Michael Scott, who had held the post since its inception in 1967, unilaterally appointed Patrick J. Murphy as his successor in September 1981.'

In 1982, the artist and gallery owner Gerald Davis contacted Pat Murphy suggesting that the Guinness brewery, a company that had employed Murphy over many years, might have a suitable building to house the next ROSC exhibition. As a result, the ROSC committee entered into negotiations with Guinness, who proposed that a four-storey disused hop store in Rainsfort Street be converted into a centre for the visual arts and a home for their Museum of Brewing. The cost involved was estimated at £545,000, of which Guinness offered to invest £195,000, leaving the rest to be obtained from public funds.

In 1983, Patrick J. Murphy and Michael Scott, who were not just members of the Arts Council but also deeply involved with ROSC, brought this proposition to the council for consideration. After we perused the plans for the conversion of the Hop Store, drawn up by Ronnie Tallon, from the architectural practice Scott Tallon Walker, we were made aware of the financial implications behind the promised £100,000 of public funding, which involved the Arts Council contributing £46,000 from its own budget. Because I was alarmed by the suggestion that such a large portion of the visual arts subvention be devoted to a single development by a private company, I considered that it was incumbent on us to ensure that the visual arts would have a permanent profile in the restored Hop Store. With that in mind, I recommended that the new venue be governed by an independent trust. Michael Scott instantly dismissed this suggestion, arguing that such a procedure would overcomplicate things and, in an effort to allay our concerns, reminded us that, 'Guinness have always had the welfare of the citizens of Dublin at heart.' In the interests of fairness the Arts Council had an in-house rule that anyone with a vested interest in a particular funding application would declare that interest and leave the room, while the rest of the council voted on the grant. So, when the Hop Store proposal came before the council, I was dismayed to observe several members, who in my opinion had an obvious stake in the project, remain firmly seated. With some embarrassment I brought this anomaly to the attention of the new director of the Arts Council, Adrian Munnelly, but before he could respond, Michael Scott blurted out, 'I don't know what Bobbie is talking about.' In response I felt obliged to remind the council that Michael's architectural firm, Scott Tallon Walker, had been awarded the design contract and as such would benefit from a positive decision. Michael immediately rebutted the charge by arguing that such a stricture couldn't possibly apply to him, as he himself was no longer a practising architect.

In the end the council voted in favour of unconditionally granting £46,000 to Guinness to facilitate the refurbishment of the Hop Store as a venue for the visual arts. The first phase of renovation was completed in August 1984 in time for ROSC '84 and Ronnie Tallon's minimal yet tasteful renovation of the nineteenth-century brick and steel structure was greeted with general approval. At last it seemed that Dublin had a suitable space for showing major exhibitions of contemporary art. Indeed, after ROSC '84 several important shows were staged in the Hop Store but after ROSC '88, in the absence of a serious art programme, it failed to become an important exhibition centre for the visual arts. In 1998, when Guinness restructured an unused six-storey fermentation plant at the brewery as a new visitor centre, the Hop Store became redundant and finally closed its doors to the public.

As far as I'm concerned the saga of the Hop Store delivered a salutary lesson in how conflicts of interest seldom represent a serious threat to doing business in Ireland.

Charlie's autocratic determination to control everything surfaced again in 1984 when a book about the role of the arts in the Irish state, *Dreams and Responsibilities*, was published by the Arts Council. It was written by Brian Kennedy, assistant director of the National Gallery of Ireland. Apparently Charlie was unhappy with Kennedy's description of Aosdána, the self-governing trust of Ireland's leading artists, in that it gave the credit for Aosdána's inception to both Charlie and the council. Haughey was furious at not being given full credit, and ordered the book to be withdrawn and subsequently destroyed.

I learned more about Haughey's imperious ways in 1988. I had been commissioned to design a postage stamp, but at a late stage in the process, I was contacted by a civil servant from the GPO. 'It has been decided not to proceed with the issuing of a stamp to commemorate the bicentenary of the French Revolution. I hope you will not be too disappointed.'

But it was not just preparatory work that was lost: thousands of sheets of the already printed stamps were shredded and the colour printing plates destroyed on the instructions of the Irish government. As Ciaran Carty noted, 'The declaration of an Irish Republic in 1916 had been inspired by the French Revolution and its stirring principles of Liberty, Equality and Fraternity. But now it seemed it wasn't worth a stamp.'

I received no official confirmation of the government's decision or any explanation as to why the design had been rejected. There were suggestions that, perhaps, admirers of Louis le Brocquy may have prompted Charlie Haughey, now back in office, to intervene and commission a new stamp from le Brocquy. I wrote to Haughey urging him to 'look into the matter'. He replied, 'There would be little point in submitting designs to the government for approval if they were not permitted any discretion.'

At that stage, the affair had already gone public, with articles in newspapers featuring detrimental headlines like 'Ballagh fails to get stamp of approval'. I decided enough was enough and contacted P. J. Mara, Haughey's loyal right-hand man. I warned him that if any stamp other than mine was issued, I would make a very public statement of my opinion.

Haughey agreed to see me in government buildings.

'What's this bruised ego, Ballagh? All I can say is that the government didn't approve the stamp.'

I told him plainly that An Post had approached me to design several more stamps, and that I was unwilling to put the work in and have them cancelled at the last minute because of unpredictable and opaque political or aesthetic disagreements.

With a nod and wink, he replied, 'Don't worry, Ballagh – you'll be all right.'

The upshot was that Ireland, along with Britain, were the only two European countries not to issue stamps to commemorate the bicentenary of the French Revolution.

Some time later I met Brian Lenihan, Tánaiste (deputy prime minister) and minister for foreign affairs in the very government that had rejected my stamp. He pulled me aside and whispered, 'Whatever happened to that lovely stamp you designed?'

That perhaps innocent query finally confirmed that the whole affair had been a solo run by Haughey.

*

One of Charlie Haughey's cherished ambitions was to transform the derelict docklands of Dublin into a financial services centre, rather like London's Canary Wharf. Part of the original promotional package was a proposal to restore the warehouse Stack A as a museum of modern art. Stack A was once used as a banqueting hall for soldiers returning from the Crimean War. Because of its open architecture and central location, I considered it perfectly suited for a contemporary museum. However, without consultation or debate, Haughey decided instead to locate the new Irish Museum of Modern Art in the recently restored Royal Hospital at Kilmainham, on the basis that it could be more easily, more speedily and certainly more cheaply turned around into a modern exhibition space than Stack A, which required a more fundamental restoration.

At the time, I believed that this represented a monumental error of judgement, and I publicly articulated that opinion. From my point of view the eighteenth-century military hospital was totally unsuitable for the display of contemporary art and its out of the way location made it incredibly difficult for most people to visit. C. J. Haughey was not pleased and, in his eyes, I became a *persona non grata*.

In 2005 the National Portrait Gallery in London contacted me, looking for a slide of my painting of Haughey for a book it was publishing. On checking, much to my embarrassment, I discovered that I didn't have one. It was a friend of Haughey's who suggested, 'Why don't you give him a call?'

By then he was long out of office and totally disgraced by revelations about his corrupt relations with banks and businessmen. I still had his private number, so I rang and explained that I needed to photograph his portrait.

'What are you doing this afternoon?' he asked.

'Nothing in particular.'

'Well, come on out, and make sure you bring some film for the camera.'

He had been diagnosed with prostate cancer and it was said that he was dying, but when he greeted me at the hall door of Abbeville I found him frail but in good form. Because the painting was badly lit, I suggested I take it down and move it to a place where the light was better.

The painting was now standing without support so I asked, 'Can you possibly hold it steady while I take some shots?'

So he did, and I took the photographs. When I sent a slide to the National Portrait Gallery I was tempted to say, 'Do you see that hand in the top left corner? That's actually his hand.'

When I'd finished, we sat down and took some refreshments, this time tea rather than stout, and had a pleasant conversation before it was time to depart. It was the last time I saw him. He died on 13 June the following year.

On a personal level Charlie Haughey was a seriously engaging character. I always enjoyed his company, his corrosive sense of humour and his often indiscreet banter. But, of course, there was much more to him than that. Without question, he was an extraordinarily complex individual. In my opinion he was one of the most visionary leaders that Ireland ever had, but, tragically, the implementation of his vision for Ireland was often undermined by the consequences of another of his characteristics: his hubris.

Despite constantly presenting himself as a man of the people, for some reason, he felt he was entitled to a philandering lifestyle, which included a Georgian mansion and a private island retreat.

Naturally, his salary as Taioseach was insufficient to cover such extravagances so he was forced to seek financial support from various private sources. Inevitably many of his political options became effectively compromised.

I often think that the narrative arc of Charles J. Haughey's life resembles a Shakespearian tragedy. It began with enormous potential only to end in disgrace and failure. Nevertheless, in spite of the ruinous outcome, sight should not be lost of his considerable achievements.

The artists' tax exemption scheme that Haughey introduced in 1969 when he was Minister for Finance marked a significant development in support for the artist in Irish society. In the 1980s when I became involved with the International Association of Art I met many artists from all over the world who commented favourably on our tax exemption scheme, remarking that it was a unique system and wishing that their own governments might introduce something similar.

Also the elderly in our society have reason to thank Charlie Haughey for introducing the free travel scheme which undoubtedly has enriched the lives of many of our older citizens over several decades.

*

I have a habit that, whenever I enter my studio, I turn on the radio. I find the background thrum of either music or talk conducive to a productive working environment. However, I do remember one particular occasion when it had the completely opposite effect. It stopped me in my tracks. In an interview with RTÉ, the businessman and newspaper tycoon Gerry McGuinness was advocating that all the monuments on O'Connell Street should be torn down and re-placed with statues of those he considered real Irish patriots: people like Tony O'Reilly, Michael Smurfit and Ben Dunne. I was aghast; surely all those businessmen had done was make a lot of money for themselves – and not always in ethical ways, as O'Reilly for one had demonstrated. Nevertheless, his outburst set me thinking. If I were going to celebrate anybody, I'd paint someone who had always acted with integrity, not self-interest. It didn't take me long to choose Noël Browne.

Browne's early life was like a Dickensian story – one of great poverty and deprivation. Many in his family, including himself, were afflicted with tuberculosis. He was introduced to an affluent Irish family in England who sent him to a good school and to university, where he qualified as a medical doctor. Back in Ireland he became interested in politics and joined a new party, Clann na Poblachta; in 1948 he was elected as a TD (member of the lower house), and became minister for health on the same day.

In office, he successfully spearheaded a campaign to eradicate TB from Ireland. He then tried to introduce a scheme for free medical care for mothers and children. The medical profession didn't like it at all, and the Catholic Church saw it as the thin end of the wedge of communism. He resigned rather than abandon the scheme. However, he continued in politics until he was nearly seventy, always insisting on seeing Ireland for what it was rather than signing up to what he called, 'the conspiracy of agreed lies'.

I had never met Noël Browne in person, although we were on the same demonstration outside the British Embassy years before, protesting against the jailing of Bernadette Devlin for her role in the Battle of the Bogside.

It was with some trepidation that I contacted him and outlined my proposition. I have to admit that I was not surprised by his initial lukewarm response. He was not the kind of person who courted glorification. Nevertheless he reluctantly agreed to meet. Before his visit to our house, I gathered catalogues and photos of my work in anticipation of a lively discussion about the putative portrait. I needn't have bothered. From the moment he arrived we talked about Ireland, history, politics and nearly everything other than my proposal.

Finally, in exasperation, I blurted out, 'What about the portrait?'

He quietly replied, 'OK, let's give it a try.'

I then realized that the purpose of his visit was not to check out my art but to check me out. I had presumably passed the test.

After his retirement, Noël and his wife Phyllis split their time between Dublin and Connemara, so, for reasons of convenience, I arranged to visit them when they were at their home in Malahide, a small seaside village in north Co. Dublin. While there I made some sketches, took some photos and met Phyllis, a warm, intelligent woman who was fiercely loyal to Noël. I took to her immediately.

Much later, I remember talking to Noël about some past controversy and him saying, 'We, of course, opposed that.'

At the time, I wondered if he was talking about one of the parties he'd joined and repudiated: Clann na Poblachta, Fianna Fáil, the Labour Party, even the Socialist Labour Party which he had founded, but then I realized he was referring to the one party he never left: his life-long partnership with Phyllis.

Back in the studio, I began working on the portrait, but to my intense disappointment, my drawings and sketches were dull and uninspiring. On my next visit to Malahide, I put the case that, in the absence of new motivations, we might take a break; whereupon Phyllis

intervened, 'Why don't you come down and stay with us in Connemara and see what happens?'

Noël's association with Connemara went back a long way, back to when he first became a minister, and as such, felt it would be hypocritical not to be able to speak Irish, the first official language of the state. Since he was educated in England, he of course spoke none, so in case any questions were put to him in the language, he opted to go to the Gaeltacht (Irish-speaking regions) and learn it.

He then kept going back. He identified with the people, 'the suffering they must have gone through to survive and the suffering of those who had to get out'. He also appreciated the hard-won landscape, the way the fields were marked out by rocks dug out of the soil, 'the bareness, the endless stone walls'.

Noël and Phyllis lived in a small thatched cottage in Baile na hAbhann, Galway, and when I turned up I was accommodated in an adjacent tiny cabin. It was June 1984 and the weather was unusually fine. Every morning after breakfast, strolling along the stony beaches, Noël and I would fall into deep conversation about his life and the many fascinating characters that had crossed his path.

It took a while, but eventually it dawned on me that these stony beaches of Connemara represented the ideal setting for the portrait. I began photographing Noël and the location from every possible point of view, hoping that, on my return to the studio, I would have sufficient material to start work on the portrait.

My initial efforts were quite conventional. I simply put Noël standing on a stony beach with a Connemara background, and then, for some reason, I decided to revert to my earlier practice of creating a large picture by joining many smaller canvases together. Once I had drawn my design onto twelve small canvases I was able to start painting. But when I'd completed a considerable amount of work, I became convinced that the composition needed something more.

Remembering that the special bond between Noël Browne and the

Noël Browne, oil on canvas and mixed media, 183cm x 137cm, 1985,
National Gallery of Ireland.

Irish people was a key factor in my decision to embark on the portrait, I decided, in order to draw attention to that connection, to allow the painted stones in the picture to spill out and deposit themselves as real stones on the gallery floor, thus linking Noël Browne with our space, public space. And I decided to add three books as well. On the spines of two are the names Samuel Beckett and Karl Marx, both supplied by Noël at my request; the Irish title of the other book, *Fód a Bhaile*, is a fisherman's expression for coming safely ashore.

Conjuring up the idea or concept was one thing; executing it proved to be entirely another matter. The depiction of a believable transition from painted stones to real stones required illusionistic or *trompe l'oeil* painting of the highest order, which, as I quickly discovered, was both troublesome and time-consuming.

After weeks and weeks painting the stones that surrounded Noël's clogs, I sat back, completely drained, and groaned, 'Fuck me, there has to be a better way.'

I looked and looked at the composition and the more I looked the more I began to speculate that the panels, with thousands of stones yet to be painted, bordering the already completed ones, could be surplus to requirements. After all, the central feature of the composition was the verticality of the standing figure in contract to the horizontality of the landscape.

Without further thought I removed the side panels and while I was at it, I also decided to remove the top two outside panels, since all they depicted was unencumbered sky. It was only then that the full impact of the resulting composition struck me. Unbelievably, without any possible contrivance or conscious intention, I had ended up with one of the most potent symbols in Western culture: the cross.

I became nervous that many people would conclude that the shape was deliberately chosen to evoke Noël's conflict with the Catholic Church, and incorrectly assume that the painting's sole concern was that particular clash. However, I decided to bide my time in reaching a final decision and in the meantime continue with other unfinished elements, which included his Aran jumper. I remember joking to a friend, 'I could have knitted several real jumpers in the time it took to paint just one.'

Ultimately I resolved to retain the cruciform layout. By using what is seen by many people as a very religious image in a totally secular way, I hoped to turn a lot of things on their head. But it was simply a formal consideration that gave rise to that image.

Once I had finished the picture to my satisfaction, I prepared myself for what I knew would be the most nerve-wracking aspect of the whole affair – showing it to Noël. I knew he would want to bring Phyllis, but I was surprised when he asked if Jack McQuillan and his wife Angela could come along. Jack and Noël had served in Dáil Éireann (the lower house) together and, at one time in the 1950s, the two of them were acknowledged by many as the true opposition to the government in parliament.

As expected, the immediate response from all of them was surprised silence, but then gradually a discussion broke out; eventually they all seemed to agree that the painting was a success.

Afterwards, in my heart of hearts, I wondered if Noël really liked it; but then, a few days later, an early edition of Beckett's *En attendant Godot* arrived in the post, along with a brief note from Noël giving his thanks, so I presumed he was reconciled to it.

Some time later, Michael Gill from Gill & Macmillan wrote to me saying they were about to publish Noël's memoir, *Against the Tide*, and that Noël had asked for my portrait to be on the cover. I was now sure he liked it.

Noël only made one suggestion to me about the portrait. He asked that, if at all possible, I ensure it ended up in a public collection. In that regard things seemed to start out well. A Fine Gael backbencher, Liam Skelly, called me saying he wanted to buy the portrait and donate it to Leinster House. Skelly, admittedly a bit of a maverick in a conservative party, argued that Noël Browne was 'one of the outstanding political figures since the foundation of the state and remembered for the eradication of TB'. Unfortunately, Dáil Éireann's powerful Committee on Procedures and Privileges turned down the offer, claiming that it was bound by a long-standing practice to display only portraits of former taoisigh. The writer Ulick O'Connor, a member of the Hugh Lane Gallery's advisory committee, then took up the issue and proposed

The History Lesson, oil on canvas, 120cm x 120cm x 120cm, 1989, Cold Spring Harbor Laboratory, USA.

its purchase for the gallery. The response by an influential committee member echoed the rejection of *The History Lesson* by the Office of Public Works committee: 'Over my dead body that artist gets bought.'

Meanwhile, *Against the Tide* had become a publishing sensation, selling well over 100,000 copies. Kenny's Gallery in Galway decided to show my portrait of Noël as part of an exhibition featuring artists and books. As it happened, Raymond Keaveney, director of the National Gallery, and his assistant Brian Kennedy saw the picture in Kenny's and decided to purchase it. However, several members of their board of trustees were adamantly opposed to their choice. Rather than have the portrait turned down, Keaveney and Kennedy kept it in storage in the gallery waiting for the right moment. After some changes to the board, they eventually got the purchase approved three years later.

The sad thing is that Noël had fallen gravely ill when the portrait was finally hung in the gallery. He wasn't well enough to come up from Connemara and see it, and tragically died before he could ever make the journey. Some time later Phyllis and their two daughters, Ruth and Susan, joined me to view Noël, standing tall and proud among the great and the good in the National Gallery of Ireland, as part of the National Portrait Collection.

After the disheartening rejection of *The History Lesson* by the Office of Public Works, I decided to keep the painting for myself; and over time, curiously, grew to value it still more. It assumed pride of place in our home.

In 2003, my exhibition *Portrait of the Artist Micheal Farrell and Other Works* took place in the Crawford Gallery in Cork, and *The History Lesson* was included. I was not best pleased to receive a call from someone who had seen the exhibition and wanted to buy it. I responded by saying, rather bluntly, 'It's not for sale.'

But he persisted, eventually travelling up from Cork to my studio in Dublin to make his case. Finally, I relented and sold this person the picture. However, you can imagine my bewilderment when just a year later, walking along St Stephen's Green, a picture in the window of James Adam & Sons, the fine art auctioneers, caught my eye: it was *The History Lesson*. I had no idea it was coming up for sale. When the bidding opened, several aspirants made their intentions clear; but when the price rose to €18,000 it became obvious that an anonymous telephone bidder would have the final say. Afterwards I tried to persuade the auctioneers to give me the name of the purchaser, only to be told, 'That information is confidential, but we can say that he is an American collector.'

I was resigned to never knowing where the picture had gone.

And there the matter rested until 2007, when I received a letter from Dr David McConnell, professor of genetics in Trinity College Dublin, telling me that the Nobel laureate James D. Watson, who together with Francis Crick discovered the structure of DNA, the double helix, was coming to Dublin to be made an honorary fellow of the Royal Irish Academy. 'He's interested in talking to you about a portrait, and, by the way, you and he have something in common. He owns a painting of yours, *The History Lesson*.'

On the morning of the Royal Irish Academy's event, Watson and his wife Liz visited my studio in Arbour Hill, where I told them that Pearse, Connolly and the other executed leaders of the Easter Rising were buried nearby. He confessed that when he bought *The History Lesson* he knew very little about Pearse or Connolly or, for that matter, me; he just liked the image. He also explained why he was on the auctioneer's mailing list. On a previous visit to Dublin he spotted in Adam's window a painting by Robert Gregory, Lady Gregory's son and the subject of the famous poem 'An Irish Airman Foresees his Death' by W. B. Yeats, and decided to buy it. We vaguely discussed the possibility of a portrait, but nothing too definite emerged from our talk.

He suggested, 'You know, you'll have to come over to Cold Spring Harbor Laboratory on Long Island and see us there.'

That evening David McConnell memorably introduced Watson as 'truly a giant of our times who was without doubt the greatest biologist of the twentieth century, just as Charles Darwin was the greatest naturalist of the nineteenth century'.

I remember thinking, *And this man wants me to paint his portrait.* So, perhaps for reasons of timidity, I didn't instantly follow up on Watson's suggestion.

But some time later, he phoned and impatiently inquired, 'When are you coming?'

In the autumn of 2007 I stayed for nearly a week at Cold Spring Harbor Laboratory, a research institute established more than a century before in an old whaling station about an hour from Manhattan. Watson became director in 1968 and in the course of the next fifty years raised sufficient government and philanthropic funding to build it into one of the most important centres for molecular biology and genetics in the world.

Cold Spring Harbor is a beautiful place with wooded meadows and fine gardens falling down to Long Island Sound, a perfect setting for Ballybung, the Watsons' home. Going there and talking to Watson was a mind-expanding experience for me, especially since I had never spent that much time with a scientist before. Scientists see the world differently. I liked that. He has a very rational, logical way of thinking. If something is provable it's fact, and that's it. That kind of intense logic was to me very fresh, because the world of art tends to operate in an altogether more evasive manner.

On one occasion, Jim confessed that there's no money in science: 'You'd be dumb to go into science for that.'

But as the author of several bestselling books, he could finance his two passions: art collecting and tennis. I understood why you would need money to buy art, but I was at a loss as to why the playing of tennis would require serious financing.

'I only play with professionals,' was his answer.

Even though he was in his eighties, he played tennis regularly; one time, I accompanied him to his club, where he knocked about energetically for two hours with a very much younger Australian professional.

One of his books, published in 1968, was *The Double Helix*, which was on the *New York Times* bestseller list for many weeks and has never been out of print. According to David McConnell, 'It is frank, witty and acerbic and established Watson as a fine writer. In it he told tales on scientists revealing them, and himself, to have all the faults and foibles of ordinary mortals. It is a terrific yarn about how great science can be done, quietly showing with minimum technical detail the key scientific contributions made by different figures in what was a real-life drama.'

Of course, the main reason I was in Cold Spring Harbor Laboratory was to come up with some ideas for the portrait. So, for a start, I busied myself taking photographs of the place. After that I asked for a session with Jim Watson himself. I began by taking fairly conventional photographs of him sitting at his desk, standing looking straight ahead, looking into the middle distance; and then the germ of an idea struck. I asked him to pose with his arms reaching forward.

'No one ever asked me to pose like that,' he nervously remarked.

'Trust me,' I replied.

Thankfully, he did.

On my return to Dublin I laid out all the material I had collected on the studio desk and began the task of trying to create an interesting composition. I knew straight away that I would place a table with Watson's books in the foreground; after all, in our many conversations, he had again and again stressed the importance of his writing: 'Someone else would have discovered the double helix, but only one author writes a book.'

The background had to be a view of Cold Spring Harbor itself. I opted to depict this beautiful landscape in a monochrome grey, since in all my photos the trees had turned to autumnal shades of orange and red and their beauty would have dominated the picture.

In some of my photos of Jim he was wearing a knitted jumper, and my immediate reaction was, *After all the torture involved in painting Noël Browne's jumper – I'm not doing that!* But then I recognized that the cable pattern on the jumper resembled the double helix, and knew I had to include it.

Using the many photos I'd taken of Jim's face, I prepared detailed working drawings for the actual portrait. In many ways they resembled a topographical survey, in that they plotted every line, every wrinkle, every spot; the accumulated consequences of a long life. Later Jim

James D. Watson, oil on canvas, 122cm x 122cm, 2008, Trinity College, Dublin.

remarked, 'It's extremely accurate. I had surgery for skin cancer fifty years ago, and my lip is asymmetrical. And Bobbie caught it.'

By this stage I had arrived at a rudimentary layout but to my dismay, it turned out to be square; an unusually static format. But as I scrutinized the square, I slowly realized that if I turned it on its axis it would become a diamond, a far more dynamic configuration.

The last and perhaps most important decision was how to deal with the double helix. I knew I had to include it; but how?

I could paint it, but that would be too awkward, too literal. I wanted to come up with an elegant solution that would appeal to the scientific mind. Finally, working with a glass artist, I designed a double helix to be etched into the glass that would form part of the picture frame. It would be there, yet not part of the actual painting – a sort of mystical presence.

At this crucial moment, my hunch about asking Watson to pose reaching out paid off. In the final composition he stands in a messianic pose with the double helix floating in space before him, as if saying, 'Look – the secret of life.'

After the finished painting was photographed, I sent a print to Jim, who replied that he was delighted with the result. He also mentioned that both he and David McConnell thought that the upcoming dinner to celebrate the fiftieth anniversary of the genetics department in Trinity would be an appropriate occasion to unveil the portrait.

At the dinner, I was placed next to Ciaran Costello who, years before, had commissioned the Laurence Sterne pictures for Clonmel. He was there because his father, Lt. Gen. Michael Joseph Costello, who ran the Irish Sugar Company, had provided the initial start-up funding of £15,000 for the genetics department.

After the black drape was theatrically drawn back, Jim, who of course had only seen a photo, went up and closely scrutinized the portrait.

As he was walking away I apprehensively inquired, 'Well, Jim, what do you think?'

'This is a marvellous painting and the beginning of a wonderful friendship.'

And so it has proved to be.

On many occasions I have travelled to Cold Spring Harbor and enjoyed the generous hospitality of the Watson family. And whenever Jim and Liz visit Ireland we always find time to meet.

There is no doubt that Jim Watson is a man of strong opinions and no stranger to controversy. He is patently humane, but has an uncompromising way of thinking out loud about genetics. On one occasion, after Watson was interviewed by a former intern in his office, he invited her to dinner. In the course of the meal the subject of Africa came up. Watson said that he was inherently gloomy abou the prospects for many African states. He suggested that because of evolution and genetics many contemporary Africans were ill-equipped to deal with the numerous difficulties that beset them. Later the intern summarized his views as racist in an article published in the *Sunday Times*.

Watson countered with a statement, 'That is not what I meant. More importantly, there is no scientific basis for such a belief.'

From all my conversations with Watson, I am convinced that he doesn't have a racist bone in his body, but the affair proved damaging to his reputation.

✶

When the Crick family sold their father's Nobel gold medal, Jim confided in me that he thought he'd do the same: 'What use is a gold medal locked away in a drawer?'

Some time after the sale, which realized over $4 million, he confessed that having already donated a sizeable amount to cancer research, he wanted to commission me to paint a portrait of Francis Crick before it was all gone; he then planned to donate it to the new Francis Crick Institute in London. I responded by saying that I'd be honoured to paint Francis Crick but never having met the man, I would need considerable help and assistance.

And thus began what essentially became a collaborative project.

For a start, Jim insisted that I portray Francis as a man in his forties, when he was at the height of his powers. This was easier said than done. Even though I had access to Cold Spring Harbor Laboratory's library and archives, I discovered very few images of Crick in his forties. Through the intercession of Ludmila Pollock, the chief librarian, the Crick family provided some private photographs; using one of them I worked up a sketch and sent it to Jim, who responded, 'No, he's too young!'

At last, in a book, I spotted a small black-and-white photograph of Francis Crick taken in a BBC recording studio in the early 1960s. I naturally thought the BBC would be able to supply me with a good-quality print, but they didn't own the original negative. Eventually, I unearthed the original in the University of California in La Jolla, and the people there provided me with a digital file. I was now able to prepare another sketch for Jim. Thankfully, this time, he said, 'OK!'

Another aspect of Francis Crick's character that Jim urged me to incorporate in the portrait was his role as a teacher. Jim contended that Crick was an incredible communicator of scientific fact. We both felt that placing him behind a lectern would underline that reality. As regards the background, a blackboard seemed an obvious choice, and above Crick's head I drafted, in his own handwriting, the genetic code: DNA–RNA–Protein.

Jim was happy with that, but when I filled in the rest of the blackboard with various other markings, also made by Crick, Jim was definitely not pleased. He said they were made much later and therefore were chronologically out of time with the period depicted. A scientist's objection; but since he was the boss, I toned down the later markings.

As the finished painting was going to hang in a scientific institute I felt it appropriate to include documentation that might prove interesting to scientists. Once again I deferred to Jim Watson. He suggested two papers by Francis Crick: one was his acceptance speech on receiving the Nobel Prize in 1962; the other was 'The Genetic Code: Yesterday, Today and Tomorrow', delivered at a symposium in Cold Spring Harbor in 1966.

In order to draw attention to these key documents I made the hands holding the documents three-dimensional; and because for obvious

Francis Crick, oil on canvas with mixed media, 2017, Francis Crick Institute, London.

DNA → RNA → Protein
ON THE GENETIC CODE
F.H.C. CRICK
F.H.C. CRICK
Cold Spring Harbor Symposium
1966

Sir Paul Nurse introduces Jim Watson and myself to Queen Elizabeth II.

reasons Francis Crick's hands were unavailable, I had my own hands cast by a fellow artist. Some say that all art is autobiographical; in this case the claim is partially true.

My predilection for the occasional inclusion of three-dimensional elements is often put down to the influence of cubism and the break-through of collage, when artists began to stick items from the real world, like wallpaper, newspaper and even pieces of furniture, onto their canvases. But I have to confess the real source of my own incli-nation to do this goes back much further, back to the fifteenth century – in fact, to Carlo Crivelli, who simply couldn't resist challenging the two-dimensional nature of the painted surface. His splendid *Demidoff Altarpiece*, created in 1476, is peppered with raised ornaments simulating gems, jewels and buttons; but Peter's massive three-dimensional keys to the kingdom of heaven, bursting out of the celestial space and into our secular world, are what compel our full engagement with the holy man. Saintly feet protrude beyond the bottom step of the altarpiece, but this time it's not a physical projection, it's an illusion, masterfully created in paint. If you ever find yourself in London, I urge you to make your way to the National Gallery and prepare to be dazzled by the virtuosity of Crivelli, an unjustly neglected artist.

In the summer of 2016 I received an invitation from the Francis Crick Institute in London to attend the formal opening in November of their new building by Queen Elizabeth II. The protocol was quite clear: the invitation was for one person only and was strictly non-transferable. However, closer to the actual date, I received a further communication informing me that arrangements had changed and, since the Queen was now going to unveil my portrait of Francis Crick, I could bring a guest. I decided to invite my daughter Rachel.

On 9 November we arrived, all gussied up, at the hugely impressive new building sited behind the British Library, along with 2,000 other guests. I was unsure of the precise arrangements for the formal ceremony but was surprised to learn, at the very last moment, that only Jim Watson and I were scheduled to meet the Queen.

On arrival she was introduced to Jim by Sir Paul Nurse, another Nobel laureate and director of the Francis Crick Institute. Jim spoke in glowing terms about Francis and his contribution to science before Paul Nurse introduced me to the Queen. We made pleasant small talk about Crick, Watson, DNA and the wonderful new building; then Paul Nurse decided to remind her that it was time for the unveiling. As she moved away I muttered something like, 'I hope you find it interesting.'

Paul Nurse made a short speech and then the Queen unveiled the portrait. Once the purple drape had fallen to the ground, she carefully examined the painting together with the Duke of Edinburgh.

The Queen almost immediately came back and commented, 'It is rather interesting' with an emphasis on the 'is' before adding, 'the painting seems to be made on two levels.' 'That's to accommodate his hands which are three-dimensional and cast from life,' I explained.

'How intriguing!'

'Of course,' I replied, 'they're not cast from Francis Crick's hands, as sadly he is no longer with us, but rather from my own hands. Oscar Wilde once said that a portrait can often amount to a self-portrait.'

However before I could deliver the relevant few lines from *The Picture of Dorian Gray*, when Basil Hallward, who painted Dorian, declares 'every portrait that is painted from feeling is a portrait of the artist not the sitter', Philip intervened, resolutely pointing at Watson, 'Have you painted him?'

'Er… yes,' I replied.

'Well, where's the picture?'

'It's in the School of Genetics in Trinity College Dublin.'

'Ridiculous,' he snorted. 'It should be here.'

With that, the royal party left the building.

CHAPTER 23

Malignant Shame

C olm O'Gorman, executive director of Amnesty International Ireland, once observed that, 'We Irish are known for our love of words, for our verbosity, but for all that, we are poor at having big conversations. When it comes to the big things, the issues that define us or make us uncomfortable, then we often become more hushed.'

And Garrett O'Connor, the psychiatrist whose speciality was the treatment of addiction, argued that this reluctance by the Irish to face up to key issues is a direct consequence of our specific history; to furnish a comprehensible explanation, he drew upon his own clinical experience. He suggested that, 'Children who are subjected to severe and prolonged abuse by parents or other authorities tend to internalize the abuse in the form of a behavioural syndrome characterized by pathological dependency, low self-esteem and suppressed feelings.' He called this 'malignant shame', and warned that, 'As adults, shame-affected children are likely to abuse their children in much the same way as they themselves were abused by their parents, thus transmitting the syndrome of malignant shame to the next generation.' He then went on to ask the question, 'Could a similar process exist at the cultural level, whereby prolonged political or governmental abuse of an entire population might be internalized as malignant shame by the institutions of society, and transmitted unwittingly to subsequent generations in the policies and conduct of government, church, school and family?' He concluded by speculating that 'There is reason to believe that such a cultural process has been endemic in Ireland for many centuries, and that its destructive consequences… for example low self-esteem, pathological dependency, self-misperceptions of cultural inferiority and suppression of feelings, are a fundamental cause of contemporary psychological, social, political and economic distress in the country.'

Without doubt the nineteenth century proved to be an extremely unsettling and traumatic time for Ireland and the Irish people. It started off badly with the Act of Union of 1801, a measure designed to inhibit further rebellions like the one staged by the United Irishmen in 1798. The act abolished the Irish parliament and transferred all power and control to London. Even though the dissolution of the parliament hardly represented a catastrophic blow to Irish democracy, since only Protestants could then stand for election, nevertheless its dissolution did represent a symbolic assault on Ireland's prestige and self-esteem.

After all, eighteenth-century Dublin, with its own parliament, had been recognized as the second city of the British empire, and boasted elegant Georgian squares, imposing public buildings and unique cultural events like the first performance of Handel's *Messiah* at Fishamble Street Music Hall; but after the Act of Union, focus gradually shifted to the imperial centre of London, and as a result Dublin lapsed into a peripheral position, simply another provincial city among many within the United Kingdom.

By 1841 the population of Ireland had expanded to over eight million and a sizeable proportion of those people, rural and impoverished, was sustained by the potato, the staple food of the poor. In the autumn of 1845, about one-third of the crop failed due to contagion by a previously unknown fungus. The Tory government in London attempted to alleviate the suffering with shipments of Indian corn, but in 1846 those shipments were stopped when the Tories were replaced by the Whigs. The Whigs were deeply attached to the ideology of *laissez-faire*, a belief that the state should not meddle in the economy and should instead leave market forces to determine the outcome. To make matters worse, they were ill disposed towards Irish Catholics, believing that the famine was a just punishment from a wrathful God for their sinful and rebellious attitudes. Charles Trevelyan, treasury secretary and the man responsible for famine relief in Ireland, wrote in 1848, 'The great evil with which we have to contend is not the physical evil of the famine but the moral evil of the selfish, perverse and turbulent character of the people.'

In under five years, a million people died from hunger, famine fever, typhus, dysentery and scurvy, and nearly two million, despairing of any future in Ireland, fled overseas. It was a calamity on a scale so vast that it probably would have overwhelmed any government, even one

An Gorta Mór, stained-glass window, 2014, Museum of the Great Hunger, Quinnipac University, Connecticut, USA.

disposed to deal sympathetically with the problem. The Whigs were not. At best, they regarded the Irish as irresponsible, and the economic theory that they espoused made Britain rich while Ireland starved. After the famine, many Irish people questioned whether Ireland could ever be governed justly by the British.

The story of Irish nationalist self-assertion after the Act of Union is a familiar one – the mass protest movements led by Daniel O'Connell for Catholic emancipation and repeal of the union; the birth of the Home Rule parliamentary party after the failure of the Fenian Rebellion; the militant agrarian campaign against English landlord power that fused with Parnell's political movement; the eventual disillusionment with merely parliamentary tactics that led to the Easter Rising of 1916, followed by the brutal War of Independence and the brief but even more destructive Civil War.

Out of the ashes a new state was born. But from the very start, its aims and objectives were the polar opposite of those hoped for by the republican men and women who rose up in 1916. In his book *Ireland: A Social and Cultural History*, Terence Brown wondered how 'a revolution fought on behalf of exhilarating ideals, ideals which had been crystallized in the heroic crucible of the Easter Rising, should have led to the establishment of an Irish state notable for a stultifying lack of social, cultural and economic ambition'.

The answer, of course, was to be found in the social forces that came to dominate the new state. Naturally, the defeated republicans, languishing at the political margins, played no part whatsoever in its formation; and elements of the left, who had helped formulate the Democratic Programme of the First Dáil were similarly deemed irrelevant to the needs of the new dispensation. Consequently, the newly emergent Catholic middle class took control of the state, described by Terence Brown as one 'in which a conservative nationalist people, dominated by farmers and their offspring in the professions and in trade, believed that they had come at last into their rightful inheritance – possession of the land and political independence'.

The Irish Free State, according to Browne, manifested 'a social order largely composed of persons disinclined to contemplate any change other than the political change that independence represented'. For example, as early as 1923, at a meeting of the Cumann na nGaedheal governing party, John Marcus O'Sullivan admitted that 'Getting rid of foreign control rather than vast social and economic changes was our aim.'

Kevin O'Higgins, a government minister and a leading ideologue of the Free State, certainly had the clearest view of the new social order. In his book *The Irish Counter-Revolution*, John Regan states that O'Higgins 'wanted to integrate into the new regime his people, the risen Catholic nationalist middle-class elite, which had emerged through politics and the professions in the nineteenth century, and which had been swept aside at the moment of their inheritance by a Sinn Féin revolution'.

Clearly what O'Higgins was advocating was not continuity with the recent revolutionary past but rather a complete break, followed by the re-establishment of the pre-existing social and economic status quo.

Unsurprisingly, the priests and hierarchy of the Catholic Church observed developments with some satisfaction. After all, in the past they had consistently clashed with Irish revolutionary and radical movements, so the slow emergence of a conservative state from the ashes of revolution provided them with a positive omen as regards their future relationship with the new rulers. Being obsessed with sexual continence, the bishops saw dangers everywhere, and in a pastoral letter warned that 'The evil one is ever setting his snares for unwary feet. At the moment, his traps for the innocent are chiefly the dance hall, the bad book, the indecent paper, the motion picture and the immodest fashion in female dress.' Hence they lost no time in making their political influence felt. One of the first pieces of legislation introduced by the new government was the Censorship of Films Act in 1923, to be followed six years later by the Censorship of Publications Act.

Terence Brown wrote that, 'The greatest crime perpetrated by censorship was not the undoubted injury done to Irish writers, nor the difficulty experienced by educated men and women in getting hold of banned works, but the perpetration of cultural poverty in the country as a whole.'

However, far more significant, in terms of the future relationship between the Catholic Church and the new Irish state, was the abdication by the government from the responsibility of providing adequate welfare for many of its citizens. Now, whether this was due to economic constraints or lack of interest is a moot point, but this obvious neglect allowed the church to step in and provide much-needed services, particularly in the spheres of health and education.

The consequences of this over-reliance by the state on the church proved to be far-reaching indeed, since, as well as providing services, the church felt free to impose strict Catholic rules and regulations in the many schools, hospitals and institutions under its care; and distressingly, many vulnerable women and children were exposed to terrible abuse.

Perhaps, however, the most dispiriting practice by the Free State was its unwillingness to innovate. When it came to the formation of institutions, the government invariably chose to imitate rather than originate. For instance, instead of drawing upon the experience gained by republican or people's courts during the War of Independence, the state instead opted to embrace the British system of justice with all its symbols of privilege: supercilious phraseology, judges and lawyers festooned in multifarious wigs and gowns, and so on. This unfortunate tendency became so endemic in Irish life that the writer Seán Ó Tuama felt inclined to write in 1972 that, 'One has only to think for a very brief moment of the various aspects of Irish life today to realize that, as a people, we have few ideas of our own, that our model in most cases is still the English, or sometimes American, model. In business, science, engineering, art, architecture, medicine, industry, law, home-making, agriculture, education, politics and administration – from economic planning to PAYE, from town planning to traffic laws – the vast bulk of our thinking is derivative.'

At about the same time, the writer and artist Brian O'Doherty coined the phrase 'doppelgänger provincialism' to characterize that same compulsion to emulate rather than originate. After all, what other explanation can there be for the monotonous habit of not adequately recognizing talent in Ireland before it has been acclaimed by others in foreign centres of culture? This need for approbation by others, considered (however unconsciously) as superior, represents, without question, a pathology of low self-esteem and self-misperceptions of cultural inferiority.' Another embarrassing habit is our rush to adopt famous international figures with the slenderest connection to Ireland in the forlorn hope that some of their glory might rub off on us. In the case of the English painter Francis Bacon, who happened to be born in Dublin, the repost to the Duke of Wellington's Irishness seems singularly appropriate: 'Being born in a stable does not necessarily make one a horse.'

Worst of all, however, is the predisposition by many Irish commissars of culture to elevate and promote only those local creators whose work most closely resembles the latest international fashion.

This enthusiastic endorsement of local artists who practise a provincial variant of the latest international success is indicative of that 'malignant shame' to which Garrett O'Connor refers.

Of course, malignant shame doesn't just impact on cultural activity; it seeps into most aspects of Irish life. Certainly the inadequate response by our leadership to the catastrophic economic collapse that followed the disastrous bank bailout of 2008 was greatly influenced by aspects of our addiction to shame. Our inept leadership seemed to approach the negotiations over our future with simply one weapon in their armoury: appeasement – the best boy in the class approach. They kept insisting that since we were 'good' Europeans, our European masters would inevitably respond to our humiliation with sympathy and fairness. Their actual response was the complete opposite. Politicians and bureaucrats in Europe viewed the Irish position as one of weakness, and imposed the severest of burdens on the Irish people. We now know that the bailout of Irish banks was imposed in order to guarantee that European banks, especially German state banks, who foolishly lent colossal sums to private Irish financial institutions, would get their money back. Because of the ineptness of our disastrous leadership, ordinary Irish citizens will now be forced in perpetuity to bear an unjustifiable burden of unsustainable debt.

We heard the boast that our bank bailout would be the cheapest in the world but it quickly turned into the most expensive bank bailout in history.

Looking back I believe that a hundred years ago, a window of opportunity opened, and for five brief years there was a real chance to reimagine Irish identity, to become more comfortable with ourselves and with others and to break the cycle of malignant shame once and for all. Unfortunately that window slammed shut in 1922 with the establishment of a state 'notable for a stultifying lack of social, cultural and economic ambition', as described by Terrence Brown.

Today, as the centenaries of momentous historical events beckon, like partition, the establishment of the First Dáil, the War of Independence, the Civil War and the foundation of the Free State, we should exploit these unique opportunities to begin a national conversation about 'the big issues, the issues that define us or make us uncomfortable' so that we might start the process of change, through revealing our faults and weaknesses – and perhaps some of our virtues as well.

CHAPTER 24

The Spectacle of the Electoral Game

I've lost count of the number of times I've been asked if I ever considered standing for public office. This curiosity reached a climax in 2011 when rumours that I was planning to put myself forward as a candidate in the upcoming presidential election surfaced in the national media. I quickly responded by issuing a statement, claiming that I had no interest whatsoever in seeking such high office; I suggested that I was in the business of painting canvases and not canvassing for votes. To tell the truth, I've never had much faith in the power of electoral politics to deliver the radical changes necessary to bring about even a semblance of equity and justice in society. In my opinion, the democratic franchise was only extended to workers and eventually to women in order to avoid challenges to power by other means. Even today, to quote Colin Crouch's *Coping with Post-democracy*, 'While elections still exist... public electoral debate is a tightly controlled spectacle, managed by rival teams of professionals expert in the techniques of persuasion, and considering a small range of issues selected by those teams. Citizens play a passive, quiescent, even apathetic part, responding only to the signals given them. Behind this spectacle of the electoral game, politics is really shaped in private by interaction between elected government and elites which overwhelmingly represent business interests.'

So even though I've had a life-long passion for politics in general, I have never felt remotely inclined to join any particular political party and participate in the electoral game. Instead, over the years, I have chosen to become involved in various campaigns that, in my opinion, stood some chance of prevailing against the odds.

When I was young I joined the multitudes across the globe protesting against the unjust and violent war being waged in Vietnam. That moral force eventually turned the tide and brought to an end a terrible cycle of death and destruction in Southeast Asia.

Around the same time I supported the campaign for civil rights in Northern Ireland, where the nationalist minority had been treated like second-class citizens by the unionist majority since the foundation of the state. If the modest demands for an end to discrimination had been met then, perhaps the subsequent conflict, which lasted almost thirty years, might have been avoided. Sadly, a deeply recalcitrant unionist government stubbornly refused to budge on the key demands of fair housing, fair employment and equal voting rights and, as a result, the peaceful civil rights campaign was superseded by those who advocated violent resistance to oppression.

In the course of the Northern conflict there were many innocent victims, including those who found themselves in long-term incarceration arising from a flawed British judicial system, which had been reshaped to bolster the political aim of defeating the enemy. Forced confessions, skewed forensic evidence and perverse legal argument resulted in the Birmingham Six, the Guildford Four and many others being given lengthy prison sentences for crimes they did not commit.

Slowly, support campaigns began to be organized, but these were fiercely resisted. In the words of Lord Denning, 'It was better that some innocent men remain in jail than that the integrity of the English judicial system be impugned.'

Eventually the strength of the campaigns was such that truth prevailed and, after far too long in prison, the innocent victims were set free.

For my part, I enthusiastically supported the various campaigns by picketing the British Embassy, attending protest marches and rallies and producing a limited edition print in support of the Birmingham Six.

*

The Afrikaans word *apartheid* means literally 'separateness', and the apartheid laws, policies and practices of the South African government gave rise to an avowedly and systematically racist country, where people of colour, comprising over four-fifths of the population, were crush-

Print published by the Irish anti-apartheid movement.

ingly oppressed. Across the globe, anti-apartheid solidarity campaigns merged to challenge this odious regime. They formed a non-violent movement where boycott became the key tactic. Interestingly, this practice of ostracization owes its name to Captain Charles Boycott, a particularly harsh land agent for the Earl of Erne in Co. Mayo.

The Irish Anti-Apartheid Movement was spearheaded by Kader Asmal, a South African lawyer who held a teaching post in Trinity College Dublin. Many Irish trade unions passed motions pledging support for the movement, but little of practical benefit occurred until a few young workers in Dunnes Stores, taking their union's pledge seriously, refused to handle South African goods. A bitter strike ensued which

Judging murals in West Belfast, 1988.

gained both national and international notoriety. At the time, whenever I walked along Henry Street in Dublin, I showed my support for the strikers by temporarily joining the picket. Finally international pressure of this kind proved too much and the South African regime was forced to release Nelson Mandela, the leader of the African National Congress, from lengthy incarceration and to agree to free and fair elections. In anticipation of Nelson Mandela's visit to Dublin in 1990 to receive the Freedom of the City award, the Irish Anti-Apartheid Movement asked me to produce a limited edition print to mark the occasion. When Mandela arrived, he requested a meeting with the Dunnes Stores strikers and in the course of that meeting Cathryn O'Reilly, one of the strikers, presented him with a framed copy of my Birmingham Six print.

✶

For the people of West Belfast, 1988 was a traumatic year. On 6 March, three unarmed IRA volunteers, Mairéad Farrell, Seán Savage and Dan McCann were shot dead in disputed circumstances by undercover British soldiers in Gibraltar; and when their funerals finally took place in Milltown Cemetery on the Falls Road, the mourners were subjected to a violent attack by the loyalist paramilitary Michael Stone. After the outrage three people lay dead and many more were injured. By the time of their funerals, beginning two days later, there was an understandable atmosphere of heightened tension, so when two undercover British soldiers drove into the cortège, total mayhem broke out as they were dragged from their car and eventually shot dead.

That terrible sequence of violence made headlines across the world, with many sensationalist articles contending that the people of West Belfast were brutish thugs with a permanent attachment to violence. I was disheartened by such vitriolic commentary, but there was little I could do about it; that is, until I received an unexpected letter. It was written by the member of parliament for West Belfast, Gerry Adams, someone I knew by reputation but had never met. In it, he pointed out how upset the people of West Belfast were with the negative depiction of their community, and outlined their determination to challenge that one-sided representation. They had decided to stage a *féile*, or arts festival, in order to bring to light the more positive aspects of life in West Belfast. The beginning of August marked the anniversary of internment when in 1971 thousands of nationalists were rounded up and jailed without any judicial proceedings. It was traditionally a time of bonfires and rioting when the RUC and the British army came in and things became violent; so the strategy of the *féile* was to present an alternative and get young people off the streets. Gerry Adams finished the letter with an invitation from the *féile* committee seeking my participation in the first festival, scheduled for August 1988.

I gave the invitation considerable thought. On the one hand I realized that, without any doubt, involvement in a festival in West Belfast would be interpreted by some as evidence of support for violence; yet on the other hand, the concept of ordinary people turning to culture appealed to my own view of the role of the arts in society. I decided to respond positively to the invitation. It was agreed that for the first *féile* I would give a talk on 'The Irishness of Irish Art', and judge a mural competition.

I drove North through the heavily fortified British army checkpoint at Newry and the openly militarized atmosphere on the rest of the

Gerry Adams, oil on canvas, 76cm x 152cm, 1997, Belfast Media Group.

journey, with more army roadblocks and armed foot patrols. I finally arrived in West Belfast in time for my first engagement, a meeting with Gerry Adams. I was fascinated by the prospect of engaging with someone who was so reviled in the media yet who, in person, turned out to be both affable and good humoured. He warmly welcomed me, and passed on the organizers' appreciation of my willingness to participate. He reiterated the reasoning behind the establishment of Féile an Phobail ('festival of the people'). It would be a genuine people's festival; on one level it would stage art exhibitions and plays, but on another level it would also be a street party. The idea was to provide a platform for the people who lived there, but also to invite others from the wider arts world, almost as an act of solidarity. Adams stressed that as far as the local community was concerned, my participation was entirely sufficient and that identification with armed struggle was neither sought nor desired.

Mary Holland in her column in the *Irish Times* recognized that reality when she wrote about how so few artists from the South, like myself, Tomás MacAnna and Ulick O'Connor, were prepared to make the journey North to participate. 'It would be even better if some politicians, who are ever ready with instant opinions on what should be happening in Northern Ireland, could also attend. They won't for fear of being branded Provo sympathisers, as though the very air of West Belfast might contaminate their reputations.'

That first night I delivered my talk in the Roddy McCorley club on the Glen Road to a fairly appreciative audience, and the following morning, nursing a slight hangover, turned up at an agreed spot on the Falls Road where I was to start evaluating the wall murals of West Belfast. I was intrigued that people with little previous aesthetic experience would turn to a specific visual art form to tell their own story. It rarely happens that art becomes a common point of reference for a social group.

The bulletproof black taxi used by Gerry Adams was waiting to take me to the various mural sites throughout West Belfast. I was joined on the expedition by Adams himself and Bill Rolston, a sociologist from Ulster University, who has published several illustrated books on the subject of murals produced by both communities in the North.

One of the first places we visited was Andersonstown to see a mural that had been painted by local lads, who were standing proudly beside their depiction of IRA volunteers. I remember Gerry Adams talking to them and asking, 'Why did you paint them with balaclavas?'

The two looked at him rather sheepishly and replied, 'We can't paint faces.'

I awarded the top prize to Gerard Kelly for a larger than life mural of Nuada, the Celtic god of war inspired by Jim Fitzpatrick the artist who produced the world famous poster of Che Guevara. Gerry was an ex-prisoner known to all by his nickname 'Macara'. Many republican prisoners used their time in jail to learn Irish, but Gerry Kelly only managed to pick up one phrase: *mo chara*, 'my friend'.

The first Féile by any standard was an outstanding success. Thankfully the week passed off without any real public disorder which, in the past, normally resulted in violent interventions by the RUC and the British army. Most activities in the programme were free of charge and were designed to ensure that the entire community had the opportunity to participate; they ranged from art exhibitions, plays, orchestral recitals and rock concerts to street parties, fun runs, arts and crafts workshops, debates, lectures and cultural evenings. All of this was achieved by a hard-working voluntary committee that received no official funding whatsoever. Nevertheless, in spite of this lack of official support, the committee was fully determined to recast Féile an Phobail as an annual event. For my part, I pledged to travel North each August and take part in what I thought was a worthy and exciting venture.

A few years later, in 1991, I agreed to mount a major exhibition of my portraits in the Belfast Institute of Further Education on the Whiterock Road, formerly St Thomas' Secondary School, where author Michael McLaverty had been the head teacher and where Seamus Heaney taught English. In planning the exhibition I decided to seek support from all the usual funding agencies, but was turned down by all except the Arts Council of Northern Ireland, who offered a small grant. I responded by thanking them, and requested that the money be paid to the festival. They turned a deaf ear to my request and stressed that the grant had been advanced to me personally, and not to Féile ad Phobail. It would be some time before the festival received any official support.

At lunchtime on a beautiful summer's day, I was hanging the portrait show on the first floor of the Belfast Institute of Further Education when Gerry Adams appeared.

'Would you like to go for a dander?'

As I was aware that 'dander' was local parlance for a stroll, I happily accepted the offer. After descending the stairs I spotted his black taxi waiting outside.

'Where are we going?'

'Have you ever been up the Black Mountain?'

The city of Belfast is surrounded by a ring of mountains that stretch from the Black Mountain in the west to Cavehill in the north. As the taxi approached the foothills, I noticed that the road was getting steeper and steeper. Suddenly the black taxi wouldn't go any further.

The driver scratched his head and declared, 'This is as far as we can go.'

It transpired that the door panels were filled with concrete as armour plating, and the massive resultant weight forced the vehicle to stagger to an embarrassing standstill. We got out and started to walk to the top; Gerry was familiar with the terrain, as he frequently walked his dogs on the mountain. On that magnificent sunny day, with all of Belfast laid out before us, it suddenly came to me: I would paint a portrait of Gerry Adams – an image of him looking out over Belfast.

In the final portrait I placed him not on the Black Mountain, looking down on West Belfast, but on Cavehill, looking at the whole city, evoking an association with the founding there by Henry Joy McCracken and Wolfe Tone of the United Irishmen. Gerry Adams stands firmly on a boulder looking out over Belfast, a posture reminiscent of the *Wanderer Above the Sea of Fog* by Caspar David Friedrich. Some time later he remarked, 'I was a bit embarrassed by it, to tell the truth. This was at a time when we hadn't made as much progress in the peace process as we have now, so it is flattering that he would have me looking from Cavehill in this sort of visionary way. There you go.'

The Belfast Institute of Further Education was also used by the Féile for drama presentations, with the premiere of a new play almost every year. *A Night in November* was written by Marie Jones, who came from a Protestant working-class background in East Belfast; it was directed by Pam Brighton, an English producer with the BBC in Belfast. It premiered at the 1994 Féile. A Protestant dole clerk, Kenneth McCallister, played by Dan Gordon, disgusted by the sectarian hatred of the loyalist fans in Windsor Park when the Republic of Ireland team qualified against Northern Ireland for the World Cup, decides to travel out to New York to support the Republic in the finals.

The minimal set, which I designed, featured a set of steps painted red, white and blue, but when the action switches to Dublin Airport, they flipped to green, white and orange. In my entire career in the theatre, I never experienced a simple piece of stage furniture repeatedly stealing a standing ovation.

Mural in Ardoyne, Belfast inspired by a print created for the 'Time for Peace. Time to Go' campaign in 1994.

Following the success of *A Night in November* and working mostly with women from West Belfast, the same team created *Bin Lids*, a title inspired by the practice that caught on during internment in 1971, when women would go out on the streets banging their bin lids to warn people that the army was coming. We staged it as a promenade production, where the audience came in and stood rather than sat. There were three different stages, and the action moved about from one stage to another. The audience were the same people whose stories were being told on stage; this was a truly powerful piece of community theatre.

In 1994, Gerry Adams's personal assistant Siobhán O'Hanlon approached me on behalf of the Féile committee, and asked if I might consider designing a poster for the festival. Siobhán was a small attractive dark-haired woman with a direct manner and a sharp Northern sense of humour. I immediately took to her. She was one of the key players involved in the Downing Street talks that led to the Belfast Agreement, and Jonathan Powell, Tony Blair's long-time chief of staff, admitted that he thought highly of her. Tragically, while still young, she was diagnosed with cancer; but to her credit, she displayed the same dedication to fighting cancer as she did to the republican struggle. At the time, I had been regularly commissioned by Sinn Féin to design the stage for their annual Ard Fheis, and each time Siobhán had my heart scalded trying to obtain daffodils, the symbol of the Irish Cancer Society, to decorate the desks on the stage – whether it was the growing season or not. Sadly, she herself lost her own battle with cancer, and when her funeral was announced I decided, along with another of her Dublin acquaintances and a close friend of mine, Gerry Keenan, director of the Irish Chamber Orchestra, to travel North and attend the interment.

We parked the car near her home on Hannahstown Hill and walked past a media scrum that was awaiting the funeral procession; a typical republican event with pallbearers carrying the coffin draped in the tricolour, accompanied by a colour party.

We stood respectfully on the pavement as it passed, only to be summoned to join the chief mourners directly behind the coffin. We had only walked a short distance when the pallbearers were changed and we found ourselves next in line to carry the coffin. I was both intensely proud to be part of Siobhán's final farewell, but also selfishly concerned that media coverage might include photographs with the by-line, 'Artist carries coffin of IRA volunteer'. I needn't have worried; the pallbearers were once again changed before we even reached the swarm of photographers. Siobhán was a very special person; as they say in Irish, *ní fheicímid a leitheid arís* ('we will not see her like again').

Back in 1994, in response to the poster request, I created an image that featured a bloom bursting free from containment in a block of concrete, while at the same time transforming into a dove of peace. As an image it resonated with the spirit of the times, when peace was longed for and soon coming. I made a graphic version of it which became the logo of Féile an Phobail for many years. The poster image was reproduced on the cover of the development plan, published in 1994, and this document successfully made the case for the commencement of official support. Since then Féile an Phobail has gone from strength to strength, to the extent that today West Belfast hosts one of the largest and most successful community arts festivals in Europe.

✳

Concerned by the lack of public debate on some of the crucial issues of the day, a group of individuals decided to form a non-party political organization called the Irish National Congress in 1989 to campaign on three main issues – peace, justice and unity in Ireland. A committee was formed and I was elected chair. Other committee members came from Fianna Fáil, Sinn Féin, the Labour Party, the Communist Party and the Green Party; some, like myself, had no party affiliation at all. A partial listing of committee members gives some idea of the calibre of those involved in the initiative: the secretary was Caitríona Ruane, who subsequently joined Sinn Féin and became a minister in the devolved Northern administration; Patricia McKenna, a member of the Green Party, was elected to the European parliament; Finian McGrath was a school principal and later a member of Dáil Éireann before being appointed a junior minister in two governments; Liam Ó Cuinneagáin was a primary school teacher before returning to his native Donegal to establish the successful Irish language initiative Oideas Gael; and when I retired as chair in 1995 I was replaced by Mary Lou McDonald, who later joined Sinn Féin. She was elected to the European parliament and then to Dáil Éireann before finally replacing Gerry Adams as leader of Sinn Féin in 2018.

Over the years, the Irish National Congress ran many important campaigns, but undoubtedly one of the most unusual was organized in response to requests for help from communities that lived along the border. For so-called 'security' reasons, many border roads had been made impassable by the British army, a policy that brought enormous inconvenience to local communities. Children going to school had to make lengthy detours, farmers trying to move cattle from one field to another often had to travel long distances through official army checkpoints, and many border towns like Clones were dying because the destruction of the roads cut them off from their hinterlands and markets. Local activists decided to take remedial action by filling in the cratered roads, and in a spirit of solidarity, the Irish National Congress decided to join them. On weekends we would hire a bus and, equipped with Wellington boots and shovels, head north to the border.

One of the first places we visited was an old stone bridge that had been destroyed. It was called Ballagh Bridge.

While we were standing there, an old farmer approached me. 'You're very good to come up,' he said. And then, 'What's your name?'

'Robert Ballagh.'

'That's a Protestant name, but we won't hold that against you.'

I had stumbled into that part of the country where my father's people originally came from. His cousin still lived in a townland near Clontibret called Ballagh's Mill, and I was later to discover that a relative, Archie Harper, married to Lily Ballagh, had been killed in the 1994 loyalist bombing in Monaghan Town.

Each weekend we would travel North, and together with local people fill in a cratered road; but it would only be in use for a day or so before the British army would return and blow it up again. On one particular weekend we'd almost finished the job when I heard a loud whirring sound. I saw two helicopters land in a field on the Northern side. A platoon of paratroopers with red berets advanced towards us, their faces blackened. Several soldiers dropped on one knee, pointing their weapons in our direction. Then I heard the click of safety catches being released.

An officer walked up and stood a foot away from me. 'I'd stop doing that, sir.'

With shovel in hand, I muttered something about European law guaranteeing freedom of movement.

He replied, 'That doesn't apply here. I have declared this an exclusion zone. I am in charge here. I would advise you to step back, sir.'

Believing that discretion is the best part of valour and taking note of the imbalance of power I, together with my fellow amateur road labourers, reluctantly withdrew, with the full intention of returning once again to help in the struggle to keep the border roads open.

CHAPTER 25

Land and Language

When I first began to paint, the dominant approach to image-making in Ireland was to depict the landscape. It was, however, a very specific approach, most memorably described by Brian O'Doherty in his catalogue essay for the 1971 exhibition, *The Irish Imagination*. He referred to painters like Nano Reid, Patrick Collins and Camille Souter as part of a 'poetic genre' in Irish painting, which was deeply affected by the landscape and the Irish light with its long twilights: 'Its atmosphere is characterized by a mythical rather than an historical sense, an uneasy and restless fix on the unimportant and a reluctance to disclose anything about what is painted, never mind make a positive statement about it.'

O'Doherty explained that the reasons behind such painting 'go back to the Second World War which forced Ireland into some of its dullest isolation, when the spiritual powers of tradition and the secular power of the Church were equally oppressive and food and intelligence were both rationed.'

This, he argued, was why many Irish artists ignored the international avant-garde. Mike Catto, an art critic from Belfast, viewed this phenomenon not as 'a reluctance on the part of Irish artists to assimilate international influences but as a basic conservatism which gives these outside influences a subordinate position'.

In the catalogue essay for the 1980 London exhibition *The Delighted Eye*, Frances Ruane further developed this analysis. 'The Irish artist has a different frame of reference and his way of feeling and dealing with the world transfer to his art. Agricultural roots, conservatism, an obsession with the past and a passion for indirect statement shape the way he expresses himself visually.'

Being an impatient artist, full of the arrogance of youth and wishing to change the world, I automatically turned my back on such art, which I saw as old fashioned, and enthusiastically embraced the alternative. I resolved that if the art around me was conservative I was going to be radical: if it was rural, I would be urban; if it was parochial I would be international in outlook; if it was imprecise I would be both precise and direct. In an interview at the time I remarked that, 'I never had any access to the culture that many people think is the Irish culture, the rural Gaelic tradition. I can't paint Connemara fishermen. My experience of Ireland is an urban one and I paint that. It would be dishonest of me to paint anything else.'

Oh! The certainty of youth!

In fact I was not alone in seeing things in such a confrontational manner. In the words of Brian O'Doherty, 'The atmospheric mode was breached in the mid-sixties by Micheal Farrell, whose work, while it indulges some romantic feeling, is aggressive and intellectually hard, giving a lead to a group of confident younger men such as Michael Bulfin, Brian King, Robert Ballagh and Brian Henderson, all untroubled by the self-inquiries of the older generation. This second generation gives to painting in Dublin a diversity and energy it did not have before and most of them show an acute political awareness.'

In addition, it's worth noting that we, as young artists, were not the only people who felt that change was necessary. When Éamon de Valera retired from parliamentary politics in 1959 and was replaced as taoiseach by Seán Lemass, according to Terence Brown, 'a way of life that had once been extolled as the authentic base upon which the nation securely rested' was swiftly abandoned. Because previous economic policies, based on notions of self-sufficiency, were judged to have failed (the fact that 408,766 people emigrated between 1951 and 1961 is eloquent testimony to that failure), Lemass and T. K. Whitaker, a leading civil servant, developed new economic policies that would open up the economy to as much foreign investment as could be attracted by governmental inducement. Obviously their main goal was to improve the material conditions of the Irish people, but there were others who would not be satisfied by an economic revolution alone. For John Waters, a controversial writer and journalist, 'It was not simply a matter of economic reconstruction, but of a total overhaul of society's self-image.' These 'self-styled modernizers', believing that the past had served Ireland badly, declared war on those values that sustained the past. Those attitudes were 'anti-rural, anti-nationalist and anti-Catholic' and they considered 'any attachment to the Irish language as a mark of backwardness'. They believed that it was necessary to 'identify all undesirable forms of thought with rural ignorance and all progressive ideas with urban enlightenment'.

I must confess that as a young hellraiser I initially felt quite at home in such disputatious company, but very quickly an issue arose which was to drive a wedge between me and the so-called modernizers. In 1968 the nationalist community in the North, which had endured almost half a century of suffering and discrimination, rose up with a peaceful civil rights campaign, only to be met by the full force of a violent sectarian state. Any opposition was met with further repression, which included one-sided internment and the murders of Bloody Sunday. This increasing repression led to armed resistance; a cycle of violence began that was to last almost thirty years.

The modernizers in the south were severely challenged by this development, because, in their view, nationalist resistance to British rule in Ireland properly belonged in the past. In addition, they were deeply concerned that a conflagration beginning in the North might easily sweep south through the whole island and irreparably damage

Overleaf: *Cuan* (Harbour), oil on canvas, sand on panel, 61cm x 122cm, 2001.

the modernization project, especially since at the start of the Troubles the majority of Irish people felt considerable sympathy with the plight of nationalists in the North. Something had to be done, and the use of violence by Northern nationalists provided the opportunity. Anything that, in their opinion, gave sustenance to the Provisionals – like nationalist history, the Irish language or even rebel songs – had to be opposed, and alternative strategies had to be constructed. The rather crude tactic of banning republican nationalists from TV and radio was adopted. Over time, the use of censorship and exclusion were enthusiastically adopted by these erstwhile 'liberal' modernizers. As John Waters wrote, 'What began as a potentially progressive and radical response to a previous hegemony ended up as neurotic and obsessive.' The policies of censorship and exclusion were fatally flawed and, sadly, many years of conflict and death were to pass before censorship was abandoned, inclusion as a policy was adopted and peace and reconciliation became a real possibility. One of the major symptoms of intellectual laziness is the willingness to portray issues in either/or terms rather than admit to any possible complexity.

Personally I must confess that as a young artist I found it both tempting and intellectually convenient to see things in such black-and-white terms; but I found that, as time moved on and a certain maturity began to seep in, issues seemed to exist in myriad shades of grey. Certainly as an artist I felt the rush to ape international trends to be both lazy and inappropriate and the rigid attachment to modernism by many artists to be strangely doctrinaire and inhibiting. Surely another approach, in line with the Irish bardic tradition, described by Declan Kiberd in *Irish Classics*, could prove more apposite: 'The effect of the Penal Laws against Catholics after 1691 was that a conservative, even aristocratic longing on the lips of the poets acquired a radical, even populist purchase because of the extensive repression: and ever since the Irish have produced a strongly traditionalist radicalism which looked back in order to look forward.'

These heretical ideas began to percolate through my work from the late 1970s on, but nonetheless, I must concede that, apart from a few small 'walk-on parts' as background to some of my portraits, the landscape remained outside my concerns. Indeed, the acknowledgement of this absence became a major theme in one of my self-portraits executed in 1983/4 entitled *Highfield*. This painting shows the artist looking out from the studio to the landscape, an obvious source of inspiration for many Irish artists; yet the interior canvas remains curiously blank. In addition, the torn Picasso poster on the studio floor warns of the dangers involved in slavishly following international cultural fashions.

The approach of the millennium provided the opportunity for much evaluation of the past as well as considerable prognostication about the future, and this atmosphere tempted me to tackle a genre that had never been a significant part of my work as an artist. After just thirty-five years of painting I decided to try and paint some landscapes. The pictures, however, ended up more complicated than I had originally intended.

I decided to paint the landscape elements with a technique that I had previously developed to create the images that were back-projected as part of the set design for *Riverdance*. Then, because I had to paint a lot of images in a comparatively short period of time, I had realized that my usual technique of layering the oil paint with under-painting and glazing would be too time-consuming; so I'd decided instead to employ the *alla prima* method. According to my art dictionary, this is an Italian term meaning 'at first' and is a method of oil painting in which the final effect is achieved in a single direct application of paint.

Also, I decided that I would not paint recognizable locations, but rather a non-specific sense of place. My intention was to engage with something more mythical and symbolic than simply the picturesque.

When experiencing the landscape there is always more to it than just the panoramic view. A valuable part of the sensation derives from the texture of materials that constitute the landscape; the litter of leaves beneath your feet, the pebbles that you pick up and cast upon the water, the sand on the beach that takes the impression of your boots. The inclusion of such textural elements became extremely important. The construct I chose to accommodate such different components was a horizontal polyptych (a painting containing several panels) with the *predella*, or lower panel, containing textural elements.

Oileán (Island), oil on canvas, gold leaf on pebbles, 40cm x 122cm, 2001.

There remained one more component that I felt inclined to include in these new pictures, and that was text. With the Irish landscape as a subject, it seemed obvious to me that the text should be in the Irish language. After all, the names of all places and geographical features originally would have been in Irish. Indeed, it was only in the early nineteenth century that the local Gaelic place names were rendered into English. The consequences of this administrative action form the basis for Brian Friel's masterful play *Translations*. The stage directions for Act 2, Scene 1 are as follows: '(Lieutenant) Yolland's official task is to take each of the Gaelic names – every hill, stream, rock, even every patch of ground which possessed its own distinctive Irish name – and Anglicize it, either by changing it into its approximate English sound or by translating it into English words.'

Because they distil the folk wisdom and popular opinions of ordinary Irish men and women down the ages, proverbs are both

ancient and anonymous, qualities that seemed appropriate to the project in hand.

There is a view that the painted image, by its very nature, tends towards ambiguity and that it frequently requires the accompaniment of text to tie down its true meaning. Consequently, I find it somewhat ironic that even though I have chosen proverbs that refer, in literal terms, to the created images, their real significance lies elsewhere. Admittedly, at times they may refer to mountains, trees, stones and tides, but of course what they are really dealing with is the human condition.

What began as a simple exercise in redressing an imbalance – no, a vacuum – in my work, became something altogether more complex. I hoped that the pictures would bear adequate witness to my respect for the land and language of Ireland. It was entirely appropriate that my exhibition *Land and Language* took place in 27 Pearse Street, the house where Patrick and Willie Pearse were born.

CHAPTER 26

Who Fears to Speak
of Easter Week?

O
n a November evening in 2014 the government of the day, a
coalition between the conservative Fine Gael party and the
Labour Party invited the relatives of the participants in the
Easter Rising and other guests to an event in the GPO, where it planned
to announce its official centenary programme.

The centrepiece was a video presentation called 'Ireland Inspires'
that airbrushed the men and women of 1916 out of history in the very
location where they had made history. No images of the signatories of
the Proclamation of the Irish Republic were on display. They had been
replaced with images of Queen Elizabeth II, David Cameron, the Rev.
Ian Paisley, Bono, Brian O'Driscoll and multi-national companies like
Google and Facebook. The relatives and journalists at the event were
shocked and dismayed. Public reaction was immediate and hostile and
the offending video was swiftly taken offline.

Those of us who had already formed a committee with the aim of
ensuring that an appropriate commemoration of the centenary would
take place were galvanized into action. This organization, 'Reclaim
the Vision of 1916, a Citizens' Initiative' was publicly launched on 4
January 2015 in the Pearse Centre, the Pearse family home in Dublin.

There was a large press turnout, probably due to the government's continuing failure to respond to the public derision of their own ill-considered proposals.

Journalists immediately launched a barrage of questions:

'Would you invite Queen Elizabeth II to your commemorations?'

'Would you have any objections to members of the British Royal Family attending the official 1916 commemorations?'

I replied that we had no intention of inviting members of the British Royal Family, but if a situation arose where other Royal Families in Europe were officially invited then it might be appropriate for members of the British Royal Family to attend. However I reminded the press that those who took part in the Rising actually went out to end British imperialism in Ireland.

James Connolly-Heron, James Connolly's grandson, was also interrogated about the British Royal Family. After dealing with roughly the same question three times, with some exasperation, he retorted,

Speaking at the seventy-fifth commemoration of the Easter Rising in 1991.

'I tell you what, let's invite the relatives of the firing squads over as well, to meet the relatives of those they shot!' This was greeted with widespread laughter. The message delivered at the press conference was that the people of Ireland could not rely on the government to mount a proper centenary commemoration, and that it was up to the citizens themselves to organize an appropriate and relevant alternative.

The launch received widespread coverage. It probably provoked the government into embarking on a programme more in tune with the public mood, which would culminate in a military parade on Easter Sunday, 24 March 2016. On the other hand the 'Reclaim the Vision of 1916' organization had always intended that its programme of activities would culminate with a major parade and pageant on 24 April, the actual calendar date of the Rising in 1916, when the GPO was captured and Patrick Pearse read out the Proclamation of the Irish Republic.

As I didn't receive an invitation to any of the official ceremonies on Easter Sunday, I vowed to avoid the city centre and, instead, spend the time with my grandchildren. A call from the BBC., several days before the Easter weekend, caused me to alter my plans.

It was the BBC. World Service in London asking me to participate in their live broadcast on Easter Sunday from the media reviewing stand in O'Connell Street opposite the GPO.

I accepted the invitation and they then inquired, 'Do you have any official accreditation?' I had to explain that I didn't, but they quickly assured me that they'd get it for me.

The next day London called back to say that my official accreditation would be available to collect at the media centre in the Department of Education in Marlborough Street on Easter Sunday morning. Oddly, they cautioned me to bring my passport. Since I live in Dublin's inner city, this particular instruction seemed, at the very least, quite puzzling, but on Easter Sunday morning, having walked the short distance from my home to O'Connell Street, the reasoning behind the precautionary advice was forcefully revealed.

An impenetrable exclusion zone had been set up around O'Connell Street, the like of which I hadn't seen since the security lockdown imposed on the city for the visit of Queen Elizabeth II in 2012. I found myself forced to make a wide detour to get into Marlborough Street and then I had to produce my passport to get into the Department of Education. Armed with my accreditation, I had to wait in the Department until it was time for the broadcast and was taken, under Garda escort, through the security cordon to O'Connell Street and took my place with the BBC team on the reviewing stand.

At midday my interview began, with the BBC presenter asking how I felt about what was planned for the day. I admitted that I was less than comfortable with the government's proposals, but to explain myself I quoted the British historian Bernard Lewis who had argued that those in power always strive to control the presentation of the past in order to make sure that their version of the past buttresses and legitimates their own authority. I told the radio audience that the purely military ceremony, where the people had no role to play other than as spectators, had little to do with commemorating or celebrating the vision of the men and women of 1916 and everything to do with providing a photo-opportunity for the political elite to clap themselves on the back.

As the official ceremony unfolded it quickly became apparent that the whole affair had been set up and stage-managed to be seen by a T.V audience rather than the general public. This perception was confirmed when I witnessed Taoiseach Enda Kenny's arrival outside the GPO being greeted by audible derision from some members of the public who were corralled out of sight above Parnell Street, but could see what was happening on huge TV screens. That small but negative response did not feature in the TV broadcast.

I was well placed to see the serried ranks of smug and self-satisfied politicians and ex-politicians filing into the VIP viewing stand sited beside the GPO and opposite the media platform. Many of them were the very ones who, through their failed policies, had destroyed the economy and the lives of so many people. On another occasion they would not have dared to show their faces in public, but on Easter Sunday 2016 they were safe: there were absolutely no members of the public in O'Connell Street.

In spite of my own reservations, I had to accept that official Ireland in responding to the state commemoration came to an entirely different conclusion. The mainstream media were stuffed with extravagant and often misleading reports describing how the commemoration had been a great success.

For example, a leading journalist wrote a glowing article in the *Irish Times* describing how 'the people of Ireland had reclaimed the streets of Dublin'. Her assertion was well wide of the mark; it was the army that took over the streets of Dublin on Easter Sunday and not the people.

Exclusion was the order of the day, and perhaps ironically that exclusion mirrored the true nature of contemporary Irish society. The exclusion felt by the unacceptable numbers of homeless people, the exclusion experienced by people on trolleys in our hospitals waiting for treatment, the exclusion and despair behind one of the highest suicide rates in Europe, the exclusion that condemns one in six Irish children to a life of poverty and the literal exclusion of those, forced by economic circumstances, to emigrate.

As far as the 'Reclaim the Vision of 1916' initiative was concerned, the controlling and elitist nature of the State's commemoration only strengthened its resolve to make sure that the events being planned for 24 April would be open to all. With that goal in mind, we opted for a parade that would be fully inclusive and that would allow the people themselves to progress through the streets of Dublin in a rousing, unfettered celebration of the vision of 1916. It also decided, since the true vision of 1916 had never been fully implemented, to choose the 'Proclamation of the Irish Republic' as the theme for the parade.

At two o'clock in the afternoon of a balmy 24 April 2016, a massive crowd began to gather in Merrion Square, ready to march to the GPO in a rousing celebration of the Easter Rising. A later time than usual had been chosen to avoid a clash with several other events scheduled earlier in the day.

On seeing the huge numbers in the square, our committee felt not only delighted that so many had answered the call, but also took comfort from the fact that extensive plans had been put in place to ensure that the parade went off safely. Many meetings had already been held with both the Garda Siochána and Dublin City Council. We were represented at those meetings by Brian Treacy, the production manager of the theatre in Liberty Hall. Bearing in mind that the 1916 Proclamation had been chosen as the theme for the parade, I designed six colourful street-wide banners emblazoned with relevant extracts that could be used to break the parade up into more manageable sections.

For example, the people from Rossport, Co. Mayo, who campaigned against the unjust exploitation of the Corrib gas field, the Right2Water campaign, AFRI (a campaign group that focuses on, among others, global environmental issues), Fracking Free Ireland and the Woodland League all marched behind a bright yellow banner with the ringing statement that, 'The Irish Republic declares the right of the people of Ireland to the ownership of Ireland.'

A green and gold banner with its assertion that 'The Irish Republic guarantees equal rights and equal opportunities to all its citizens' was followed by Clerys workers, who were sacked from the famous Dublin store that closed with half an hour's notice in 2015 after 150 years of trading; the Dublin Council of Trade Unions, Dunnes Stores workers, all the leading trade unions, the Irish National Organization of the Unemployed, the Housing Action Network, the Repeal the Eighth Amendment campaign and several Irish language organizations.

The Irish Anti-War Movement, Shannonwatch, PANA (the neutrality alliance) and the People's Movement all fell in behind a blue and yellow banner with the clarion cry 'The Irish Republic declares the unfettered control of Irish destinies to be sovereign and indefeasible.'

The oft-quoted slogan, 'The Irish Republic cherishes all the children of the nation equally' welcomed contingents from the Irish Travellers Movement (with a horse and a barrel-topped caravan), SARI (the anti-racist sports organization), a support group for recovering addicts, the gay community, the Irish Cuba Solidarity Campaign, Palestinians living in Ireland, the Romanian community, the Kurdish community and people living in direct-provision hostels.

Finally, behind a bright red banner that proclaimed 'The Irish Republic declares its resolve to pursue the happiness and prosperity of the whole nation and all its parts,' marched various political organizations including Sinn Féin, People Before Profit, the Communist Party of Ireland and the Workers' Party.

It took enormous patience on the part of the voluntary stewards not only to impose some coherence on the gathering, but also to insert over thirty noisy bands into the great throng. At around three o'clock the excitable crowd, having been marshalled into a reasonably orderly parade, set off with St Joseph's Longstone Pipe Band from Co. Down leading the way, followed by a colour party bearing the Irish tricolour and flags of the four provinces. Next came Crióna ní Dhálaigh, the lord mayor of Dublin, followed by girls from Craobh O'Toole GAA Club, in team colours, holding seven large gold medallions that featured portraits of the seven signatories of the Proclamation.

Then, marching in procession, fifty women from both Ireland and abroad carried between them a huge version of the 1916 Proclamation printed on cotton. They were wearing Irish Volunteer, Cumann na mBan and Citizen Army uniforms that they had made themselves in the months preceding the parade.

Meanwhile, behind a banner printed with James Connolly's celebrated slogan, 'We Serve Neither King nor Kaiser, but Ireland,' the 1916 Relatives Association marched together with the Liverpool 1916 Group, the Tom and Kathleen Clarke Association from Brooklyn, New York, a large contingent of lawyers and trade unionists from Australia, the Connolly Association from the UK and the Cabra Historical Society in their Irish Volunteer uniforms. They were followed by the 1916–21 Club, the Save Moore Street campaign, the Flames not Flowers street theatre company, the Raging Hormones singing group and the large, colourful Limerick Soviet banner.

As the parade slowly made its way through the streets the Dublin, crowds began to gather at the stage that had been erected in front of the Spire. A film of the seventy-fifth anniversary commemoration was shown on a large screen installed at the back of the stage, while the singer and musician Don Baker entertained the crowd. There were performances from pipers Tiarnán Ó Duinnchinn, John O'Bríen

Overleaf: *Birth of the Irish Republic*, a print inspired by Walter Paget's illustration in the National Museum that was produced to raise funds for the restoration of the 1916 plot in Glasnevin Cemetery.

and Emer Maycock and harpists Laoise Kelly, Michelle Mulcahy, Úna Monaghan and Paul Dooley.

By that time, even though the tail-end of the parade was only just leaving Merrion Square, the women carrying the Proclamation arrived in O'Connell Street to join the huge crowd in front of the stage. The towering historical document was passed over the heads of onlookers and hoisted up to the accompaniment of deafening cheers.

It was now time for the pageant to begin. Unfortunately, we were sadly unable to call on the services of Tomás Mac Anna, who had devised the satirical pageant for the 1991 commemoration, as he had passed away in 2012; but Joe O'Byrne, the writer and director, agreed to oversee the 2016 pageant.

At roughly four o'clock the actor and narrator for the day, Adrian Dunbar, walked on stage, welcomed the massive audience in O'Connell Street and then introduced Lorcán Mac Mathúna and Íde Nic Mhathúna who sang extracts from the *Book of Invasion*s, and Sibéal Davitt who danced to images from the Daniel Maclise painting, The *Marriage of Strongbow and Aoife*. They were accompanied by music played by Dónal Lunny, Daire Bracken and Brian Fleming, and then, to the accompaniment of plaintive music played by Cormac Breathnach on the low whistle, Adrian Dunbar described the tragedy of *An Gorta Mór*, the Great Famine, preparing the way for actor David Herlihy to recite, with the thrum of percussion, a heartrending poem entitled 'The Song of the Famine'. Adrian Dunbar than spoke about the Literary Revival and the role of W. B. Yeats, who was not just a poet of mythology and mysticism, but through his work also reflected on the events of his day. His potent poem, inspired by the Dublin Lockout, 'September 1913', was recited by David Herlihy. This was followed by a short film clip featuring Rory O'Neill, aka 'Panti Bliss', reading a brief extract from Oscar Wilde's 'The Ballad of Reading Gaol'.

Throughout the pageant, striking images provided by Luis Poveda and Conleth White were continually being shown behind the performers, and when several colourful depictions of Patrick Pearse appeared, the actress Fionnula Flanagan, taking her place centre stage, delivered a powerful reading of Pearse's poem 'The Fool', and concluded with his famous oration at the graveside of Jeremiah O'Donovan Rossa.

Just as Pearse's words spoke eloquently about his own time, the young poet Stephen Murphy in his caustic poem, 'Was It for This?', challenged current reality:

> Was it for Biffo citing Lisbon as the only show in town
> Inviting Europeans to kick us while we're down
> Inciting fear amongst a people in need of some relief
> From the systematic slaughter of our nation's self-belief?

It was at this point that the most spectacular sequence of animated images was shown, illustrating the succession of executions in Kilmainham Gaol. The disturbing and powerful visuals were reinforced by trenchant drumming by Brian Fleming. Then, with a slight change of mood, Lorcán Mac Mathúna sang Pearse's '*Fornocht Do Chonac Thú*', (Naked I saw you) followed by Íde Nic Mhathúna with '*Róisín Dubh*', (Dark Rosaleen), accompanied by Daire Bracken on fiddle.

Adrian Dunbar reminded the audience that, even though many songs commemorated the events of Easter Monday 1916, the most popular by far is 'The Foggy Dew'. He then invited Frances Black on stage, who sang her version with heartfelt sensitivity, accompanied by Jimmy Smith and Eoghan Scott.

This was followed by Patrick Galvin's stirring ballad about the last man to be executed, 'James Connolly', sung with real emotion by Damien Dempsey accompanied by Sean McKeon on pipes. His great performance of this moving song preceded the rousing oration delivered by James Connolly's grandson, James Connolly Heron, in which he castigated the current political leadership for its failure to implement the vision of 1916. He reminded the attentive audience that the men and women of 1916 were prepared to sacrifice their lives for their country, whereas today there are politicians who seem prepared to sacrifice the country for their lifestyles.

Adrian Dunbar then thanked all the citizens, the many organizations and the bands who took part in the parade, as well as the performers and crew; in conclusion, he invited Zeenie Summers, a young black woman from South Africa, to lead the assembled multitude in the singing of the national anthem, 'Amhrán na bhFiann' ('The Soldier's Song').

The events that marked the actual centenary of the Easter Rising were an outstanding success. Our driving ambition was to organize a citizens' initiative, and what happened on the day was certainly that: huge crowds enjoyed themselves without a hint of boisterous or disorderly behaviour. In fact, the police didn't have to deal with a single incident during the parade and pageant.

According to some estimates, at least 80,000 citizens gathered in O'Connell Street to watch the pageant; that particular evaluation represented 80,000 more members of the public than were present, in the same place, for the official commemoration on Easter Sunday. For many citizens it was a day to remember, a day when they had an opportunity to express their pride in their history and their sense of national identity in a truly unapologetic manner.

CHAPTER 27

The Ties that Bind?

S omething that has always puzzled me is my almost Pavlovian tendency to root for the underdog in any sporting fixture, or to instantly sign up in support of some marginal or unpopular cause. Today I can draw some comfort from the fact that many of the controversial campaigns that I backed, with the passage of time and the disclosure of the truth, have been vindicated; nonetheless, this eventual justification provides no real clue as to why I felt driven to support those vexatious issues in the first place.

I notice that many people look to their family history to uncover possible inherited traits that might explain their own behaviour, but in my case such retrospection provided very few clues. My maternal grandfather, Augustus Edward Bennett, known as Eddie, was one of the Westropp Bennetts, a long-established Limerick family of Protestant landowning stock; and I clearly remember, when I was about five or six years old, being taken to 'Ballymurphy', the family home of the Westropp Bennetts in Crecora, Co. Limerick. This was my very first holiday.

At the time, my great-aunt Ada lived there on her own. To my eyes the house seemed enormous and was reached by means of a long

Billy McNamara and myself in my aunt's farmyard.

winding driveway; a ruined gate lodge forlornly kept watch over a dilapidated iron gate. On entering the house I was astonished by the array of exotic objects that adorned the old place. On either side of the hall door there were receptacles for umbrellas and walking sticks fashioned from hollowed-out elephants' feet, and on the walls, stuffed heads of various unfamiliar beasts gazed mournfully down on the inhabitants. My great-aunt's husband had been a colonel in the British army and had shipped these trophies home as a permanent memento of his overseas imperial adventures.

By today's standards the house itself, though spacious, had two distinct disadvantages: it had neither electricity nor running water. To a six-year-old boy, these shortcomings meant very little, but for adults they were more than a little inconvenient and it was only through the toil of servants that domestic existence was rendered bearable. For me, however, each day offered new and fascinating adventures, beginning literally at daybreak when I was woken by the jagged strains of the rooster, whereupon I rushed downstairs and dashed outside to greet Billy McNamara, the farm labourer, who would be ushering the cows into the byre to be milked. Billy sported straight dark-brown hair and a face that seemed to be permanently creased in a toothy grin.

The art of milking a cow by hand is more difficult than you might think, but Billy managed to teach me how to coax a squirt of milk from an udder into a bucket, a skill that sadly I found little use for back in Dublin. Another enjoyable task involved trudging through the fields on an ass and cart, with Billy alongside, to fill a large milk churn with fresh clean water from a bubbling spring that lay some distance from the house. It was this regular supply of clean water that allowed Maureen, my aunt's maid, to do her many chores. When not cooking, making beds or cleaning the house, she was up to her elbows in the large kitchen sink washing dishes or clothes.

The lack of running water created other difficulties. When my mother decided I needed a bath, poor Maureen had to ferry upstairs countless copper vessels containing hot water, heated on the kitchen stove, to fill a hip-bath that sat in the middle of a room with no plumbing whatsoever. There were, of course, no inside toilets, so anyone who was short-taken had to exit the hall door, walk along a path through the trees beside the house and enter an outside toilet or 'privy', strategically built over a running stream. Here they could sit and defecate to their heart's content. Because of the distance to the privy from the house, a somewhat bizarre signalling system was employed, so that when it was occupied the door was to be left open, but firmly closed when the convenience was available for use. Another equally puzzling aspect to the set-up was the interior layout, which had a wooden bench with two polished holes positioned side by side. I wondered, *Why on earth would two people take a shit together?* None of the adults seemed prepared to respond to my many questions on the subject. I decided that the complexity of the toilet arrangements could only give my relatives constipation.

The absence of electricity must have been frustrating for my parents but, as a small child, I adored the moment when darkness fell and oil lamps began to shimmer throughout the old house. For me it was a magical experience that gradually drew to a close at bedtime when I climbed the staircase, illuminating my way by candlelight. The candle was fixed in a big brass candlestick holder, equipped with a funnel-like snuffer, which I used to extinguish the flickering flame before finally falling asleep. In the course of that first holiday we took the opportunity to visit several other fine homes occupied by more of my mother's relatives. Her cousin Zillah lived in Milltown near Bruff, a splendid house with a granite portico and adjoining stables, where Zillah bred racehorses. We also called in on Raheny near Hospital, which was the home of my great-aunt Jane. There I was introduced to the arcane delights of croquet by distant cousins. By this stage of the holiday, I had formed the distinct impression that the major difference between city and rural folk was that people from the country resided in rather large homes. My parents and I, after all, occupied a fairly dingy rented basement flat in Dublin, and nearly all my friends also lived in adjoining rented accommodation. It was only later that I became acquainted with people who actually lived in houses.

Even so, before the end of the holiday, I was forcefully disabused of the idea that country people all lived this way. One day my parents

My parents enjoying their honeymoon.

decided to go golfing and left me in the care of my great-aunt, who promptly fell fast asleep. I was so bored I decided to take action. I made my way along the driveway, out through the huge rusty gates and on to the public highway. I hadn't gone too far when somebody stopped me and inquired as to my intentions. When I replied that I was walking back to Dublin, he wisely decided that a diversion was in order. I was taken to a tiny whitewashed cabin with a clay floor, and seated on a stool beside a smouldering fire. At first the interior seemed pitch black, but as my eyes adjusted to the darkness I realized that I was surrounded by a crowd of strangers, all crammed into this modest space. Everybody wanted to know who I was, what I was doing and where I came from. Eventually an elderly woman broke through the crowd and offered me a mug of milky tea and a cut of home bread.

The Blackrock rugby team with the 1936–7 Leinster Trophy. My father is seated second from the right.

I think I was on my third mug of tea when I was amazed to observe, silhouetted in the doorway, the familiar form of Billy McNamara. He took one look at me, grabbed me by the hand and safely delivered me back to my great-aunt Ada, who was still snoozing away on a seat in the front porch.

I began to develop a curiosity as to why some people ended up in very modest circumstances while others lived lives of plenty. Even though I was only six years old, I already sensed that this was terribly unfair. It was years later, however, that I began to comprehend the complex role played by class in Irish society, a task made extremely difficult because we Irish like to think of class as an English phenomenon and, as the English departed nearly a hundred years ago, we have adopted the ruse of not recognizing class as a significant or relevant factor in Irish life.

A few years ago I was surprised by a phone call from someone called Bruce Andrew Finch, who disclosed that he was my cousin Natalie's son and that he had been researching the Westropp Bennett family. He told me that the following night he was giving a talk on my great-uncle Tom in the Stephen's Green Hibernian Club and invited me to attend. Until then my only recollection of my great-uncle Tom was of a tall, distant old man with a bushy moustache, so what I learned that night was a revelation.

Thomas Westropp Bennett was born in 1867, the son of a British army captain and the first Catholic in an old Limerick family of Protestant gentry. He was elected to serve in local government, but was unsuccessful when he stood for East Limerick in the 1910 Westminster election. Eventually, however, he was elected to the senate for Cumann na nGaedheal in 1922. This was a time of bitter internecine conflict in Ireland, and Westropp Bennett faced a campaign of both arson and intimidation from anti-treaty republicans. The Anglo-Irish treaty had brought to an end the war of Independence; but some opposed the terms of the treaty and this led to a bitter civil war. In 1922 an IRA raiding party arrived at 'Ballymurphy' intent on burning it to the ground, yet even though he was unarmed, Westropp Bennett successfully convinced them to spare the old house. In 1925 he stood for the position of *cathaoírleach* or chairman of the senate, and was unsuccessful; but three years later, after setting out his vision – summed up by his declaration, 'It is the duty of the second chamber to prevent violent change' – he was victorious.

Westropp Bennett believed that his primary role was to maintain the stability of the state. Even though he was a strong supporter of William T. Cosgrave's Cumann na nGaedheal government, he was his own man and pursued a bipartisan policy as chairman of the senate. But after Fianna Fáil won the 1932 election, and fearing the possible establishment of a revolutionary government, Westropp Bennett chaired a series of private negotiations between opposition leaders W. T. Cosgrave and Eoin O'Duffy, which resulted in the rebranding of Cumann na nGaedheal as Fine Gael and the formation of the Blueshirts, Ireland's very own fascists.

Meanwhile tension mounted between the Fianna Fáil government and the senate chaired by Westropp Bennett. While Westropp Bennett strove to maintain the senate's independence, de Valera claimed that it had attempted to 'mutilate government measures or wilfully delay them'. De Valera's frustration culminated in the introduction of a bill in the Dáil to put an end to the senate and, as a result, with its formal abolition on 19 May 1936, my great-uncle's political career was over. Later, in 1945, he became chairman of the Irish Agricultural Wholesale Society as well as vice-president of the Royal Dublin Society. He died in 1962 at the age of ninety-five.

I congratulated Bruce Andrew Finch on his hugely informative talk but, as I was leaving, he surprised me once more by drawing my attention to an elegantly framed oil painting, hanging in prime position at the base of the grand staircase. It depicted a rather ample, self-assured gentleman. Bruce informed me that he was my great-great-grandfather, Edmund Smithwick, a founding member of the club. Now, I was aware that my maternal grandmother Helen was a Smithwick but I knew very little about the family history. I discovered, when I researched this branch of the clan, that Robert Smithwick, who was born in Hertfordshire, came to Ireland in the 1620s and that his son Lt. Col. Henry Smithwick was a soldier in the Cromwellian army. His grandson

The Irish Ladies Hockey team in Germany in 1936.

John arrived in Kilkenny in the early eighteenth century and founded the brewery at St Francis Abbey. His grandson, Edmund Smithwick, bought a freehold lease of the brewery in 1827 and Smithwick beers became very successful in his lifetime. As a close associate of Daniel O'Connell he was active in the campaign for Catholic emancipation. He was also involved in Kilkenny politics for nearly forty years, and served as mayor of the city on three separate occasions. In 1876, the year he died, Edmund Smithwick was listed as owning 800 hectares (2,000 acres) of land in Kilkenny.

The stories of my distinguished ancestors were fascinating, but unfortunately, as far as I was concerned, the lives of those pillars of the establishment failed adequately to explain my own contrarian behaviour. Nevertheless I persisted with the search for further enlightenment.

The union of the Westropp Bennetts with the Smithwicks in the marriage of my grandparents was unusual, to say the least. I learned,

My mother playing golf on the lawn in 'Ballymurphy'.

long after both of them had died, that my grandfather had been married previously, and that his first wife, on her deathbed, had begged her best friend Helen Smithwick to marry Eddie and to look after him. Helen obliged, but the marriage was soon tested by the Civil War, during which Eddie sided with the Free State whereas she supported the anti-treaty forces. I remain convinced that the memory of this bitter personal divide was the main justification for my own mother's reluctance to allow any political debate in her home.

This political vacuum, however, didn't result in domestic silence; on the contrary, my parents' flat resonated with endless discussions and arguments about sport. I suppose this was to be expected, since it was sport that originally brought them together. My mother played hockey for Ireland, and I recollect as a child finding an old photo, taken in Cologne in 1936, of the Irish team in a line-up with their German equivalents. The Irish women are standing rather sheepishly with their hands by their sides while the Germans are defiantly giving the Nazi salute.

My father, on the other hand, excelled in tennis, cricket and rugby, representing his country in the first two and his province, Leinster, in the third. On one occasion, having lost some childhood game, I remember my father cautioning me against being too disappointed by defeat, by recalling an episode from his sporting past. Ireland were playing against Japan in the Davis Cup and against all the odds, my father managed to beat their number one player. This unfortunate individual, unable to deal with the perceived disgrace of defeat, threw himself overboard on the return voyage to Japan. My father cited that tragic outcome as a warning against taking sport too seriously.

My father attended the High School, Dublin, which catered for Protestants and other minorities, so the intake of pupils was necessarily small. This state of affairs was probably beneficial when it came to pupil–teacher relationships but on the playing field, it was an unmitigated disaster. The numbers simply weren't there to make up a half-decent team. More than once my father recalled the misery of playing rugby against the big Catholic schools and inevitably suffering ignominious defeat.

On leaving school, perhaps to avoid future humiliation, my father made the unusual choice of joining the Blackrock Rugby Club. I say unusual because most of the members of that club were past pupils of Blackrock College, one of the big Catholic schools that excelled at the sport. In 1936–7 that strategic decision was rewarded when, for the very first time, Blackrock Rugby Club won the Leinster Senior Cup. According to my father, there was only a single occasion when his religion became an issue. He recalled that one day during practice, the trainer, Wally Finn, a Holy Ghost priest, in urging the forwards to get down lower in the scrum whacked any player whose arse stuck up with a prickly stalk that he had cut from a nearby garden. My father felt that this behaviour was totally inappropriate, so when his own arse got a lash he promptly stood up and felled the reverend father with a single blow. Obviously, being a Protestant, my father didn't harbour quite the same level of respect for a Catholic priest as his teammates, who were shocked by what they saw as a grievous assault on a man of the cloth. They were convinced that his playing days with the club were over. To his credit, Fr Finn arose, dusted himself down, threw away the stalk, continued with the practice session and never mentioned the incident again.

Many say that sport is a great leveller, and certainly my father was warmly accepted by the members of Blackrock Rugby Club. However, when my parents decided to get married, his experience of the Roman Catholic Church was much less cordial. Because the proposed union was what they called a mixed marriage – that is, one between a Catholic and a non-Catholic – Catholic regulations insisted on a Catholic religious ceremony; but the actual wedding service was not allowed in the Catholic church chosen by my mother. Instead my parents were married in the sacristy, the small ante-chamber normally used by the priest when preparing to say mass. My father felt this was an unnecessary humiliation.

Another more serious abasement was the *Ne Temere* decree. This was a promise extracted from the non-Catholic partner in a mixed marriage that all prospective children would be brought up as Catholics. The moment my father agreed to this insidious condition, my future fate was sealed, and I wasn't even born at the time. Coming from a Presbyterian background, where liturgy is somewhat spare, my father confessed to feeling rather dismayed by Catholic ritual. He quipped that, from his perspective, the mass, with the ringing of bells and Latin incantations, smacked of some primitive tribal ceremony. Nevertheless, when I was still quite young, he made the fateful decision to become a Catholic. I was always convinced that this surprising choice was due not to some Pauline conversion, but to a desire to please my mother, who was herself a devout Catholic.

My mother was a very pleasant, well-liked person; but, being both middle class and quite conservative, she was obsessed with appearances, always concerned with what others might think. Unhappily, as an only child, I often found myself the focus of that preoccupation. For some reason my mother hated straight hair, and to her great mortification I was born with the straightest hair imaginable. As an infant she was able to keep it in check with various hair clips, but when I grew up and began to play with other children, acute embarrassment provoked me into removing them, much to my mother's consternation.

Not to be outdone, she opted for a more permanent solution. When she was having her next home perm, she persuaded me to accept the imposition of a few curlers. The result was ridiculous, and I couldn't wait for the humiliating permanent waves to grow out. After that disaster, there was a truce on the hair front, only to be broken many years later when I was about twelve or thirteen.

As an initial salvo my mother proposed, 'Would you like a real American hairstyle?'

Thinking of Elvis Presley's magnificent quiff I immediately accepted the offer, but, after what seemed like an eternity in the barber's chair, I was shocked to observe in the facing mirror an almost bald head looking back at me. It was an American hairstyle all right, but one that was obligatory in the US armed services: a crew cut. My mother was delighted with the result; no unruly hair left standing. But as ever, I couldn't wait for my hair to return to normality.

By the time I was sixteen I had long abandoned the Catholic Church, but so as not to upset my mother, every Sunday I went for a walk and on my return pretended that I had been to mass. One Sunday, whom should I bump into, sauntering through nearby Herbert Park, but my father – who, as it turned out, was engaged in a similar subterfuge.

I'm not sure that my father gained any real spiritual benefit from Catholicism, but I do believe that he found his involvement with the local branch of the society of St Vincent de Paul very rewarding. There was huge poverty in Dublin in the 1950s and I'm sure that he took considerable personal satisfaction from helping the many poor families in the parish.

My father also loved parks, and firmly believed that they, along with libraries and museums, were there for the edification of all the people. An unforgettable childhood memory is of my father slipping out of the hall door, followed by me yelling, 'Where are you going, where are you going?'

He calmly replied, 'I'm going to the National Gallery to see my pictures.'

Confused, I spluttered, 'But they're not your pictures.'

I was left to ponder his parting shot, 'They may not be my pictures, but they're *our* pictures.'

Following that original encounter when we were both playing truant from mass, my father and I took to going on occasional walks together; a practice that persisted long after I got married and even after his grandchildren began to accompany us. I always enjoyed those walks and the conversations that naturally arose in the course of them – some trivial, others more serious. Probably as a result of his own background, my father, in analysing any issue, always imparted to me a sense of the importance of an informed conscience and of not accepting situations blindly. I shouldn't have been so surprised when one day he informed me that he had just resigned from the committee of Elm Park Golf Club. I was surpised because I knew how much he enjoyed playing golf and the camaraderie of the clubhouse, but when he outlined his reasons I immediately appreciated them. He said that he could no longer serve on a committee that discriminated on the grounds of gender, religion, race and class.

I remember saying, 'What do you mean?'

He replied, 'Women are only associate members with no voting rights, and Jews, blacks and working people are denied membership.'

This principled stand, however, did not extend to resigning from the club itself; he rejoiced in playing golf and refreshments at the nineteenth hole far too much! The Irish Anti-Apartheid Movement was established in 1964 to campaign against the scandalous discrimination practised by the South African government against the majority of its people, so when the Springboks, an all-white team, arrived in Dublin in January 1970 to play a match against Ireland, a major protest was planned.

On the actual day of the fixture, over lunch at my parents' flat, my father casually remarked, 'I suppose you're going to the protest at Lansdowne Road?'

Aware of his love of rugby and the fact that he usually attended all home internationals, I cautiously responded, 'Well, yes.'

To my delight, he replied, 'Good. Can I come with you?'

Together we joined the 10,000 protesters who marched from the city centre to the rugby ground at Lansdowne Road. The game went ahead and resulted in a draw in front of a small crowd, and was played behind barbed wire to prevent protesters disrupting the game. I was extremely proud to have protested, together with my father, against the iniquitous South African regime. Sadly my father did not live to see the end of that regime and the election of Nelson Mandela as president of the new South Africa.

*

Reflecting on those formative years, I find myself forced to conclude that the presumptions that inform my own dissenting behaviour, in all likelihood, are not inherited from my complicated family background but were picked up, unconsciously, over many years from a single source: my father – a quiet contrarian.

In 1979, when Pope John Paul II came to Ireland, the whole nation ground to a halt. But not exactly the whole nation. In my own case, as a seriously lapsed Catholic, I felt no affinity whatsoever with the unfolding religious hysteria, so when the day of the papal mass in Phoenix Park arrived, I was determined to ignore the whole affair by spending the day painting in my studio. On the morning in question, however, having walked the short distance from my home to the end of Capel Street, I was astonished to find my passage across the Liffey to my studio in Parliament Street completely blocked by a sea of humanity slowly advancing along the north quays in the direction of the park.

A policeman on duty, who witnessed several of my unsuccessful attempts to breach the phalanx of the faithful, snorted, 'What the hell are you up to?'

I replied, 'I'm trying to cross the bridge.'

'Why on earth would you want to do that?'

I explained, 'I'm going to work.'

Somewhat irritated, he growled, 'You should be going with the rest of them to Phoenix Park.'

However, he then rather reluctantly began to clear a way through the crowd so that I could cross the bridge, muttering at the same time, 'And you call yourself an Irishman.'

That was not the first and certainly not the last time I found myself swimming against the tide.

CHAPTER 28

Bearing Witness

S elf-portraiture is a curious business. When we visit a gallery and find ourselves transfixed by the unblinking stare of an artist, we often find that our response is quite different to our experience when confronted by other pictures. From the deep recesses of our mind a question slowly emerges, 'Why has the artist painted this particular picture?'

We never seem to ask ourselves the same fundamental question about other paintings. We may wonder about the subject of the painting or the location depicted, but we rarely question why the artist made the picture in the first place. There is a reason for this. As we continue to view a self-portrait, it slowly dawns on us that the artist isn't looking at us at all, and that the picture almost certainly has been created by the artist studying his or her own reflection. Thanks to our own complex relationship with our reflected image, this realization renders us slightly uncomfortable. After all, over-indulgence in our own reflected image has always had negative connotations, from Narcissus to the Queen in 'Snow White', with her plaintive, 'Mirror, mirror, on the wall, who is the fairest one of all?'

So our uneasiness may be due to a fear that the artist has succumbed to vanity, or at least an excessive self-regard in the creation of the work. Undoubtedly there are examples of such narcissism in the history of self-portraiture, but most artists seem to be after something else entirely when they seek to record their own likeness. As the novelist Arundhati Roy observed, 'For an artist, a painter, a writer, a singer, introspection – contemplating the self, placing yourself in the picture to see where you fit – is often what art is all about.'

Certainly, when great artists like Rembrandt trace life's journey through their self-portraits, they remind us all of the fragility of life and the nature of the final destination that awaits us all. Laura Cumming notes perceptively in her book about self-portraiture, 'There is surely integrity involved in acknowledging one's shortcomings and flaws and tendency to decay.' In the studio you could argue that the self-portraitist's work takes the form of a soliloquy or monologue; however, once the painting enters the public domain and is seen by another person, the monologue is transformed into a dialogue and in this way the creative process is finally completed. This special, almost intimate, relationship between the self-portrait and the viewer recalls George Berkeley's '*Esse est percipi*' ('to be is to be perceived') – his idea that we only exist when we are perceived by others. In the same way, you could argue that the self-portrait only becomes a true work of art when it is viewed by someone else on the gallery wall.

Laura Cumming writes: 'Self-portraits catch your eye, they look back at you from the crowded walls as if they had been waiting to see you.' Other paintings or portraits do not require quite the same engagement. When an artist paints a portrait of another person, a dialogue of necessity develops between the artist and the sitter, to the extent that when the portrait is finally exhibited this lively conversation can effect a degree of exclusion. We, the viewers, can feel that we are almost intruding on someone else's private talk – a scenario utterly different to the unique dialogue between the self-portrait and its special audience of one. Nevertheless we must accept that until the arrival of photography in the mid-nineteenth century the self-portrait required the artist to develop an almost obsessive relationship with the mirror, a relationship both complex and contrary. For example, when we view a self-portrait that has been painted using a mirror, we tend to accept the resultant image as an accurate representation of the artist, yet the laws of physics would tell us otherwise. When we look in a mirror we find that our right-hand side is on the right-hand side of our reflection and because we have become so accustomed to our reflected image, we judge this representation to be perfectly normal. It's only if we happen to be wearing clothing with some text that we begin to realize that something strange is going on, because the lettering in the reflection appears back to front or, to put it more correctly, laterally

Kilkenny Kite flying in the Hendriks Gallery, Dublin.

reversed. Most of the time we pay scant attention to the contrariness of our laterally reversed reflection, but on occasions our familiarity with it can cause us problems. For example, most men have learnt to knot a necktie by observing themselves in a mirror, yet if asked to knot a tie on someone else, they find themselves completely flummoxed! One solution is to stand behind the person in question, thread the tie around his neck and then make the knot following a procedure that has been learnt from years of practice in front of a mirror. This particular experience clearly points out the variance between what we can see when we directly observe someone and what we see when we look at that person's reflection in a mirror. As previously noted, when we look at ourselves in a mirror our right-hand side appears on the right-hand side of our reflection whereas if somebody else looks directly at us they will discover that our right-hand side is directly opposite their left-hand side. These realities raise certain issues when we look at self-portraits that have been made using a mirror.

Consider Van Gogh's famous *Self-Portrait with a Bandaged Ear*. Most observers could be excused for believing that Vincent mutilated his right ear, but it is most likely that he used a mirror to paint this portrait, so the image must be laterally reversed and therefore the bandaged ear is, in reality, his left one. Certainly, the greatest self-portraitist of them all, Rembrandt understood this left/right conundrum, for when they X-rayed his splendid self-portrait in Kenwood House, they discovered that he had changed his mind when painting the picture and had switched his palette and brushes from one hand to the other. He obviously wished that future generations would know whether he was left- or right-handed. Of course, the left/right conundrum is not the only factor at play when artists use a mirror to create a self-portrait. There is also the thorny question of 'likeness', which bedevils all portraiture.

How often have we heard someone remark about a photograph 'It doesn't look at all like me' when, in fact, what they probably should be saying is that the photo does not resemble the self-image that they confront, on a daily basis, in their bathroom mirror, an image that is, of course, laterally reversed. Now, if our features were truly symmetrical this would not pose a problem, but unfortunately this is not the case. There is a simple test that explains the situation. If we cut a frontal photograph of someone's face down the middle, discard the right-hand side, and then copy and flip the left-hand side to make a new right-hand side and put these two halves together we should have a reasonable likeness of the person's face, that is, if human physiognomy were symmetrical; however, instead we end up with a bizarre face that doesn't remotely resemble the person in question.

This test tells us that not only are our faces asymmetrical but as a consequence, a face seen in a mirror will appear quite different from the same face directly observed. Throughout art history, however, most artists seem to have ignored the issues raised by the employment of mirrors and to have chosen instead to simply get on with their self-appointed task of trying to record some evidence of their own existence. However, for those artists concerned by the complexities raised by the reflected image, the development of the photograph, which could be printed the right way around or, to put it another way, not laterally reversed, offered a real breakthrough. For the very first time self-portraitists were provided with the opportunity to see themselves as others see them, and as a consequence were able to make pictures of themselves that might accurately resemble the perception of others.

There is an argument that it was only with the creation of large flat glass mirrors in Murano in the fifteenth century that true self-portraiture became a reality, in that detailed self-examination became easier. Certainly, previous to this technical development, an artist wishing to record his likeness had to rely on small discs of highly polished metal or small convex glass mirrors first manufactured in the thirteenth century. By the way, such a convex mirror is centrally positioned in Jan Van Eyck's extraordinary painting *The Arnolfini Wedding* and contains a tiny self-portrait.

Whether such small and distorting reflective surfaces inhibited the production of self-portraits or not is a moot point, but certainly up until the fifteenth century artists only gave themselves walk-on roles in their pictures rather like the way Alfred Hitchcock slipped his own image into his movies. A typical example would be Masaccio's

The Tribute Money where the artist paints himself wearing a red cloak, standing to the right of the main group, barely part of the action.

Towards the end of the fifteenth century however, things began to change and some artists, perhaps impatient with their cameos decided instead to cast themselves in 'starring' roles. Albrecht Dürer's powerful self-portraits represent a clear exposition of this new tendency. Yet, surely it was more than just the availability of bigger and better mirrors that motivated this fundamental change of attitude? In his book *Sincerity and Authenticity* the American critic Lionel Trilling questions 'whether man's belief that he is a "Je" (an individual) is the result of Venetian craftsmen having learned how to make plate-glass.' Trilling is in no doubt as to the answer. 'At a certain point in history men became individuals. Taken in isolation, the statement is absurd.

With Seamus Heaney at the unveiling of a bench designed for Child Vision, the National Education Centre for Blind Children. It features a poem written by Heaney.

How was a man different from an individual? A person born before a certain date, a man – had he not eyes? Had he not hands, organs, dimensions, senses, affections, passions? But certain things he did not have or do until he became an individual. He did not have an awareness of what one historian Georges Gusdorf calls internal space. He did not suppose that he might be an object of interest to his fellow man, not for the reason that he had achieved something notable or been witness to great events, but simply because as an individual he was of consequence.'

It was the development of this new sense of self that allowed artists to paint true self-portraits and writers to create autobiographies. 'The subject of an autobiography is just such a self, bent on revealing himself in all his truth. His conception of his private and uniquely interesting individuality, together with his impulse to reveal his self, to demonstrate that in it which is to be admired and trusted, are, we may believe, his response to the newly available sense of an audience, of that public that society has created.'

So we may reasonably conclude that before this extraordinary historical moment of psychological change artists felt no real inclination to engage in introspection or self-examination and certainly, even if they had, the public would have little understanding of the products of such soul searching.

Certainly I have been no stranger to the practice of self-portraiture, in fact one of the very first paintings I made, when I was still in school, was a monochrome self-portrait in a jacket and tie holding a freshly sharpened pencil. However many years were to pass before I returned to such an autobiographical approach with the painting *Number 3*. Although, to be honest, with that particular picture the term 'self-portrait' might seem contradictory, as my face is obscured by a book. In fact, in several paintings from that series my face is either missing altogether or concealed from view. Nevertheless, in all the pictures, I feature in one way or another, but within the context of a wider *mise-en-scène*. I am just one player in an extended cast list.

∗

My 1997 self-portrait, *The Bogman*, is clearly a different proposition. It shows me in Wellington boots, doing something I have never done in my life – digging for turf in a bog. So what's going on here? There is surely ironic humour at play. The obvious metaphor is that of an artist digging for inspiration in ancestral terrain. Seamus Heaney's poem 'Digging' makes an intuitive analogy between his own creativity as a poet and his father and grandfather cutting turf:

> Between my finger and my thumb
> The squat pen rests; snug as a gun.
> …
> My grandfather cut more turf in a day
> Than any other man on Toner's bog.
> Nicking and slicing neatly, heaving sods
> Over his shoulder, going down and down
> For the good turf. Digging.

The Bogman is framed with a stone surround inscribed with lettering spelling out the Irish proverb, *Briseann an dúchas tré súilibh an chait*, literally 'heredity dawns or breaks out in the eyes of the cat', which could be interpreted loosely as, 'You can take the man out of the bog, but you can't take the bog out of the man.'

*

When my artist friends Campbell Bruce and Jackie Stanley returned from a holiday in Italy they presented me with a souvenir from Florence, a pair of underpants embellished with an image of David's genitalia as sculpted by Michelangelo. As it happened, this practical joke provided me with a key to unlocking something that had been troubling me for some time. A few years before, I had visited an exhibition of Lucian Freud's work in London and was struck by a wonderful late

The Bogman, oil on canvas, 200 x 122cm, 1997.

THE BOGMAN

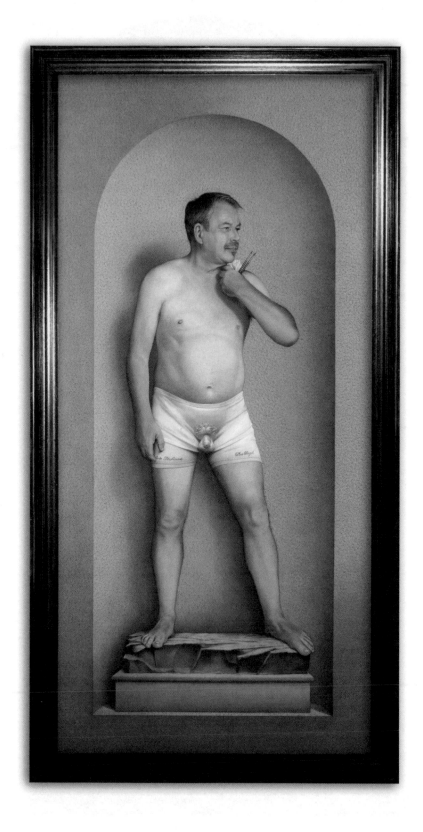

self-portrait. He's standing with a palette and holding a palette knife aloft, and is naked, wearing just a pair of old boots. It's a defiant picture, sort-of saying, *I may be an old fucker, but I'm still painting.* At the time, it definitely tempted me to try another naked self-portrait, but I was reticent on account of previous difficulties with such themes. But with my Italian underpants, I quickly realized that they would create the illusion of nudity, and therefore I could go ahead and paint a nude self-portrait that in fact wasn't nude. Obviously, my physique doesn't resemble David as sculpted by Michelangelo, which is an idealized portrayal of a handsome youth. But I thought there was a certain irony in replacing the beautiful young man with a pot-bellied ould fellow, and the sling shot, which was David's weapon of choice, with paint brushes. I am posed in a classical architectural niche, standing on exactly the same sort of plinth that David stands on in Florence.

Because I've always had a problem with extravagant signatures, I've often surreptitiously incorporated my name into the composition of the picture in hand, rather like the cameo roles played by Alfred Hitchcock in his movies. In this case my name is inscribed as part of my Florentine underpants. Even though the initial inspiration for *Self-Portrait in the Italian Style* was Lucian Freud's provocative self-portrait, I ended up with something utterly different and probably more light-hearted and humorous.

✳

When, on a TV arts programme Declan McGonagle, director of the Irish Museum of Modern Art, remarked that, 'Robert Ballagh is not a real artist, he is a mere illustrator,' a friend, the actor Fionnula Flanagan, picking up on his put-down, made me a present of a book about the artist David Hockney with a personal dedication: 'To the merest illustrator of them all!' It took some time for my own thoughts on the subject to crystallize into a self- portrait, which I finished in 2008,

Self-Portrait in the Italian Style, oil on canvas, 2006.

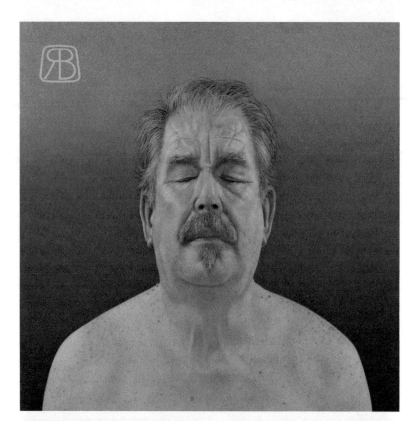

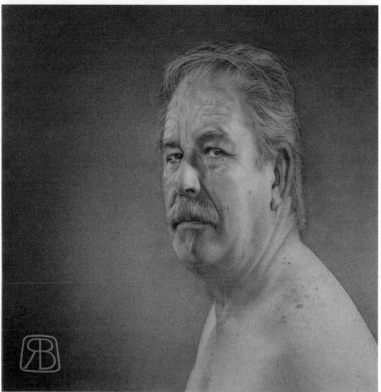

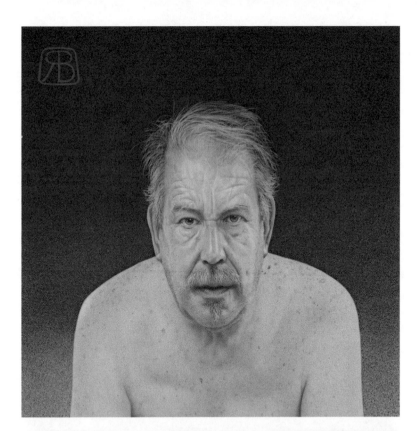

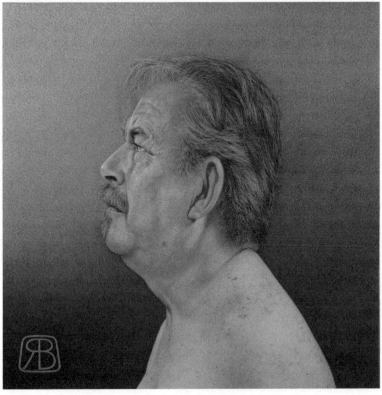

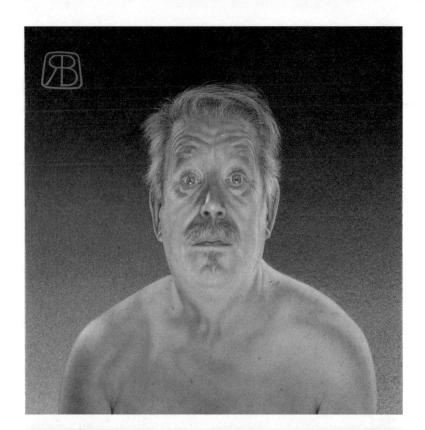

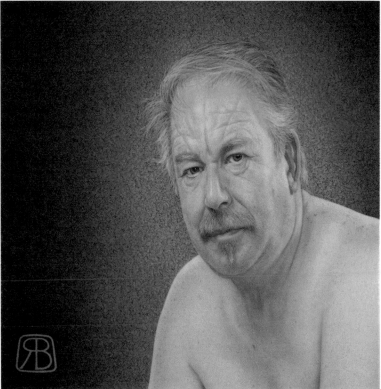

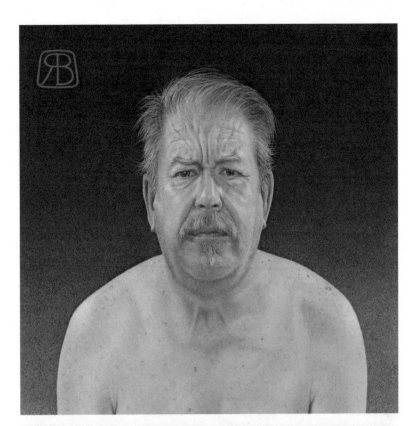

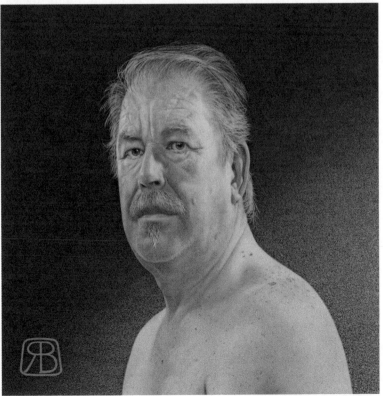

defiantly yet proudly entitled *The Illustrator*. In the painting I stand confronting the spectator, arms akimbo to fit the narrow diamond shape of the composition, holding three paint brushes and wearing glasses. The only other item of note is the white T-shirt I am wearing, which features the slogan 'Fuck the begrudgers'. Brendan Behan's caustic counsel is surely eternally relevant, particularly in Ireland. By the way, even though the painting itself failed to sell, I did receive several inquiries about the availability of the T-shirt.

✶

When Wexford Arts Centre approached me about the possibility of exhibiting during the Wexford Festival Opera of 2010, they inquired whether there was anything I hadn't already done or perhaps something that I might like to do. Sadly, having failed to come up with any tangible ideas when Anya Von Goslin and Karla Sánchez O'Connell from the Wexford Centre, noticing the Castro portrait leaning against the studio wall, suggested a series of self-portraits executed in a similar manner. This prompted an exhilarating yet radically disquieting voyage of self-discovery that lasted about a year. It started with a day-long photo session involving my regular collaborator, the photographer David Davison, in order to create a range of images to use as references for the eventual portraits.

I simply pulled faces and we tried different lighting effects. For the first few I had a shirt on; but since there's no such thing as neutral clothes – they're all tied to time and fashion – I discarded it. For the same reason I took off my glasses. It slowly dawned on me that I was engaging with portraiture in a way that was timeless, avoiding anything that would associate it with a particular period or place. According to Laura Cumming, the author, 'Rembrandt deliberately painted himself out of time, set himself free of the moment.'

This paring away of anything that might provide a clue to my life other than my own unadulterated image was a radical departure for me. Previously my portraits included many objects and allusions that contributed to an understanding of the person portrayed, but now everything was jettisoned to leave only a head and shoulders close up, without any clothes or any other prop, and observed with a forensic precision that laid bare the process of ageing. We took perhaps sixty photographs from which I made sketches, which were then distilled into working drawings for the final paintings. There are eight different poses in the series of self-portraits. Some are looking sideways, others are head on, one with eyes shut. Philip Vann, an English writer and art critic, wrote in the catalogue essay, 'There is a liberating kind of seriousness to these pictures, matched by a more intense and searching painterliness than ever seen before in Ballagh's oeuvre.'

Whether the seriousness is due to being diagnosed with leukaemia is a moot question. However, being told that you have cancer does bring your own mortality into sharp focus. As 2017 approached, I felt it was time to have another close look at myself; after all, a lot had happened in the previous half-dozen years. Once again I booked a photo session with David Davison and was slightly surprised that in spite of all the vicissitudes, I didn't look too bad; admittedly the hair was greyer and thinner and there were a few more wrinkles, but all in all, I seemed to be wearing quite well. This time, I felt that just one self-portrait would be sufficient, so, having transferred an acceptable drawing to the canvas, I began painting what was to become *Man with a Silver Earring*. The title is an obvious tribute to Johannes Vermeer, but it is much more than that. Years before, taking advantage of working with *Riverdance* in Oklahoma, I purchased a pair of silver earrings from a Native North American craft shop. They featured a flute playing hunchback, a figure called Kokopelli – the deity responsible for agriculture, music and fertility. On my return, I gave them to Betty. She adored them. They never left her ears from that day forth. So, when she died, I went and had my left ear pierced and, in her memory, have worn Kokopelli ever since.

The portrait is finely detailed and quite intense, evoking a certain melancholy, due no doubt to the fact that ageing inevitably anticipates the dreadful reality of the steady loss of family and friends. I sincerely hope that I have sufficient time and energy left to complete several more self-portraits, each bearing witness to the passage of time, until, inevitably, my span together with this story will grind to a shuddering halt. Yet if I'm fortunate, I might still be able to grasp a pencil in my shaking hand and make some rudimentary marks on a sheet of paper as that moment approaches; perhaps a faint primordial swirl containing a frail scratch and two smudges, readable even to infants as a primitive face, indicating that this was an artist – once.

INDEX